S0-AVM-052

Indian and Eskimo Artifacts
of North America

Charles Miles

with a foreword by FREDERICK J. DOCKSTADER

Bonanza Books • New York

© MCMLXIII Henry Regnery Company, Chicago, Illinois

Manufactured in the United States of America

Library of Congress Catalog Card No. 62-19386

This edition published by Bonanza Books,
a division of Crown Publishers, Inc.,
by arrangement with Henry Regnery Company

(I)

Foreword

There are many fine books about the American Indian which consider his cultural variations, and in greater or lesser depth treat of those qualities which make him what he is. Many of these volumes regard his culture in social terms, many inspect his artistic achievements, and some delve into extremely specialized fields of interest. But most of these are general in scope, and treat a tribe or an area in comprehensive terms.

In such studies, material culture, or, what the Indian makes, is of major importance. An examination of this phase of his life is based upon a review of the environmental resources—those materials which are used by the individual; the techniques and processes employed —how the article is made; and the decorative elements which are added to an object for identification, to make it more attractive, or for increased efficiency. The native terminology, economic implications, social forces at work, or ways in which the article is used usually complete the monograph.

While some of these volumes present the reader with a large amount of illustration, such examples are quite rare indeed. All too often, a fine study will be accompanied by only a handful of illustrative examples, and the reader must visualize for himself from verbal description. Needless to say, the ability to create such a mental picture varies tremendously with individuals, and one man's house may well be another man's mansion.

The need for an illustrated compendium of material culture has long been recognized. In earlier years, a few scholars produced such works, but these are now extremely scarce; they were often illustrated only by pen-and-ink sketches, or, in some instances, by photographs which were not too successfully reproduced.

Furthermore, teachers were often frustrated in trying to teach Indian units without adequate pictures, artists needed basic visual reference materials for their sketches, collectors sought for identification of their treasures, and museum personnel employed illustrative catalogs for comparative purposes.

It was with these thoughts in mind that the author has accumulated the present collection of photographs of Amerindian artifacts. Using only a minimal text— for this is primarily a pictorial catalog—he has amassed a tremendous variety of examples, and presents them under several functional headings. Such an arrangement permits a wide latitude for the user, as well as making it easy to find a given object. In many instances, close-up photographs present technical details of manufacture which are not readily seen in larger photos.

The author has endeavored to include all of the more familiar types of Indian objects in this collection. In addition, he has presented many examples which have never before been published, other than in the occasional out-of-print ephemeral monograph.

It is expected that this volume will go far toward supplying most of the needs of teachers, artists, students, collectors, and others interested in the Indian. Museum people will find much of value in the great variety of subject matter included; unfortunately, since many of the examples do not bear tribal identification, it will be possible to use these illustrations only as a guide to the areal origin of a given specimen. This is the most serious flaw in the present organization of the work.

In the mind of the author is the hope that this method of presentation will suggest to readers the tremendous range of materials used by the aboriginal inhabitants of this continent, their wealth of ingenuity in employing those resources to the utmost, and the astonishing variety of cultural expressions which resulted.

A simple introduction into the richness of Indian art is provided by the many illustrations showing the variety of motifs, techniques, and materials which the Indian used in achieving true artistic triumphs. This alone cannot help but whet one's appetite for further reading in specialized fields.

The form of organization adopted by the author can be employed to advantage by collectors in displaying their prizes. Curators of small museums can often find suggestions for special exhibits, or particular storage arrangements, by incorporating some of the groupings. It will be of interest to the reader to review the manner by which a variety of peoples accomplished the same end: the comparison of Pueblo moccasin with desert sandal and Eskimo boot, or the water transportation of the Seminole, Aleut, or the Mandan. All were successful developments to meet a given need; each was quite different in design, material, and construction.

If such a wealth of pictorial matter succeeds in arousing and stimulating the reader to further investigation, or helps a teacher introduce a class to another way of life, then this book will have fully served its purpose. It is certain to serve as a source for a large amount of visual reference. With appended bibliography and listing of museums and private resources available to the individual student, it is likewise sure to be a valuable reference tool for many years to come.

FREDERICK J. DOCKSTADER

Preface

Limitation of the artifacts shown in the book to those of North America is for the convenience of North American readers, who are accustomed to thinking of Anglo-Saxon America separately from and to the exclusion of Latin America. It is recognized that the actual flux of cultures and populations in prehistoric America was not so separated.

The implied separation of Indians and Eskimos is a similar concession. Seemingly, the Eskimos with their fur-bundled persons and as yet distant, treeless homeland of ice and snow, are partially foreigners, whereas the Indians, though quaintly and sometimes romantically eccentric by contemporary standards, are and have been neighbors in the kinds of homelands we know. Actually, of course, the Eskimos are an integral part of the body of Asiatic pioneers who peopled the Americas before 1492.

By "artifacts" is meant, for the specific purposes of this book, all human-altered objects made and/or used by Indians and Eskimos; distinction between ethnological and archaeological being ignored in the makeup of this presentation. Some raggedness of definition has been unavoidable regarding size and origin: When does an object become too bulky or immovable to be considered an artifact—a totem pole, a canoe, hut, or house? Likewise, when is an artifact Indian or Eskimo in a *native* sense, not simply made by an Indian or an Eskimo?

In meeting the first difficulty—that of classification as to size—the author has perhaps dodged a little in some cases; for instance, canoes and totem poles, which are represented by native-made miniatures.

A regrettable omission of an example of human alteration of natural materials is that of houses; the structural details alone would lead one far afield from the main areas of concern in a book on artifacts.

Difficult arbitrary decisions were also necessary regarding the meaning of "Indian" and "Eskimo" as adjectives. All modern Southwest pottery has been regretfully ignored for these reasons: the creation of such pottery has been too much due to white man's "nursing"; it is the product of individuals rather than of folk (a distinction similar to that recognized in the character of ballads); and it imitates rather than carries on aboriginal spirit. Beadwork, however, although completely dependent on the white man's trade beads, is treated rather fully, with the feeling that it is a completely Indian folk expression in spirit and execution. On the other hand, trade goods in general, with the exception of metal tomahawks, have been omitted.

A major trial in the creation of a book such as this is the constant knowledge that it will have to turn out imperfect else it will not turn out at all. Such imperfection is a disappointment to the author as well as to readers. Therefore an apologia may be in order to offset to some extent the inevitable shortcomings involved.

First there is the matter of illustrations; why aren't there more; and/or why aren't there more of these, fewer of those, and some examples of this?

The answer to the first is cost and room—to keep the price of the book within reach of the general public. The second is less easily disposed of because it involves the author's personal judgment, for which criticism is always in order. However, decisions had to be made, or, as already pointed out, there could not have been a book. It is just hoped that the over-all result is good enough to alleviate whatever criticism there may be.

Similarly, some of the textual discussions may be thought to be too brief; possibly even leaving out what the critic thinks is essential. But, just as the book could not portray all artifacts fully, so it could not go into more than essential discussion. Again, the consequent omissions are open to criticism. Furthermore, the book is intended to stimulate interest, and there is a wealth of literature to extend and expand the information here given in brevity.

Dr. Dockstader in his foreword has noted yet another inherent shortcoming, too frequent omission of tribal identifications. The defense for this is implied in the reason for its importance. It is because so very many of the surviving artifacts of American Indians and Eskimos are without such tribal identification that readers, particularly museum curators, collectors, and anthropologists, want to see them attached to pictures of artifacts in a book. They hope for clues to or full identification of the unidentified objects of which they themselves are bound to have a plethora. The author ventures to remind them that he was in the same fix, only more so because such identification printed in a book is a responsibility which, if muffed, can lead to misinformation or deception. It was thought to be much better to leave out all uncertain identifications than to risk this possibility. (It is sincerely hoped it hasn't crept in anyway. As the late E. W. Gifford, curator of the University of California Museum of Anthropology, used to remark sadly, "We fish in very muddy waters indeed.")

Exact provenience of prehistoric objects is of similar importance. Frustrated archaeologists sometimes declare that its absence makes an artifact worthless, but their annoyance moves them too far. There is always value in a "genuine" artifact.

Perhaps it is pertinent at this point to remark on a moral about all artifacts: always record their origin and history when known, and keep the record associated with them.

The word "genuine" above reminds us of a disagreeable subject inevitably associated with artifacts—faking. It is certainly hoped that no fakes are depicted in this book. But so numerous and ubiquitous are they that such a misfortune is possible. On the other hand, the reader is warned not to take too seriously possible statements such as are made by authorities who claim they can "spot" spurious objects every time. It is commonly forgotten that it is a serious matter to succumb to intuition and feeling, however strong, and charge that an object is a fake when it isn't. Such sensationalism does malicious injury.

These are some of the hazards inherent in compiling a book such as this. There are others. One is noted in the text, that of including and excluding artifacts involving modern or European materials and ideas. Though other examples could be given, it is hoped that enough has now been said to put this matter of inevitable imperfection in an adequately revealing light and by so doing mitigate it somewhat. With this explanation, possibly readers and critics will be pleased to go on to the merits and pleasures of the book.

Acknowledgements

As John Donne said, "No man is an island entire of itself; . . ." So in the preparation of a book of this nature no amount of effort to be independent and not bother anybody can be effective. Thus, the author finds himself amazed at the number of acknowledgments of help that are due, and fearful lest he overlook some.

First of all it must be acknowledged that the encouragement of Miss Pearl Ann Reeder of the Lightner Publishing Corporation and Allen Brown, veteran dealer in Indian material and commercial artist, kept the author from collapsing at the prospect of the extent of the work to be done—which became obvious only after the book was already started.

While much of the photography was learned the hard way, a number of friendly experienced photographers gave invaluable impetus with tips and advice, and the expert services of the Oakland Camera Corner darkroom staff were a vital factor in obtaining good results.

Most of the artifacts illustrating the text are in the author's collection, so were available at all times for rearrangement and rephotographing. More than two thousand 35-millimeter photos were taken, mostly with Panatomic X film. Photos taken by the author of artifacts in other collections are by courtesy of the Oakland Public Museum, the Indian Museum at Sutter's Fort in Sacramento, Dr. H. H. Stuart of Eureka, California, Professor Winfield Scott Wellington of the University of California, and Mrs. Jeanette Counter of Berkeley, California; many of the artifacts were collected by the late Edward C. Counter for one of the most extensive collections ever gathered in the West.

Photographs furnished by courtesy of others have been indicated and come from the files of:

The Museum of the American Indian, Heye Foundation, New York, N. Y.; The Smithsonian Institution, both the Bureau of American Ethnology and the National Museum, Washington, D.C.; The Milwaukee Public Museum, Milwaukee, Wisconsin; The Robert H. Lowie Museum of Anthropology, University of California, Berkeley, California; The Southwest Museum, Los Angeles, California; Binfords and Mort, Portland, Oregon, publishers of *Stone Age on the Columbia River* by Emory Strong; and B. W. Stephens, librarian of the Illinois State Archaeological Society, Quincy, Illinois.

Specimens of photography were also loaned by Willis G. Tilton, Topeka, Kansas, and Allen Brown, Chicago, Illinois, from their respective stocks of Indian artifacts.

Suggestions and help have also come from these individuals, from the curators of the museums, and from many other courteous and generous persons, among whom are: Dr. Harold E. Driver, Indiana University; Mrs. James B. Watson, Seattle University; Dr. J. B. Griffin, University of Michigan; Dr. Edward P. Lanning, and the late Dr. A. L. Kroeber of the University of California; in the past, the late Dr. David Banks Rogers of Santa Barbara; and Clark Wissler of the American Museum of Natural History, who explained and encouraged the use of functional classification in assembling the author's collection.

Further detailed acknowledgment of help in assembling the collection used must regretfully be foregone, but not from any lack of gratitude to the many amateurs, professionals, dealers, and other friends who have helped and participated in the enterprise of collecting and identifying material.

Another notation of thanks is due Allen Brown for the use of his professional skill in touching up the photographs to insure their sharpness and clarity, a vital service for a book predominantly of pictures.

Contents

continued

Contents, continued

Who Are the Eskimos and Indians?

When Europeans first began wondering about the origin of the Indians, a number of theories were constructed, largely out of imagination: Indians had always been here, just as Europeans had always been in Europe; they had come from somewhere in the Old World as descendants from the Ten Lost Tribes; in one version, they were, at least partially, descendants of an ancient Welsh migration; or they had come from the survivors of the mythical Atlantis or its less-known sister continent Mu, which were vanished lands under the Atlantic and Pacific, respectively; lastly, by theory they had come from somewhere in Asia.

Only one of these theories has held up under anthropological study and has been accepted by all anthropologists. This is the theory that traces Indian origins to ancient men in Asia, with supplemental migrations from less and less ancient Asiatic peoples until today, when, subject to Communist interference, the movements still go on with contact and interchange between Alaskan and Siberian Eskimos.

Two major sets of evidence have brought about expansion and acceptance of this theory, one negative and the other positive.

The negative evidence is that while increasing numbers of "missing links" in the development of man have been found in the Old World, none at all has been found in the New World. Although some very old skeletal material has been unearthed in the Western Hemisphere, none of it has been as old or as primal as *Pithecanthropus erectus* and Peking man. Finally, no fossil remains of anthropoidal primates have yet been found in either of the Americas.

The positive evidence is that physical anthropologists have analyzed the bodily characteristics of thousands of Indians in both of the Americas and found that the Indian characteristics are basically Mongoloid—the same as the basic bodily characteristics of the bulk of Asiatics in the vast area adjacent to North America. This does not mean that physical anthropologists do not see what we all see—the many physical differences between Indian groups: tall or short bodies, dark or light skins, flat or Roman noses, long or round heads, and so on. Such differences are also evident in Asia.

The qualities on which anthropologists base identification of the Indian with the Mongolian racial strain constitute another set of evidence which, in general, is less obvious to the uninitiated and requires more precise observation. One of the more evident characteristics which is common among Eskimos, and to a lesser extent among Indians, is the epicanthic fold, a fold of skin over the inner canthus of the eye. Another characteristic, which is rather spectacular, but which does not occur as often, is what is called the "Mongolian spot," a purplish bruiselike mark at the base of the spine which appears frequently among Indians and Asiatics of Mongoloid strain but rarely among other peoples.

The evidences in skeletal material are, of course, much more limited than testimony which can be given by the full body. About the only easily discernible skeletal evidence is the presence among the teeth of shovel-shaped incisors, a form confined to the Mongoloid strain.

When Did They Come?

As archaeological evidence has accumulated and been more expertly studied, the period of time that human beings are estimated to have lived in the New World has become somewhat longer than what the earlier anthropologists were willing to admit. A great many former arguments have been silenced by discovery of the Carbon 14 method of dating. Without going into detail as to its nature, we can describe Carbon 14 by saying that it measures the age of once-living materials back many thousands of years with an accuracy within a few hundred years. With the aid of this technique archaeologists have been able to agree on a date of slightly more than 11,000 B.C. for Clovis-style Lehner fluted blades. Some archaeologists have been convinced of even earlier dates.

The paths of migration of these ancient men are being intensively studied by archaeologists, but as it takes much evidence to achieve reasonable certainty, the paths are still rather dim. However, it is believed by archaeologists and geologists that men must have crossed from Asia at the same time that many now-extinct animals were passing to and fro over the land bridge that once existed between Asia and North America. This was during the Ice Age while there was still so much water impounded in the icecap that the level of the oceans was lowered, thus leaving dry land where Bering Strait now is. It is further believed that, as the icecap spread irregularly, there was an open lane of land through Alaska and down east of the Rockies into the ice-free reaches of the continent. It was through this lane that ancient men and animals passed.

After traveling into more favorable country, these early human beings began to multiply and to roam about in the same fashion as Europeans did in the New World—or in the Old World, for that matter.

Culture Areas

A culture area is a region in which are found artifacts that reflect or are associated with a particular way of life. Two kinds of culture areas interest anthropologists. One is an area in which evidences of some prehistoric culture are found; the other is an area in which similar ways of life can be observed as having existed at the time of Columbus' discovery or during the subsequent conquest of post-Columbian America. Those areas concerned with prehistory are of interest to the archaeologists; the other areas are the concern of the ethnologists. The geography of cultures of living peoples is ethnography.

Although anthropologists manage to keep their thinking clear within this dualism, it tends to confuse the average person and the amateur anthropologist. The confusion is increased by the tendency of museums to mix the two in their presentation of exhibits. Therefore, it is well to examine each area to better understand their separate bearing.

Considering the archaeologists' culture areas first, we find that the literature of their reports is filled with words such as "horizons," "complexes," "phases," and so on, which have a special meaning within the context of the science. Accordingly, it is somewhat difficult to simplify current archaeology properly. However, it can be understood that the areas they talk about have as much temporal as geographical significance. For instance, the earliest area might be understood to be that in which the earliest kinds of artifacts have been found. When the first fluted point was found in connection with extinct animal remains, it was associated with Folsom, New Mexico. For a long time similar points found elsewhere were known as Folsom points, and a search was on to find how far away such points appeared. Meanwhile, other forms of ancient points were discovered together with artifacts and conditions which could be assembled to constitute a pattern of life: Clovis points, Sandia points, Yuma points, and others. One after another, more and more culture areas were identified and reported.

Some of these cultures had a wider spread than others. Consequently, when cultures are assembled in chronological sequence in a particular area, one culture may be limited while another may be comparatively widespread. That is, one may be located entirely within the area or even within a part of it while a former or a subsequent one may be identified as spreading a considerable distance beyond its modern political and geographical boundaries.

Results of archaeological study of the central part of North America in the region of Ohio illustrates the nature of such a prehistoric sequence of cultures. Broadly speaking, there were five culture stages in this one area. Each stage had its typical ways of living, and, in general, each showed an advance in complexity and variety of the adjuncts of living.

The earliest stage began with the appearance of the first wandering human beings, presumed to have been the same sort of nomads who followed the grazing herds of prehistoric animals as they passed to and fro between Asia and the Americas. Their trails are dim indeed and are marked only by the charcoal, debris, and crude artifacts of Folsomoid nature left where they camped or killed and feasted on creatures, some of which are now extinct.

The second stage, called the "Archaic" stage, seems to have begun about 8000 B.C., and to have continued until about 1000 B.C. It was a period when the men coming from Asia were tending to stay in North America and were beginning to wander less and multiply more, although they continued to be simple hunters and gatherers of food.

The third stage, called "Woodland," was somewhat complicated in the Ohio Valley by the overlapping of two culture types: Adena and Hopewell. In this stage the Indians of the Ohio Valley had learned agriculture which induced them to adopt a sedentary life. They lived in permanent villages, cultivated foodstuffs and tobacco, learned to make and use pottery, and discovered the delights of smoking. They also developed the practice of building mounds over the graves of their dead, and hence were known to pioneer anthropologists and to the public as the "Mound Builders." The Hopewell Indians are notable for their fine craftsmanship and artistic skill evidenced in the artifacts they buried with their dead, or that they otherwise left behind.

The Adena culture endured from about 1000 B.C. to about A.D. 200 or 300 and the Hopewell culture from about 400 B.C. to A.D. 300 or 400; the latter developed a little later and lasted a little longer than the former, although the two coexisted for some time.

The fourth stage, called the "Late Woodland" stage, lasted from about A.D. 400 to A.D. 1000, and was less localized than the three previous stages, probably because the population of Indians had increased to the point where there was continuous contact, much travel, and imitation of neighbors' discoveries and ways. The Late Woodland stage repeated the agricultural sedentary character of the Early Woodland stage—though with changes of form in artifacts and in ways of life —and continued the building of mounds.

The fifth stage, called the "Fort Ancient" culture, was the last stage of Ohio Valley life in the pre-Columbian spirit. At its end, this stage saw the beginnings of adoption and adaptation of white men's artifacts and customs. It began about A.D. 1000, and its somewhat violent breakup is set at about 1680 to 1690. Since then the culture in the region around Ohio has been that of the conquering Europeans, progressing from the pioneer stage with its log cabins and long rifles to the present with TV and rockets—a culture in which the First Americans have been marooned and steadily cajoled into abandoning and forgetting their old ways until only such mementos· as the artifacts depicted in this book remain as visible evidence of ways that were.

This sketch of the past in terms of culture sequence in the Ohio region is quite like what could be written in similar sketches of successive ways of life in other areas. Some names of such cultures in other parts of North America are:

1. Lamoka, Frontenac, Orient, Point Peninsula, Owasco, and Iroquois in the northeastern area around the St. Lawrence Basin, New York, and New England.

2. Sandia, Basket Maker, and Pueblos I, II, III, and IV in the Southwest, with a plethora of other rather sharply identified cultures in different parts of the area, such as Hohokam, with its own periods and dates, Mogollon, Mimbres, Three Circle, Pine Lawn, etc.

3. Lauderdale, Copena, and Middle Mississippi in the Southeast, the lower Mississippi area, and the Gulf states.

4. Oak Grove, Hunting People, and Canalinos in the Santa Barbara coastal region, with hints of primal cultures more ancient than these.

5. Old Bering, Koniag and Late Koniag, stages of Aleut, and other cultures defined and named through archaeological exploration in the Arctic.

Only another book could begin to name and define all the cultures in detail with their technical differentiations.

The ethnologists' divisions into cultures are not so difficult for the general reader to follow, although they are extensive to cover properly in detail. In 1492 and during the years before dissolution of native ways by white men, Indian and Eskimo cultures were divided into a number of large, fairly homogenous groups with rather distinct differences, because many of the elements that created such groups were strongly geographical. Each of these groups had its own roster of artifacts. Many of these artifacts did not occur at all in other groups, and many more differed radically from artifacts used for like purposes in other groups.

Analysis of each of these groups would take too much space for this book, so they will just be named:

1. The Eskimo-Aleut group along the Arctic top of North America, which can be subdivided into Eastern, Central, and Western areas, with the latter divided into the Bering Coast Eskimos without wood, the southern Eskimos with wood, and the Aleuts on their treeless islands.

2. The Northwest Coast Indians, whose common culture traits extended from Alaska into northwestern California. Within this group are certain conspicuous regional traits that differ among the northern, central, southern, and California areas.

3. The intermountain area, sometimes called the "Plateau" area, which roughly covered the country between the Sierra Cascade ranges and the Rocky Mountains. This group has been somewhat vaguely divided into a northern wooded and watered area and a southern arid and barren area.

4. The California area proper, having two distinct subdivisions, one in the central valley drained by the Sacramento and San Joaquin rivers and one on the southern coast and its offshore islands, where a semimaritime culture flourished.

5. The Southwest, sometimes called the "Anthropologists' Paradise," because in its area are living cultures and prehistoric cultures enough for both ethnologists and archaeologists to "anthropologize" in almost limitless detail. Most of this area is in Arizona and New Mexico, but its elements extend into California, Nevada, Utah, Colorado, and Texas.

6. The Northwoods, or Subarctic area, in northwestern Canada. This is a rather bleak home for hardy but sparse Woodland Indians who, in consequence of their somewhat harsh lives, have a culture pattern that is quite simple and limited.

7. The Plains area, extending from the Northwoods in Canada in a broad grass-dominated belt through the west-central part of the United States between the Rockies and the Eastern Woodlands almost to the Gulf of Mexico. It was the home of the "horse Indians," but in prehistoric times was rather lightly populated by pedestrian Indians.

8. The Eastern Woodland area, differing from the others in that much of the culture associated with it is prehistoric as most of the historic Indians wasted away, or were driven out, or were "pushed around" with little interest taken in their culture patterns until it was too late to record much about them. This group can be subdivided into a Northeastern area, dominated by the Algonkins and Iroquois; a Mississippi Basin area; and a Southeastern area. Literature about the Eastern Woodland area is generally concerned with its prehistoric culture periods in which it had quite similar elements throughout: agricultural tools; elbow pipes; tools made of chipped flint or similar stone; banner stones, birdstones, and other stones of unknown use; pecked-stone axe and adze blades; and so on.

Language Groups

The anthropologists study not only the culture groups of the pre-Columbians of North America but also the linguistic groups of that period.

After Europeans had been in the New World a while and had begun to pay attention to aboriginal speech, they discovered that not only did the Indians speak different languages but they also spoke more languages than were used in Europe; some two thousand in all—two hundred north of Mexico and eighteen hundred in

Latin America. This means, of course, native languages, not imposed or borrowed European languages.

A map compiled and drawn by C. F. and E. W. Voegelin (*Map of North American Indian Languages*; published by the American Ethnological Society in collaboration with Indiana University; Publication No. 20 of the Society) presents a graphic panorama of the situation in North America. The map shows more than fifty major language groups or families containing some two hundred individual languages—a family being a group of closely related languages, such as the Romance languages which are composed of Italian, French, Spanish, Portuguese, and Romanian. Following a classification by Edward Sapir, these language groups are presented in six divisions of linguistic families having structural resemblances. Each of these divisions is shown in a different color, so that the map has the appearance of an irregularly marked patchwork quilt. Only the Eskimo-Aleut group appears as a single color band; the others show major areas with smaller scattered patches, some far distant from the main group.

That linguistic divisions are not suited to arrangement of artifacts is obvious because tribes in a single linguistic group appear in several cultures in separate areas. For example, the Sioux of the Plains, the Iroquois of New York, the Caddos of Arkansas, the Pomos of California, and the Natchez of the South are all in Sapir's Group VI. However, this map does stir up speculation on how such widely scattered members of a language group got where they did and where their original home was when their language was developed.

Summary

This, then, is the background of Eskimo and Indian artifacts of North America. The artifacts were made by people of Mongoloid origins who came across a now-extinct land bridge from Asia or, later, in boats across Bering Strait which eventually replaced that land bridge. They were people who migrated about in both Americas, lived long in some places—where they developed cultures and constructed languages—and migrated again en masse or in small groups up to and after the appearance of white men. They were people who spoke some two hundred languages, which have been reduced in major group numbers to six, and who dwelt in some eight culture areas, each with its different ways of life.

Artifacts and a few dwellings and mounds are the major visible mementos of the many cultures of the Indians and Eskimos, some few living and millions dead, whose span of life in North America can be measured back thousands of years into the misty past of extinct animals and the last ice age.

1 Food

From "Is there anything to eat?" to "When do we eat?" the food problem has been and still is the number-one problem for all mankind and for all other animate creatures. Solution of the problem is always the same —find and gather the food; then, if the food isn't eaten on the spot, transport it to where it is to be eaten; if the food isn't ready to eat as gathered, prepare it, perhaps serve it, and maybe store some of it. This routine is followed by the lesser creatures as well as by lordly man himself.

Indians and Eskimos were no exceptions to this routine. They obtained food by hunting game, by fishing, by gathering wild plant foods, and during their last few thousand years on the continent, by harvesting cultivated plant foods. Hunting was the chief means of supporting life in that large part of North America which formed a vast triangle based on the Arctic Ocean and extending its apex almost to the Caribbean. Fishing predominated in part of Alaska, in the territory of the Northwest Coast Indians, on the coasts of southern California, and on the coasts of the states bordering the Caribbean. Wild plant foods were the mainstay of the southern part of the intermountain plateau west of the Rockies and of most of California. Farming, although more than four thousand years old in the Americas in 1492, was carried on by only about a quarter of the North American Indians, the Eastern Woodland Indians, and the Pueblo Indians of the Southwest.

However, no area was dependent upon just one kind of food. The Arctic Eskimos, though severely restricted by their icy and snowbound homelands, dug roots whenever they could get at thawed-out open ground. Also, in many areas the inhabitants had to be ready to meet breaks in the usual routine of their staple foods—buffalo herds changed their usual schedule or route, or drought dried up more edibles than usual. All Indians and Eskimos were experts in harvesting anything and at any time necessary to keep themselves alive.

Harvesting

Although "harvesting" applies to all foods that occur in quantity or numbers to constitute crops, including fish, buffalo herds, grasshoppers, and ducks, it has been a popular custom to apply the term to the gathering of static foods, such as grains, fruits, shellfish, plants, roots, and, among the Indians, grubs and insects in season.

Gathering Receptacles

The gathering of small foods required portable receptacles in which to drop gleanings as the harvesters moved about. These receptacles were of various kinds, but mostly baskets, which were light and not easily broken. Most baskets had handles or slings for suspension to leave the bearer's hands free while he clambered about and picked the food.

Carrying Baskets and Nets

The gathering grounds were often at some distance from homes, therefore to economize on walking, the harvesters took receptacles which would hold as much as the harvester could carry.

When the load was too heavy and the distance too great for the harvester to carry it in his arms, he had to devise a pack that could be placed on his shoulders or on his back. This left his hands and arms and legs free.

Packs for portage of grain, nuts, berries, and, of course, other small items besides food, took the form of carrying baskets among the Indians. There must have been such burden baskets everywhere in North America, except in the Arctic or on the Plains after the coming of the horse, but the bulk of surviving pack baskets come from the West where their use has continued even to the present day among tribes clinging to the old ways.

The standard method of attaching carrying baskets to the body was by a sling that looped over the forehead rather than over the shoulders as we do it. Slings or tumplines were frequently attached to handles or to some parts of the carrying baskets, but often they were merely passed around the burden. To provide security for this latter method, pack baskets were made more or less conical in shape if the load was to travel any distance. California- and Nevada-type burden baskets were perfect or nearly perfect cones. Elsewhere, the cone was rounded off or cut off and truncated at the bottom. The coast Salish liked rectangular rims as well as rounded ones.

Another factor in the shaping of burden baskets, and also in their use or nonuse, was the usual distance to be traveled. As the distance diminished, the conical shape had less value and the size less point until there was no need for a burden basket at all. A third factor was the character of the loads to be carried. In predominantly hunting areas, the loads were mainly meat. Therefore, the carrying basket was replaced by a pack frame, or the animal or a large part of it formed a pack in itself.

Carrying nets displaced baskets in only one area—the territory of the Papago Indians of southern Arizona who, with Mexican neighbors, constructed and used a net in a frame. This was a combination of net and pack frame. The nets by themselves, and sometimes in place of tumplines, were used jointly with baskets in the wild-plant food area of the West.

Other Gathering Utensils

Besides berry and clam baskets and burden baskets and nets, Indians and Eskimos used bags, seed beaters, poles, fruit hooks, sap catchers, headrings, breast yokes, and, as previously noted, tumplines in the activities of gathering and harvesting.

Digging Tools

The digging stick, just about the humblest of prehistoric artifacts, is one of the most dramatic to contemplate. Since the digging stick is merely a simple stick, sharpened at one end, it is a tool that has rotted away by the millions. In large part the remains when found have been ignored or hardly noted even by archaeologists. It is the Adam of an imposing host of mankind's most used tools. It has developed into picks, spades, hoes, shovels, and mattocks; into plows, harrows, fresnos, steam shovels, and bulldozers. Today its gigantic grandsons, the behemoth earth movers, fascinate us as they nonchalantly change a whole landscape in a few days.

Even in pre-Columbian North America the digging stick had made considerable growth into complexities, though in its primary form it still remained in use everywhere, even in the farming belts where stone-bladed tools had become familiar.

Primitive digging sticks were so simple that there were but two variations: round, pencil-style points and flattened points. Some of the Southwest Indians added footrests to the digging sticks by leaving a branch stub near the digging end; south coastal Indians of California used digging-stick weights; and a number of tribes in the western intermountain plateau put horn or bone cross handles on the butts of their root diggers.

The Eskimos found that small, elbowed tools were very handy. They made pick, adze, and mattock blades of ivory, horn, or bone. The resemblance of these blades to some of the assumed adze and chisel blades in the Eastern Woodland area arouses suspicion that many of these latter are being misnamed, particularly those that were polished from use. Sometimes the polish on Eastern agricultural tools was so extensive that it obliterated the marks of flaking and chipping. Think of the work such a tool did in its time!

It is customary for collectors, in the areas where hundreds, perhaps thousands, of these farming tools have littered the sites of ancient cornfields and villages, to classify them as oval- or fan-shaped spades and as stemmed or notched hoes. Some of the flint spades attained imposing sizes—well over a foot in length.

Although chipped flint and kindred stones were the usual material, there are enough pecked and ground stone blades and shell and bone blades around to tell us that there may have been more of them in use than the preponderance of flaked implements indicates.

Small Receptacles

1.1 Two Eskimo twined basketry bags woven with grass
1.2 Aleutian woven-grass basketry bag with colored yarn squares, extremely fine openwork construction
1.3 Northwest Coast Indian berry basket, elongated pyramidal form, rigid fine-twined open weave
1.4 Coiled Salish basket, imbricated, with a sling loop of unusual tubular construction decorated with buckskin fringe trimmings
1.5 A berry basket plaited with ribbons of inner cedar bark by an aged Hoh Indian woman as an example of "the way they used to do it"
1.6 Tightly coiled Puget Sound Indian basket, hard and rigid as wood and completely watertight
1.7 British Columbia rectangular-rim style, woven native cloth sling attached, hard-coiled and imbricated in colors
1.8 Quinault-style design (band of birds around rim and interlocking crosses), twined weave
1.9 Klikitat-style berry basket used in the middle Columbia River Valley area, late-style design with figures of horses and women
1.10 Another Klikitat berry basket but with old-style (simpler) chevron design, loops on rim for tying on covering
1.11 Salish-style clam basket, roughly twined of strips of wood, for utility use, particularly on beaches and riverbanks
1.12 Diegueno cactus fruit basket, coarsely twined
1.13 Apache-style harvest basket in diagonally twined weave, with danglers and fringed buckskin reinforcement on bottom
1.14-1.15 Pitched water-carrying jugs used by desert Indians and in the Southwest wherever pottery was likely to be broken, built-in lugs and buckskin slings

1.1

1.2

1.3

1.4

1.5

1.6

1.7

1.8

1.9

1.10

1.11

1.12

1.13

1.14

1.15

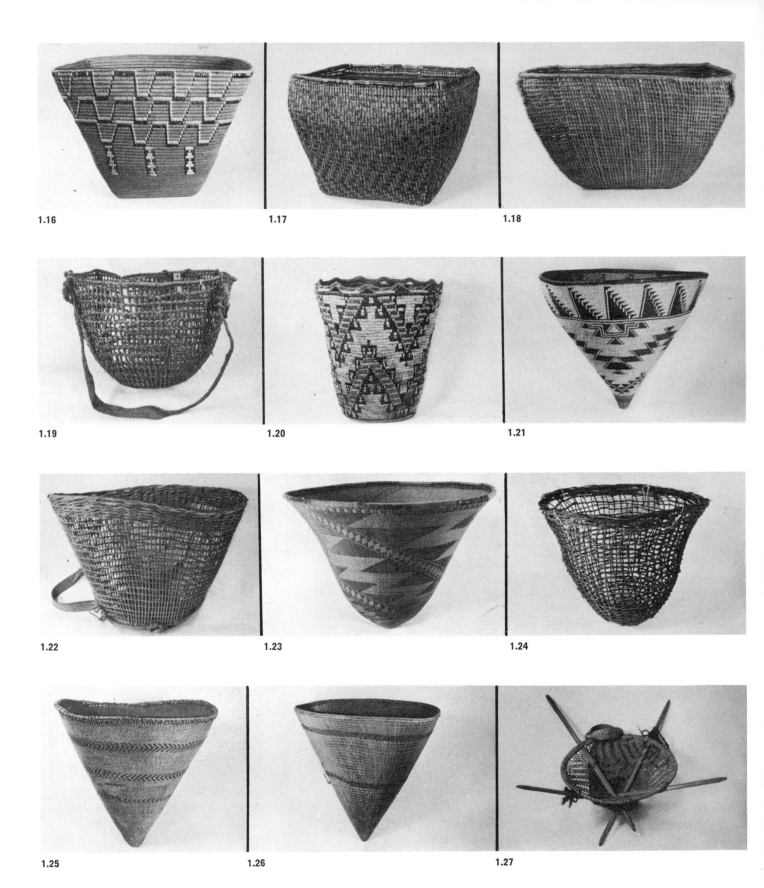

1.16   1.17   1.18

1.19   1.20   1.21

1.22   1.23   1.24

1.25   1.26   1.27

4

Carrying Baskets and Nets

1.16-1.18 Three Salish Indian burden baskets from British Columbia: (1.16) coiled with a design in colored imbrication; (1.17) plaited in herringbone pattern; and (1.18) twined in a fine open weave; all with rectangular rims

1.19 A typical utility carrying basket in coarse open weave, used by Salish tribes in general for miscellaneous cartage

1.20 A coiled and imbricated basket in what is commonly called Klikitat style, with a late form of colored decoration and, as usual in the middle Columbia River area, with rim loops woven in for attachment of covering on a load of berries or nuts

1.21 A Pitt River Indian twined basket of the typical California conical shape, design in black on a white background

1.22 The Yurok-Hupa version of a coarsely woven utility burden basket

1.23 Bell-shaped Pomo basket in diagonal twined weave (one of the largest of Indian burden baskets)

1.24 Pomo version of a coarse utility carrying basket, woven of grapevines; quite rare because collectors spurned it in favor of its beautiful sister (1.23)

1.25-1.27 Two Yokuts twined baskets of perfect cone shapes: (1.25) tightly woven to carry seeds and other fine cargoes; (1.26) fine open-weave; and (1.27) a Papago Indian net on a pack frame, the net woven like lace in a decorative design, the whole equipped with a plaited back shield and forehead band

1.28 Typical Apache-style burden basket, commonly trimmed with buckskin fringes and reinforced with leather bottoms

1.29 Kutenai burden receptacle made of outer bark sewed and lashed together with buckskin; made and used by Pretty Otter of the Kutenai tribe

1.30 Central California-style carrying net without a forehead band

1.31 Central California-style carrying net with a forehead band

1.32 Two such nets showing the forehead bands in more detail, the left one being the band (1.31), with disk-form shell beads woven in to act as rollers on a forehead pad, the other band designed for ventilation; both bands native woven cloth from native materials in aboriginal style

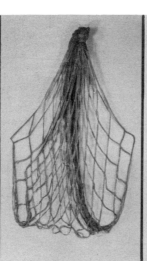

1.28   1.29   1.30   1.31   1.32

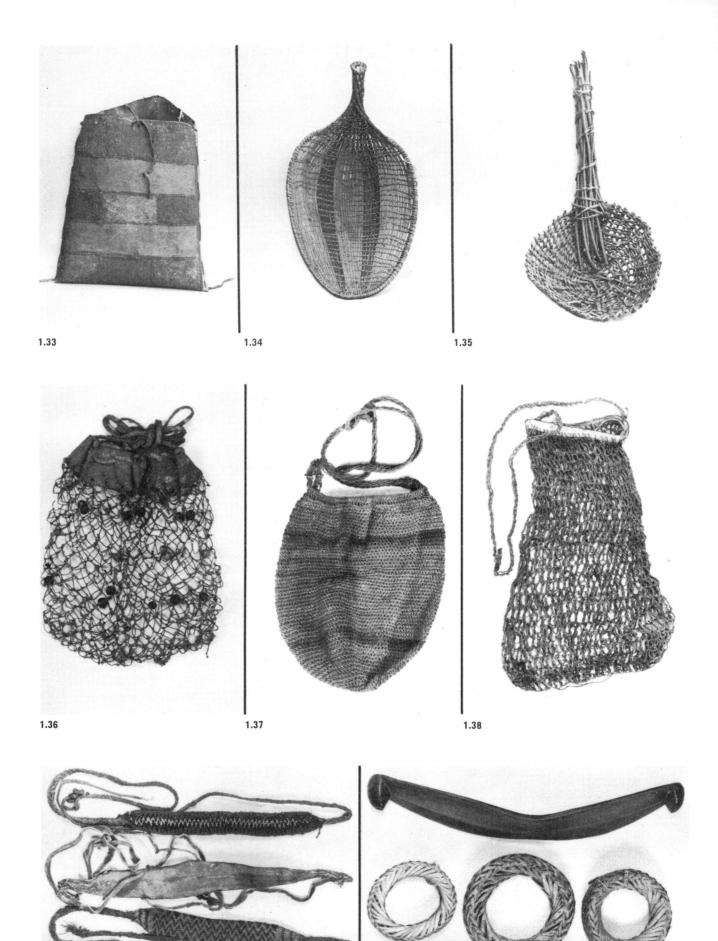

1.33

1.34

1.35

1.36

1.37

1.38

1.39

1.40

6

Other Gathering Utensils

1.33 Rawhide bag, Sioux, painted red and green, used in gathering chokecherries and other crops

1.34-1.35 Seed fans or beaters, used to shake off and sift seeds; characteristic of the California-Nevada area: (1.34) a Yokuts Indian form, and (1.35) Pomo. Sticks were used in other areas, and poles served for harvesting from trees

1.36-1.38 Carrying bags, the hand and shoulder form of the carrying net: (1.36) North Woods (Canada) Indian style, woven with narrow leather cordage called "babiche" and by coiled looping, ornamented with large glass beads; (1.37) closely meshed netting bag, origin unknown; (1.38) Yurok-Hupa style knotted netting bag with buckskin rim and sling

1.39 Tumplines; top and bottom Columbia River Salish, finger-woven cloth headband with colored zigzag designs, and braided pack cordage; center, Chippewa, with rawhide headband (hair left on), and rawhide pack straps

1.40 Eskimo wooden breast yoke (top) with hooks for draglines, and (bottom) Southwest Indian headrings to hold pots steady and cushion the head

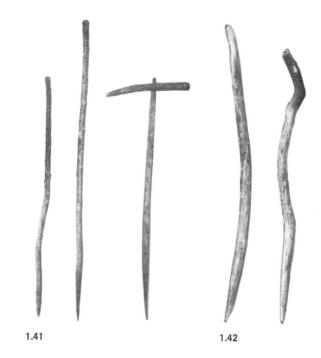

1.41   1.42

1.43   1.44

Digging Tools

1.41 Digging sticks; left to right, two small ones from a cave near Cottonwood, Arizona, with round and flattened points, respectively; one crutch-type from the middle Columbia River area, trade iron "stick" with horn handle

1.42 Two big mountain mahogany sticks from the interior of southern California

1.43 Four Chumash whalebone tools, diggers, or possibly levers to pry off abalones

1.44 Two Chumash "doughnut stones" suited to use as combination stick weights and lever fulcrums

1.45 Crutch-type stick handles of horn, bone, and stone

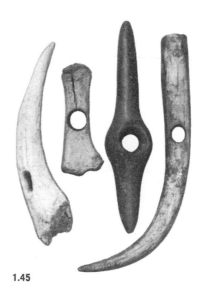

1.45

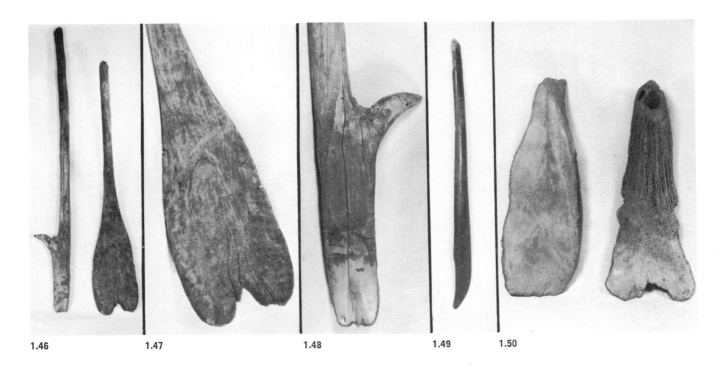

1.46   **1.47**   **1.48**   **1.49**   **1.50**

1.46   A Zuñi foot-rest stick and a Shoshone
wooden shovel
1.47-1.48   Close-ups of the blades of each
1.49   Southwest Indian weeding "sword"
from the Four Corners area
1.50   Buffalo bone (scapula) and horn hoe
blades from agricultural village sites west
of the Mississippi River

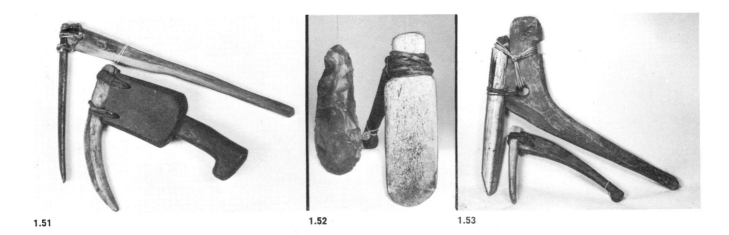

1.51   **1.52**   **1.53**

1.51   Eskimo root adze and root pick with
bone and ivory bits
1.52   Comparison of an Eskimo whalebone
root adze blade with an Eastern flint blade
(left), suggesting a mode of attachment for
the latter
1.53   A heavy Eskimo mattock with a
walrus-tusk blade, and side view of the
root-adze blade in (1.52)

1.54   Oval-type flint spade blades from the Ohio-Valley
1.55   A fan-shaped blade from Tennessee
1.56   Polish on two spade blades as compared with polish on a "chisel" (pick?) and an "adze" (hoe?) blade, all from Tennessee
1.57   Two notched hoe blades of Mississippi Valley type
1.58   Two chipped-flint and one ground or pecked (above) hoe blade, stemmed type
1.59   Comparison of Eskimo ivory pick bit and a "hump-back" stone chisel, suggesting an attachment and use for the latter

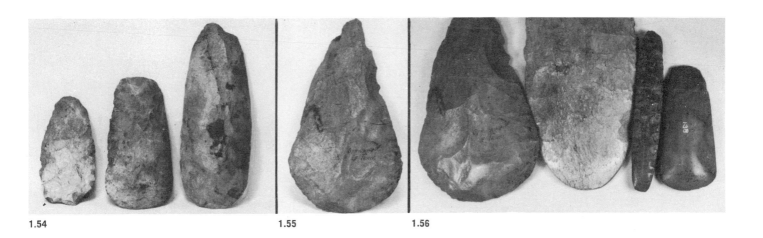

1.54   1.55   1.56

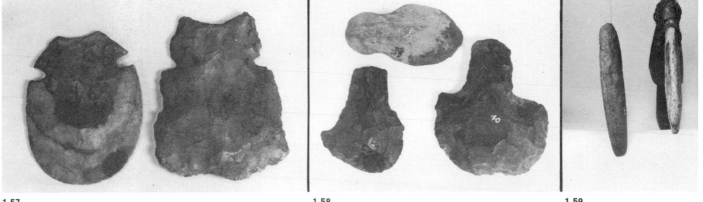

1.57   1.58   1.59

Hunting

As already noted, the pre-Columbian Indians and Eskimos of North America depended chiefly on game for food. Game was harvested by hunting with spears, harpoons, bows and arrows, clubs, bolas, and slings and by trapping in nets, deadfalls, snares, lassos, pits, and game corrals. Indians also drove game over cliffs, stampeded game with fire, and ran animals into water where they could be speared from a canoe.

Hunting was considered work, not sport, inasmuch as meat from game and also much of the material for clothes, tents, utensils, tools, and other necessities, came from success in hunting. Privation and death came from failure in hunting. The prehistoric Americans harvested crops by any effective method available to them. At the same time they did not wantonly waste the crop. The invading Europeans were the ones who exterminated passenger pigeons, nearly did away with buffaloes, and in general looted and wasted North America's natural game resources. This wholesale slaughter was halted only by enlightened fellow citizens through use of police power. A deplorable result of the conquest of the continent was the killing off of game, leaving the people who lived on it to starve.

Clubs, Rabbit Sticks, and Bolas

A thrown rock and a thrown club, even though just a stick and a rock, are probably the oldest weapons. The club is still in use as a police weapon, but its roles in hunting have faded. The Indians and Eskimos, however, kept clubs in constant use by dealing lethal blows to trapped game and caught fish. The clubs were of many shapes and sizes, but they tended to be of only three kinds: the basic bludgeon club, the slung-shot club, and the rabbit stick.

The basic bludgeon was used everywhere. Less used was the slung shot, which is a stone on a leather or sinew cord or loop, sometimes called a "braining club." Inasmuch as grooved and holed stones, "anchor stones," large "net weights," and the like were used in such clubs, there were probably more in use than is generally realized because we do not recognize the remains. The rabbit stick, too, may have had more use than its remains would indicate. About the only prehistoric rabbit sticks collected have been dry-cave finds in the Southwest. In fact, rabbit sticks are still in use in that area.

Bolas may have developed from slung-shot clubs, using two or more weights on cords, and they, too, may have had more use than is recorded. Use of the bolas among the Eskimos and some California Indians has been recorded. There are indications that some stones buried in pairs and some grooved and spool-shaped pottery artifacts may have been bolas weights.

Spears

Spears are poles with sharp points, for thrusting or throwing with intent to kill. It is common practice to call spearheads, spears. Two kinds of spears were used by pre-Columbian Indians: conventional spears with a single head, generally not barbed, and fish and bird spears, with either barbed heads or barbed tines.

Conventional spears are recorded ethnologically as being in use by Eskimos and Plains Indians and in a short dagger form in northern California. Archaeologically, spears appear to have been much more widely used, but such a conclusion is probably a popular fallacy due to calling all stone artifacts that could have been spearheads, spears. It is likely a fallacy because any spearhead, even on a shaft, could become a knife by simply cutting off the pole a handbreadth from the end. As knives were both more convenient and more useful than spears, there is a great deal of likelihood that most, if not all, such artifacts were actually knife blades.

The Eskimos used two kinds of conventional spears: one a short stabbing spear for wounding or killing swimming animals; the other a heavy lance to kill wounded, trapped, or cornered game. A specialized form of the latter consists of a pole with a socketed end into which a short, small spear could be affixed and renewed as its predecessors were left in the victim. Extra small spears which were used as spare points were carried in a bag.

The Plains Indians used a long lance which was wielded from horseback to bring down buffaloes and sometimes foes in battle. Impressions of the popularity of this weapon have become exaggerated, however, because of its conspicuous appearance in paintings and drawings of the Buffalo-Bill type of pageantry—an appearance instigated by the picturesque looks of lancers on horses. Actually, the long lance was clumsy in comparison with bows and arrows and guns, and was better for parades and ceremonies. Whether or not the lance came into use with the acquisition of horses is not on record. But from the stabbing, rather than thrusting, manner in which it was wielded, it may have been adapted from aboriginal spears used in the Eskimo fashion. A few surviving lances have stone heads, but most that now exist are supplied with more practical steel or iron points.

The California Indian spear hardly qualifies as a spear. It is short and more of a dagger, though as a rule it has a regular spearhead. It may have been a weapon in the past, but ethnologically it is connected with the paraphernalia of dance and ceremony, particularly among the lower Klamath River tribes.

In contrast to conventional spears, fish spears were in wide use. The two varieties were a shaft with a single head and a shaft with two or more barbed tines on the end. The single-headed spears were favored by the Eastern Woodland Indians; the pronged kind preferred by the Eskimos and Northwest Coast Indians. Both varieties and a somewhat hypothetical third type are known archaeologically in California. The third type is a reconstruction of bone spike-and-barb combinations assumed to have been lashed to a shaft as spearheads. A fourth type has also been hypothesized from examples in other primitive areas. This was a shaft to which a curved and a double-pointed bone were lashed diagonally as a head.

Bird spears similar in form to the fish spears and with a similar mission—to hook as well as to pierce—were in use by the Eskimos. They are better classified with darts because of their lightness and the fact that they were thrown with atlatls. Such weapons in spear form may, however, have been used by the Eskimos as they are or were used until recently not too far south of the Mexican border.

Harpoons

A harpoon is a spear with a detachable point attached to a line. The head is barbed or shaped to pivot sidewise inside a victim, such as a fish, so as to hold it on the line and pull it in or play it in water. Much hunting of sea mammals would have been impossible without the harpoons which were the mainstay of the Eskimos before they obtained guns.

Harpoons were also used quite far inland from the coasts. Points are picked up occasionally in the Great Lakes area, some of which are made of native copper rather than the usual bone or ivory, or horn.

The makeup of harpoons varied from the butt of a point stuck into the end of a shaft to the development of a quite complicated weapon. A typical Eskimo harpoon of the latter type might have a bone or ivory head. To construct this type, a socket was made in the end of the shaft. Into this was fitted a foreshaft of double-pointed bone or ivory, then the head mortised to the foreshaft. All of the head and foreshaft were lashed together in such a way as to come apart at a blow instead of breaking. The point might also have a tip fitted into a slot. Sometimes this tip was provided with its own line.

In the center of the shaft, the Eskimo would place a finger rest for security in throwing and perhaps a bladder float with its valve and plug. On the shaft butt, he would put a spur, or ice pick, of bone or ivory. Finally, the point lanyard might be coiled onto and attached to an anchor board that would be jerked out into the water to further impede the animal's swimming.

Less common, but put to considerable use, was another kind of harpoon with one and sometimes two composite points consisting of two barbs and a center point glued and lashed together to contain a socket and a line attachment. Most were small, but a bigger size with the addition of a special shell, copper, or iron blade was used to harpoon whales by the Indians in the neighborhood of Vancouver Island. Pieces of such harpoons found archaeologically might not be recognized by one unaware of this type because the lashing and glue, if not cared for, soon disintegrated.

It should be added that the pivoting device which was achieved by constructing the point with a spur on one side and placing the hole so as to give toggle action was often used along with barbs. This made effective action doubly certain.

Harpoons also involved a number of auxiliary artifacts besides those already noted, such as wooden scabbards and furred-skin wrappings for the tips, line attachers and detachers, bracket rests for kayaks, and bags for spare parts.

Arrows

Arrows are shrunken darts propelled by bows instead of by hands or atlatls. The superior force and speed imparted by the bow make the smaller and lighter projectile not only possible but necessary. Nevertheless, there are arrows that approach darts in size, and vice versa.

Inasmuch as arrows correlate with bows, and their use is not certainly evidenced by artifacts of North America before A.D. 500, it follows that the size of stone projectile points offers a clue to the adoption of bows and arrows in various places. Also, archaeological findings accompanying arrowpoints indicate that the smaller chipped points are really the only arrowpoints, the hosts of larger ones having been dart- and spear-points, or knife blades.

Besides their points, which may be just the sharpened front ends of the shafts, typical arrows consist of shafts, nocks, and feathering. Both Indians and Eskimos varied each of these parts and combined them in several ways so there are numerous forms of arrows, many of which identify their origins. However, extinction of a tribe or lack of data makes identification of many arrows uncertain.

Some common attributes of arrows which help identify their source are shape of nock, attachment and length of feathering, kind of bird feathers used, ownership bands and other marks, kind of shaft (many were in two parts), wood used in shaft, mode of lashing and/or gluing (feathers, points, and joints in composite arrows), and, of course, the kind of point used.

Arrowpoints, Spearheads, and Knives

The illustrations of the arrowpoints, spearheads, and knives show five ways of looking at them.

First are some of the major divisions and subdivisions of a classification plan devised by Dr. Thomas Wilson of the United States National Museum and illustrated in the annual report of the Smithsonian Institution for 1897, and repeated in *Prehistoric Implements* by Warren K. Moorehead in 1900. Second are examples of products from some of the commoner materials used in making these artifacts. Third are groups of local types recognized west and north of the Rockies. Fourth are a few of the types identified for localities through detailed data assembled in a report by Robert E. Bell in *Special Bulletin No. 1* of the Oklahoma Anthropological Society. And fifth are a few of the favorite types whose names are familiar to amateur collectors and dealers.

Text continues on page 36.

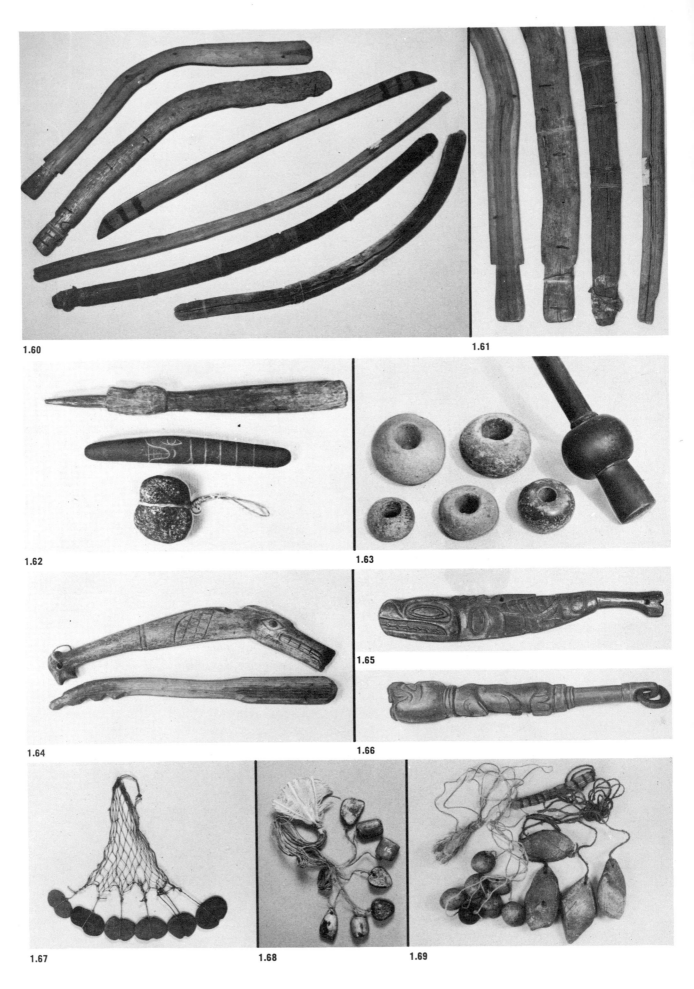

1.60

1.61

1.62

1.63

1.64

1.65

1.66

1.67

1.68

1.69

Clubs, Bolas, and Rabbit Sticks

1.60-1.61 Rabbit sticks of boomerang type (but not returning): (1.60) top to bottom, three historic-period Southwest types, two with boomerang curves and one (may be a loom batten) with propeller twist; and three prehistoric types, two grooved, Basket-maker types and a California stick from a San Bernardino County cave; (1.61) close-ups of two historic rabbit-stick handles, Navajo and Hopi, and two prehistoric, Basketmaker grooved types (Note repair reinforcements of sinew, and wire lashing.)

Rabbit sticks were thrown with the inside of the curve toward the victim and their shapes caused them to bounce and jump about instead of sliding. The Australian returning sticks united curve, propeller twist, and cambered cross sections to achieve their properties.

1.62 Three game clubs: top, old Quinault wooden club with duck head carved above handle; middle, Northwest Coast stone fish effigy club; bottom, Eskimo braining club, granite head, rawhide looped handle

1.63 California "doughnut stones" and a South Sea Island "doughnut stone" club head suggesting one mode of North American use (See also 1.44)

1.64 Northwest Coast whalebone effigy club with abalone-shell eyes, and a modern Salish Indian fish club picked up at Celilo Falls on the Columbia River

1.65-1.66 Two Northwest Coast Indian game clubs, the effigies said to represent the fish or other animal the club was intended to kill (from the Professor Winfield Scott Wellington collection)

1.67-1.69 Bolas, which the Indians and Eskimos threw into flocks of birds to bring down game: (1.67) Pomo Indian bolas with net-webbed cords and "net sinker" weights (this may be a fragment of a net); (1.68) and (1.69) Eskimo bolas with bone and ivory weights, two with feather and one with straw rudder. In both form and use, these are like bolas thrown by the ancient Egyptians and were most effective when thrown into bird flocks. Three-weight bolas are also familiar as weapons used by South American Gauchos. It is likely that some grooved and holed stones and baked-clay artifacts were bolas weights instead of net weights or charm stones.

Spears, Darts, and Lances

1.70 Four Eskimo spears: top, a leister, or fish spear with three barbed tines; the other three are short stabbing spears, the kind used to spear swimming game

1.71 Close-ups of the points in (1.70), showing lashing with leather and baleen

1.72 Eskimo "repeating" lance; the foreshaft with its tip set in the socket of the whalebone headpiece so as to come out when thrust into prey

1.73 Close-ups of three points for "repeating" lances, showing flint (top) and slate tips

1.74 A Plains Indian lance of the type familiar in parade and combat pictures but most steadily used for stabbing buffaloes from horseback in the same fashion as game was stabbed from canoes (Note feather and fur trimmings and a metal tip made of an old bayonet lashed on as shown in the close-up below.)

1.75 Close-up of lashing in (1.74)

1.70

1.71

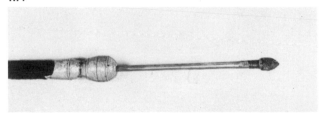

1.72

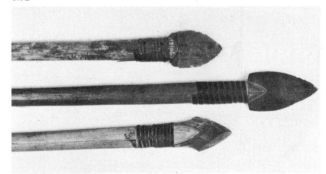

1.73

1.74

1.75

Food 13

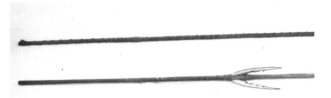

1.76

1.77

1.78

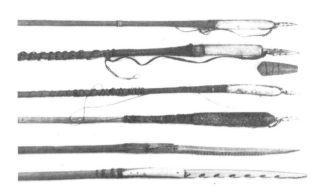

1.79

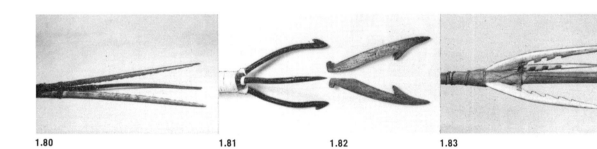

1.80   1.81   1.82   1.83

1.76-1.77 Two Eskimo bird darts: (1.76) handles of the leister type, and (1.77) with three barbed tines, see (1.83), set in the middle of the shaft to provide a second chance at snagging a bird in a flock

1.78 Typical dart butts, some cupped for reception of an atlatl hook: Note top one fletched in two places and bladder float on bottom dart. (These are not the butts for the point next them.)

1.79 Typical harpoon and bird-dart points and the wooden scabbard for one tip. All are Eskimo.

1.80 Bird-dart (Eskimo) assembly: This and assemblies in (1.81-1.83) all show same leister technique.

1.81 Metal tip from a bird spear of sort in use until recently by Indians in Mexico

1.82 Bone double barbs, perhaps also used with a center spine; from central California mounds

1.83 Eskimo bird-dart shaft barbs

Harpoons

1.84-1.85 Center and front assemblages of two Eskimo harpoons: (1.84) showing finger rests and line wrapping; (1.85) showing, top, a heavy-duty head with foreshaft only; below, a medium-duty head with point directly in head socket

1.86 Spurs, or ice picks, for butt ends of harpoons

1.87 Close-ups of harpoon shaft centers with finger rests, lanyards, and lashings

1.88 Spur-shod butt of heavy-duty harpoon

1.89 Toggle-type head of (1.88) on foreshaft rod, with retrieving lanyard attached

1.90 Miniature of a float board with harpoon, atlatl, and coiled retrieving line

1.91 Whalebone and ivory front-assemblage pieces, showing (second) anchorage of foreshaft to head, and toggle-type whale point with socket placed on foreshaft

1.92 Bladder float attached to harpoon shaft, showing method of fastening valve and bladder neck, and wood or cork plug

1.93 Siberian-type ivory harpoon head as used on the coast and islands of Bering Strait, decorated with red painted dot pits; and three kayak harpoon brackets

1.94 Point scabbards made of wood and sinew, a harpoon bracket, a float valve, and two finger rests

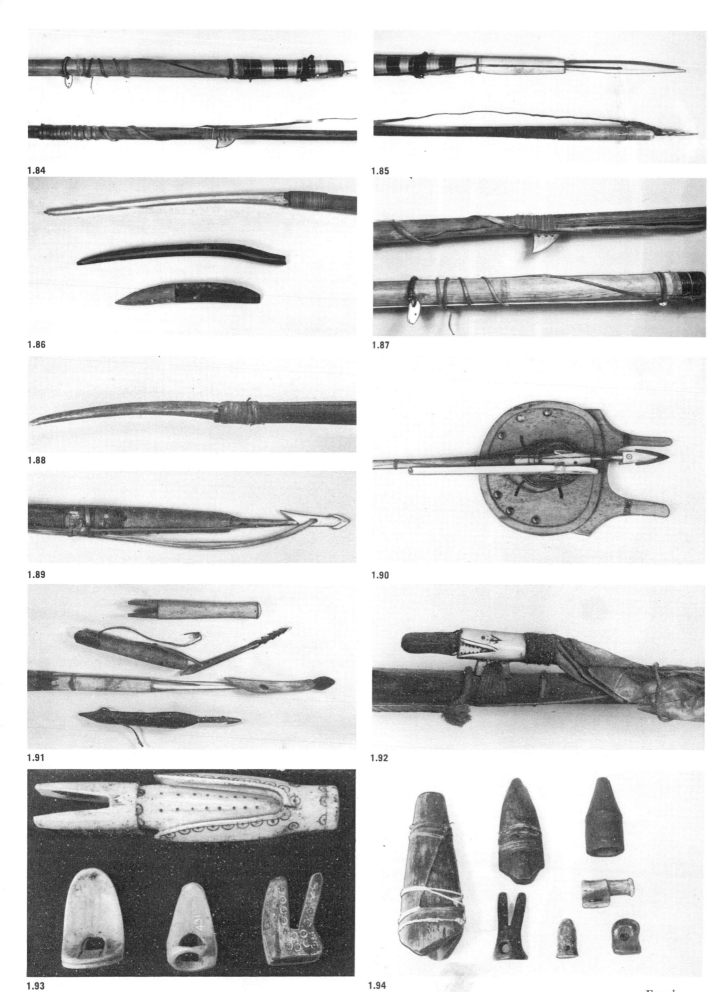

1.84

1.85

1.86

1.87

1.88

1.89

1.90

1.91

1.92

1.93

1.94

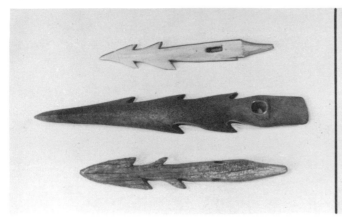

1.95

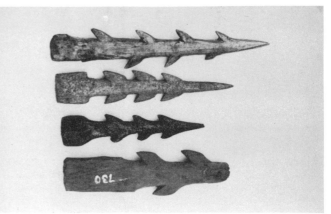

1.96

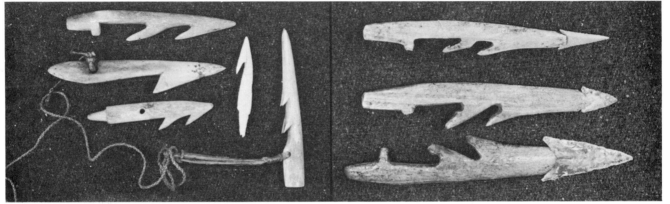

1.97

1.98

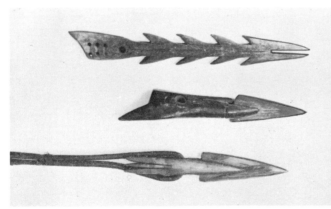

1.99

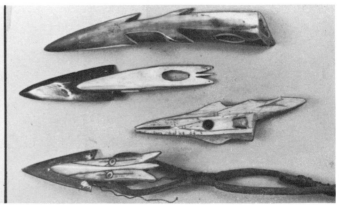

1.100

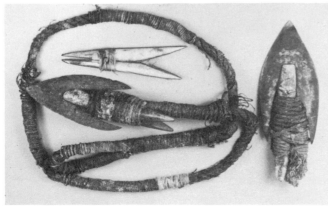

1.101

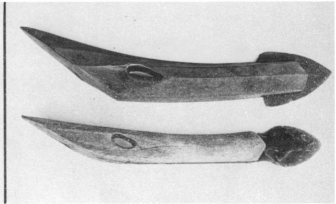

1.102

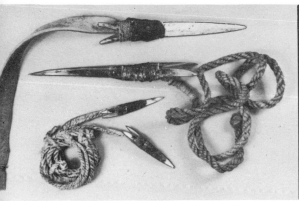

1.103

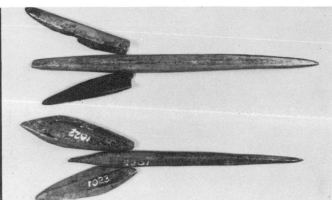

1.104

1.95 Eskimo bilaterally barbed ivory harpoon points with differently placed and shaped line holes, and pin- and flat-shaped butts
1.96 Central California bilaterally barbed bone points with flattened butts and shouldered for line attachment
1.97 Side-barbed forms; top, northern California; below, Columbia River; bottom, Alaska; center, southern California; and right, of unknown origin, made of ivory, with two sets of twin barbs
1.98 Sea lion harpoons, northern California coast Indians, with tips fitted in slots, two lower tips glass

1.99-1.100 Eskimo toggle-and-barb types of harpoon points with shoulder spurs of different kinds and positions: Six points have deep, narrow slots for blade-type tips; (1.99) center with slate tip; (1.99) bottom and second on (1.100) with tips of some sort of shell or bone resembling tortoise shell; (1.100) bottom has a copper tip with holes for line attachment.
1.101 Makah Indian whale-harpoon assemblages of three-part composite type, showing one pair of bare barbs or spurs, and two complete points with copper and iron blades, one with sinew rope lanyard partially wrapped with a cordage casing

1.102 Eskimo toggle-type harpoon points, with socketed butts, upper with ground slate tip and lower with chipped flint tip
1.103 Small composite types of harpoon points with bone awl or pin-shaped centers and bone barbs; northern California coast and coastal Salish Indian types above and, bottom, a pair for use on a Y-branched shaft; made with pockets, or sockets, for tips of shafts
1.104 Archaeological specimens; upper, north California coast, and lower, Oregon coast

1.105-1.107 Eskimo and Indian pictures relating to harpoon use: harpooning whales from open boats (umiaks), some with sails; showing use of one hand for hurling, one for lanyard
1.108 Harpooning walruses, showing use of inflated sealskin floats and operation from a decked kayak (The bird on the left has been caught in a trap, apparently baited or concealed with leaves.)

1.109 Whale-carrying float (top) and (below) Makah Indians home from a successful whale hunt traveling in a dugout canoe with sail
1.110 Harpooned seal or walrus, harpooner braced cowboy fashion, with float in reserve; lower, three hunters in a three-hole kayak

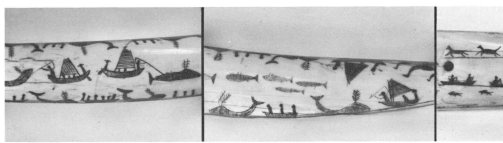

1.105   1.106   1.107

1.108   1.109   1.110

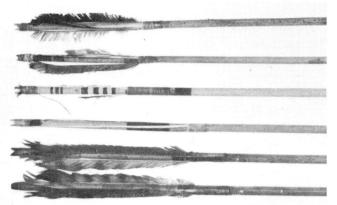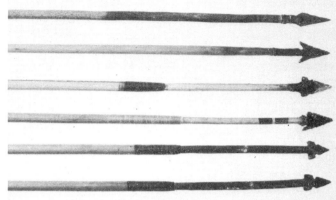

1.111

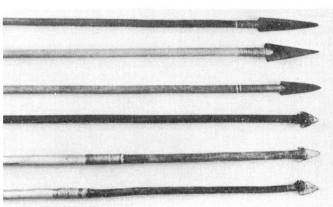

1.112

1.113

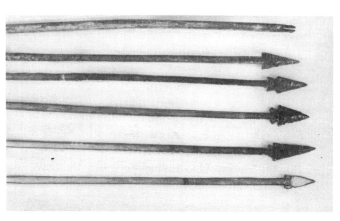

1.114

Arrows

1.111-1.114 Twenty-four arrows: (1.111) six California arrows; 1 and 2 central; 3 to 6, north and northeastern; (1.112) 1, Ohio; 2, 3, 4, northern Plains; 5 and 6, Apache. Origin of others (1.113 and 1.114) not recorded. All have stone heads except (1.111) 1, (1.112) 1, 2, and 3, which are iron, and (1.114) 1, from which the head is missing out of a shouldered slot.

More than half have ownership marks composed of encircling lines and bands of various colors, mostly red and black. There are two sets of such marks on (1.111) 4, 5, 6, (1.113) 3, 6, (1.114) 5 and 6. So-called "blood grooves" on (1.111) 4, (1.112) 1, 2, 4, and (1.113) 5. Burn marks, perhaps from grooved heat straighteners, on (1.113) 1 and 2.

Half of the shafts are in one piece, and half are composite; wood foreshafts on wood shafts except (1.112) 5 and 6, which have jointed cane main shafts and wood foreshafts. Nocks are all U-shaped except

(1.112) 2, 3, and (1.114) 1, which have expanded V notches. Lengths of shafts in inches as follows:

1.111	1.112	1.113	1.114
31¼	23	29	26¾
30	26¾	28¾	38
32¼	26¼	42¼	32
30	22¾	32½	23¼
34	33½	29	30¾
34	30	29¾	30¾

The feathering is all split vanes in threes, 4 and 15 spiraled; feathers from various kinds of birds. Lengths of feathers between sinew bindings are:

1.111	1.112	1.113	1.114
4¼	6¾	4¼	4
4	9	4¼	4
3¼	4½	6½	5½
6	8	9½	4½
6	5	4½	3
6	4	6	3

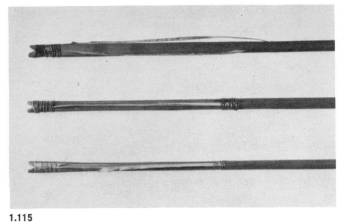

1.115

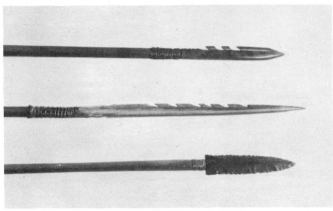

1.116

1.115-1.116 Two Eskimo deer arrows with bone and ivory tips supplied with many notches and barbs to create rankling and bleeding, and a flint-tipped arrow for bears (1.115) butts, and (1.116) points: the explanation of difference being in the different behavior of the two kinds of animals when shot; just as hunters today use different calibers and cartridges for different kinds of game

1.117 Six Northwest Coast Indian arrows; bone points carved in different ways on four, and copper harpoon arrowpoints with lanyards for the other two

1.118 Feathering and nocks of (1.117): Two center Northwest Coast arrows have no feathering and they and the following two have expanding and bulbous nocks. The Eskimos often feathered their arrows with two instead of three feathers.

1.119-1.120 Eskimo fish arrows; two of leister type; three of harpoon type, with ivory tips supplied with lanyards, and a heavy-tipped bird arrow; (1.120) butts of (1.119)

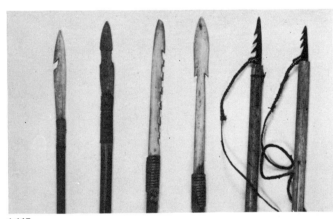

1.117

1.118

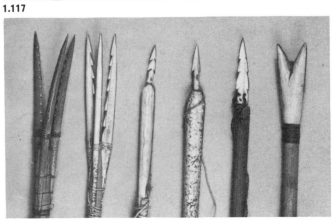

1.119

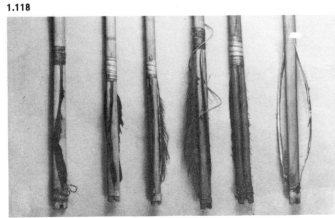

1.120

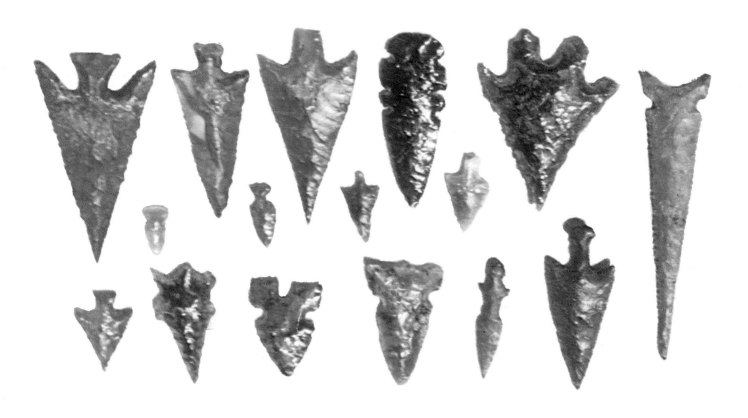

*Arrowheads made by Indians west of the Rockies
showing extensive use of obsidian, agate, and jasper*

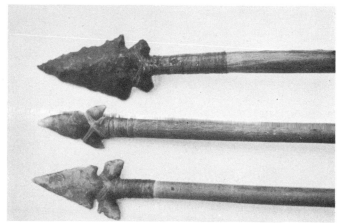

1.121

1.121 Three stone-tipped points showing mode of crossing the sinew threads through the side notches

1.122 Top and bottom, elkhorn tips from northern California, and, center, bone arrow used by eastern Sioux

1.123 Two serrated slate tips with lashing over the barbs; ownership bands on shafts

1.124 Some unusual tips; (a) bone with incised chevron decorations (or ownership marks); (b) Eskimo ivory tip which may have been the mounting for four leister-style tines; (c) tiny flint tip on an old Plains arrow; (d) bulging wooden tip for a bird arrow of Indian rather than Eskimo character, all of a piece, the shaft having been whittled down from the tip; (e) bone bipointed pin lashed at an angle to the point of the arrow; does not appear to be a North American arrow, but pictured to show how this mode of pointing could have been used with bone "pins" found in North America

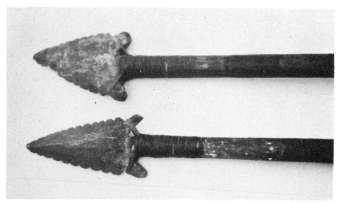

1.122

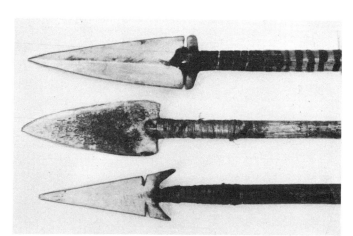

1.123

1.124

1.125

1.126

1.127

1.128

1.129

1.130

1.131

1.132

1.133

1.134

Arrowpoint Shapes

1.125-1.126 Following the plan of Dr. Thomas Wilson of the United States National Museum, these are arrowpoint examples of his Division I (1.125), Leaf Shapes, and II (1.126), Triangular Shapes. Under I, his subdivision Class A is pointed at both ends; Class B has concave, convex, or straight bases; and Class C is similar to B but narrower. His Division II has no subdivisions.

1.127 Continuing the Dr. Wilson plan, these are subdivisions of Division III titled Stemmed. Classes A, lozenge-shaped, and B, stemmed and shouldered

1.128 Class C of Division III is stemmed and barbed.

1.129 In Dr. Wilson's Division IV, Peculiar Forms, Class A (1.129) has beveled edges. Bevels of this class are one to each edge, usually the left one.

1.130 Class B of Division IV has serrated edges. The serrations vary greatly in different areas, in character and in size, as indicated in the examples shown.

1.131 Class C, bifurcated stems, of Dr. Wilson's Division IV from east of the Rockies, mostly flint

1.132 The eight obsidian points, also of Class C, are from the southern intermountain plateau west of the Rockies. Possibly such stems seated the point more firmly and checked its rocking on the shaft.

1.133 Departing now from Dr. Wilson's plan, with the exception of a Class D, Division IV arrowpoint with squared barbs (near Celilo Falls, Columbia River), miscellaneous unusual forms are shown, mostly with marked exaggeration of various parts of the simpler forms.

1.134 Five Folsomoid forms are shown here, distinguished by flutes on the sides. (This type had not yet been recognized in Dr. Wilson's day.) The point in the center is from Goose Lake in northeastern California. The origin of the others is unknown.

1.135

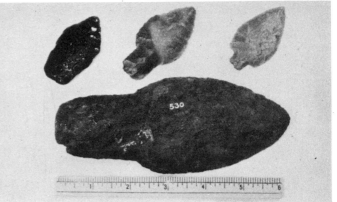

1.136

1.137

1.138

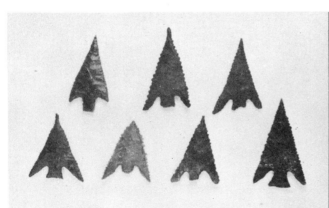

1.139

1.140

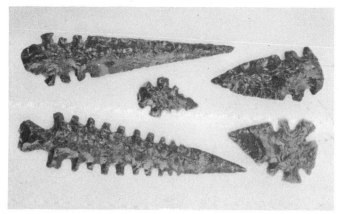

1.141

1.142

Western Regional Types and Forms

1.135 Bering Coast Eskimo arrowpoint forms identified as flint bear arrows in distinction from horn, ivory, and bone points used for deer and other game. Note similarity to Yuma and Scottsbluff types.

1.136 Harpoon points at the top and a lance head, bottom; the former are fitted into slots in the ends of large whale harpoon points.

1.137-1.138 Columbia River types, mostly gem material. The various forms of smaller points (1.137) all have definite areas of major distribution in localities adjacent to the river. The three large examples (1.138) are called by local collectors "mule ears" and are considered to be knife blades.

1.139 "Beach arrows" from blows in sand dunes at the mouth of the Mad River in northwestern California. These points are unusually thin, of a local brown and greenish stone that looks like jasper. They commonly have long barbs, fine serrations, and elongated needle tips.

1.140 Bifurcated-stem obsidian points already shown (1.132), originating in the southern portion of the intermountain plateau west of the Rockies

1.141 Distinctively serrated obsidian points from the delta area at the mouths of the San Joaquin and Sacramento rivers in central California

1.142 The obsidian spear (or knife) and accompanying arrowpoint were found in the hands of an individual burial near Oakley, California. The points in (1.141) were in or near the same site. The nearest source of obsidian is some fifty miles distant.

1.143-1.144 The three common shapes of Canalino (historically, Chumash) Indian points found in the southern coastal and island area of California: The small points (1.143) are in the two shapes shown, made of a dove-gray stone and of a brown stone resembling jasper. The larger artifacts (1.144) are what Dr. Wilson calls "lozenge shape" and were knife blades or spearpoints, made of a local variegated flintlike stone.

1.143

1.144

1.145

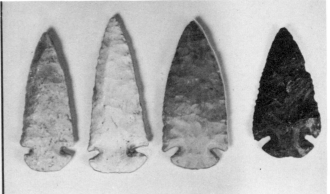

1.146

1.147

1.148

1.149

1.150

1.151

1.152

1.153   1.154

Eastern Types and Forms

1.145 Arkansas "willow leaf" points, cited in Dr. Robert E. Bell's report as Nodena; A.D. 1400 to 1600; reported almost exclusively from Arkansas

1.146 Dovetail or fantail points, a variety not cited by Dr. Bell. Most specimens are credited to the upper eastern Mississippi Basin. (Courtesy Willis Tilton.)

1.147 Indiana "broad stems" corresponding to Dr. Bell's Adena-type points, credited to the northern states of the Ohio Valley and Tennessee. He dates them as 800 B.C. to A.D. 800.

1.148 Another type not cited by Dr. Bell; might be called "square tails"; all from Misssouri

1.149 Also a familiar Mississippi Valley form which might be termed "wedge tails"

1.150 A Texas type, sometimes called "Comanche points" and cited by Dr. Bell as Pedernales points; from 5000 B.C. to A.D. 500 or 1000; originating in what is now central Texas

1.151 An Arizona type, distinguished by being beveled on each side of both edges

1.152 So-called "war points," Will County, Illinois

1.153-1.154 Stemmed and shouldered (1.153), and (1.154) side-notched points: All thirteen came from the same farm in Will County, Illinois, as the war points in (1.152). Their variance illustrates the fact that several shapes of points may all be popular in the same locality.

1.155

1.156

1.157

1.158

1.159

1.160

Arrowpoint Materials

1.155-1.156 Flint points: Flint was a popular stone among the chippers of both the Old and New Worlds, but freely as the name is used, there is considerable disagreement among the users as to exactly what constitutes flint. Without getting into the arguments, flint is a variety of quartz and its colors are caused by impurities. Wilson gives as colors gray, yellow, green, blue, and smoky black, and indicates that white in flint is caused by weathering. He adds "tints of red and brown." Shown are: (1.155) solid-color flint artifacts, and (1.156) flint arrowpoints in variegated colors.

1.157 Obsidian points: Obsidian (volcanic glass) is a favorite material west of the Rockies, where, mineralogists say, there is no flint. Use of obsidian tends to predominate in areas where it is easily obtained. Points shown are of unpatterned solid-black obsidian.

1.158 Jasper and petrified wood points: Jasper is used all over the United States, but petrified wood is more familiar in the West. Jasper is commonly red or yellow, sometimes having both colors in one point. Petrified wood occasionally shows the rings of the original tree wood.

1.159 Agate points: Agate varies greatly in color and general appearance, but is lustrous and colorful, hence the term "Oregon gem points" (although agate points are also found in great numbers in Washington State).

1.160 Straight quartz points; clear "rock crystal" and "sugar" quartz; the clear three from California and the sugar specimens from the Atlantic Coast

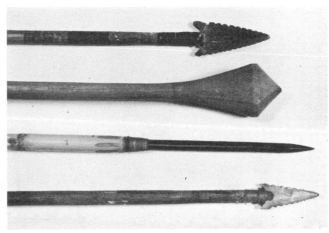

1.161

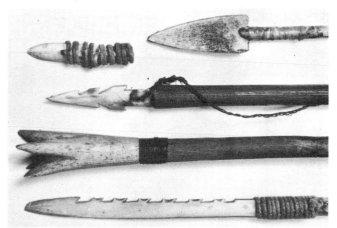

1.162

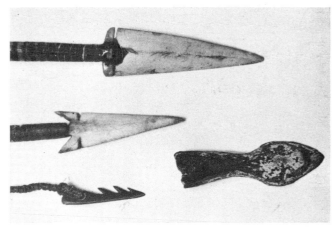

1.163

1.161 Four points of: slate (top), wood (two center), and shell (bottom)
1.162 Bone and ivory points from the Eskimos, Northwest Coast Indians, and Sioux
1.163 Elkhorn points (two upper), north-western California; and lower, copper points, bottom left Northwest Coast and bottom right Wisconsin
1.164 European post-Columbian materials; upper, two iron and, lower, three glass; the bottom one made by Ishi, last survivor of the Yahi tribe in central California, using milky jar glass. In earlier times Indians sometimes knocked the red glass from railroad switch standards to make what were to them excitingly attractive arrowpoints.

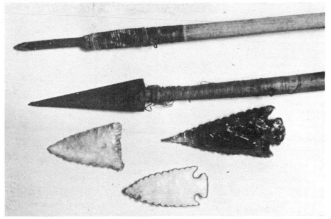

1.164

Food 29

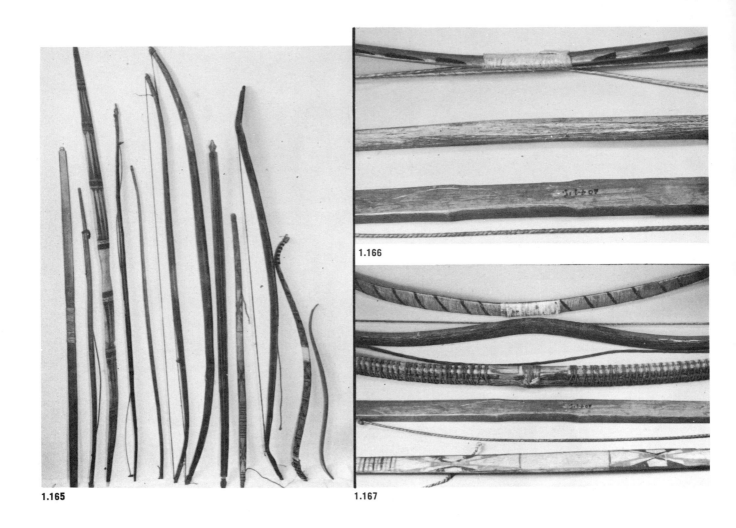

1.165

1.166

1.167

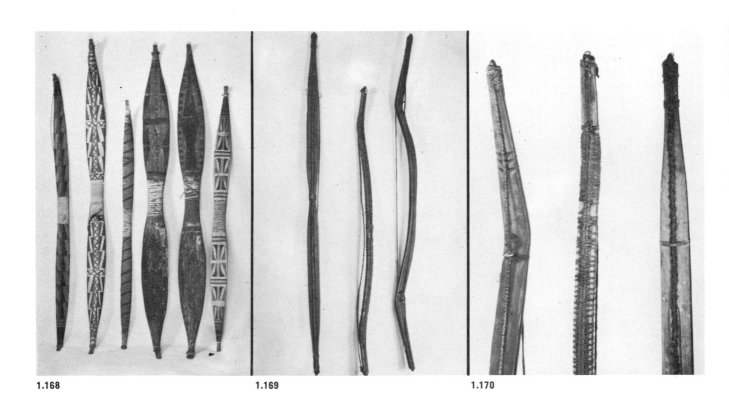

1.168

1.169

1.170

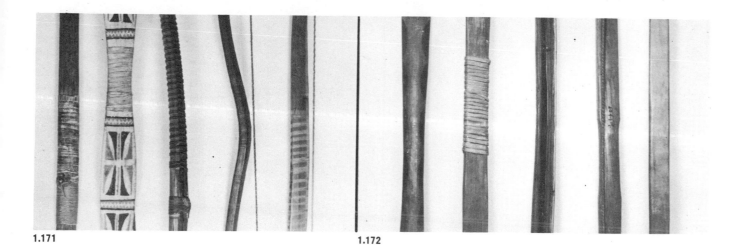

1.171   1.172

Bows

1.165   A dozen Eskimo and Indian bows, showing the variations of lengths and silhouettes; the two longest, Kutenai and Southwest Indians, and the two shortest, lower Colorado River Indians

1.166   Flattened, oval, and rectangular cross sections of bows

1.167   Centers of two sinew-backed bows, an Eskimo cordage-reinforced bow, and two self bows

1.168   Six northwest California bows of the Yurok-Hupa type, made of yew wood with glued sinew backing painted with area designs; quite flat and lens-shaped in cross section

1.169   Three Eskimo bows with different versions of cordage reinforcement

1.170   Closer view of the preceding bows in (1.169), showing wrapped cable cores and cordage lashing

1.171   Bow grips and wrappings for reinforced bows

1.172   The same for self bows. Two of these bows are painted.

1.173   Eskimo picture (lower) on ivory showing Eskimo hunter placing an arrow correctly into a caribou

1.174   Bowmen on land and water stalk beavers in a pond

1.175   Various forms of bow cord notches and attachments; that on the right showing a somewhat unusual method used by central California Indians of building up a notch with sinew and glue

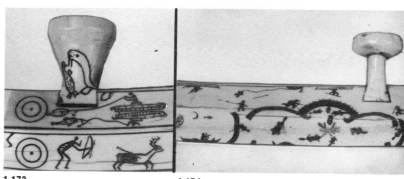

1.173   1.174

1.175

1.176

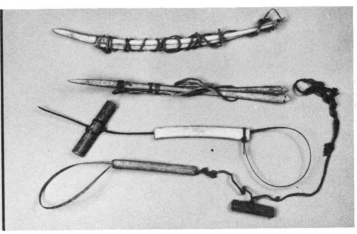

1.177

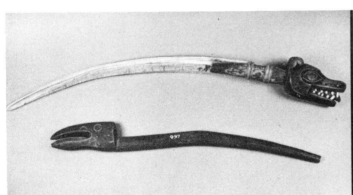

1.178

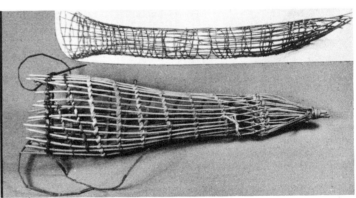

1.179

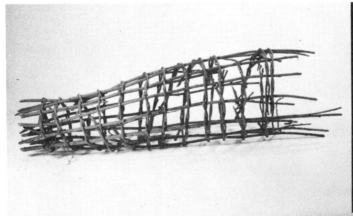

1.180

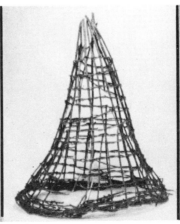

1.181

1.182

Traps, Snares, and Decoys

1.176 Model of an Eskimo trap. Tension and spring are provided by twisted cordage inside the cylinder. When the trigger is pulled, the spiked arm snaps over to impale the victim.

1.177 Two Eskimo trap triggers, above, and two marmot snare traps to be set in burrows. The bone tubes keep earth from fouling the lines.

1.178 Northwest Coast Indian trap stakes, used to mark and hold traps

1.179 Stocking-type fish traps, upper Pomo Indian, to set in a stream; lower, model of a coast Salish trap towed between two canoes to scoop up fish

1.180 Pomo Indian trap entrance, woven with grapevines

1.181 Pomo grapevine fish or eel trap

1.182 Yurok model of an eel trap. A mouth similar to (1.181) is inside the cage.

1.183 Eskimo hunters driving caribou into a corral which apparently has openings set with nooses, in one of which a caribou stands with its antlers entangled. Note that the men are on snowshoes and armed with bows and arrows.

1.184 Picture of a deadfall trap. The man appears to be setting the trigger. The animal present in the trap may be simply to show what is caught there (perhaps a fox).

1.185 Br'er Rabbit has taken the first fatal step to a larder via noose trap, and perhaps the bird is also bound thither. The picture is etched on an ivory comb.

1.186 Eskimo animal trap and a fish trap like the Pomo upright trap (1.181). Hunter below is shooting a gun at a seal on an ice block.

1.187 Eskimos operating a seine from boat and shore; one Eskimo with dip net

1.188 Continuation of (1.186) showing a gill net in operation; below, a man clubbing a caught fish

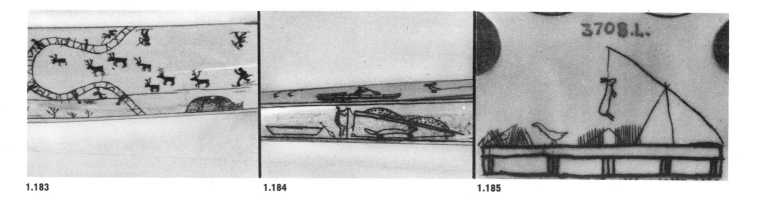

1.183   1.184   1.185

1.186   1.187   1.188

1.189

1.190

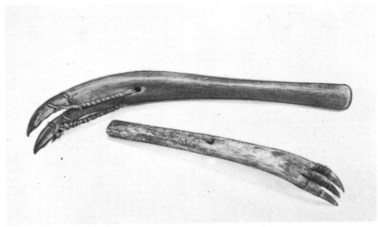

1.191

1.189 Auditory game decoys made and used by the Northwest Coast Indians; the two longer ones, from Vancouver Island, emit a blast when blown; smaller one with totemic decoration is for use with a ribbon strip of grass, leaf, or bark, blown as schoolboys learn to blow a blade of grass between the thumbs; the sound said to resemble the thin bleat of a fawn
1.190 Double whistle emitting the "voice" of a widgeon (fresh-water duck) and a horn or trumpet to project game calls
1.191 Seal scratchers; used by Eskimos to scratch on ice and cause seals under the ice to think there was "company" overhead; equipped with real seal claws
1.192 Yokuts Indian cage for carrying a decoy pigeon used to lure wild pigeons within reach of capture

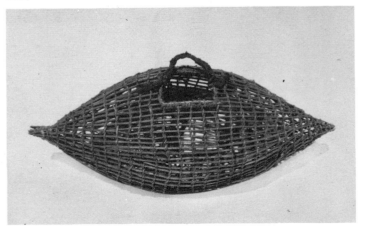

1.192

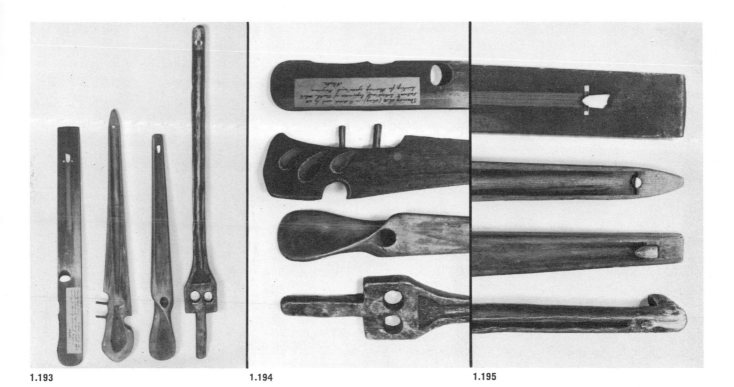

1.193   1.194   1.195

Atlatls, Slings, and Blowguns

1.193 Four styles of atlatls (spear throwers); left, Northwest Coast Indian; center, two styles of Eskimo throwers; right, approximate two-finger form found in prehistoric debris in caves, this specimen, however, obtained while in use by Mexican Indians not far south of the border; remarkable for combination of two atlatl forms, grooved on one side and ungrooved on the other, a hook in each case

1.194 Close-ups of the preceding

1.195 Close-ups showing the Janus nature of the Mexican specimen, right, in (1.193)

1.196 Baked clay spool and grooved artifacts which may have been weights for bolas, central California

1.197 Canalino grooved stone which Dr. David B. Rodgers judged to have been bolas weight

1.198 Lemon-shaped baked-clay objects duplicating the shapes of sling projectiles used in the South Seas; northwestern California

1.196   1.197   1.198

The three kinds of artifacts are treated together because without the original dart, spear, arrow shaft, or knife handle it is commonly impossible to distinguish one from another. The practice is to separate arrows from spearheads at a length between three and four inches, and to name as knives those which by shape or construction (by personal opinion) seem to be unsuited for other use.

This is not an exhaustive coverage of all the different kinds of arrowpoints, spearheads, and knives, but it is hoped that some ways of looking at them coherently are shown.

Bows

Bows had been used in North America for only about a thousand years by 1492, and somewhat less in some localities, although they had been used in Europe since 7000 B.C. It either took the bow a long time to reach Siberia, or it was held up somewhere before crossing Bering Strait. One theory is that moisture conditions were such in the Arctic that the bow became impractical and dropped out of existence before it could penetrate into climates that were more favorable to it. Continued use of the atlatl by Arctic Eskimos bears this out. Another adverse factor in the Arctic was the lack of suitable wood for self bows. Once the bow reached North America, however, it seems to have taken hold rapidly so that before the discovery of the continent its adoption was complete.

Construction of bows divides into three kinds: those of one stave of wood only, called "self bows"; those with the addition of reinforcements, usually sinew strands or strips glued on the wood, or sinew cordage lashed and wrapped around the wood, called "reinforced bows"; and bows made up of parts, characteristically three, called "composite bows."

Composite bows can be dismissed briefly because there were so few such bows made. They were a forced development in the central and eastern Arctic where there were no single pieces of appropriate material large enough to make a bow. They were made now and then with horn ends, in a limited area in the northern Plains and intermountain plateau area. Of the few that were made, only a few survive.

Self bows were used everywhere, even where reinforced bows were made. Cordage reinforcement was characteristic of Eskimo bows, being a solution to the problem of unsuitable bow wood. Sinew backing was used by the Indians on the Pacific slope of the Rockies from British Columbia south and for some distance into the Plains.

Within these three forms were all sorts of sizes and silhouettes which were more easily noted but less easily analyzed. Most of these variations originated in the uses intended and in the materials used. The reasons for some of the details are puzzling, perhaps being no more than a whim or fashion in a tribe. However, the details furnish a key to the origin of certain bows, providing, of course, that the kind of bow made by that tribe is on

record. Here are eight identifying criteria of an Indian or Eskimo bow:

1. Self, reinforced, or composite
2. Curved inward, straight, or curved outward when unstrung
3. Silhouette or pattern of profile
4. Shape of full-face aspect: lens shape, straight, or constricted
5. Shape of cross section at center and between center and end
6. Shape of bowstring notches or manner of cord attachment if not notched
7. Kind of wood or other material used
8. Design of decoration, if any

Uses of letters and figures to represent these attributes could provide a code for identification of a bow when the characteristics of bows made by the same tribe or group are known.

Traps, Snares, and Decoys

Because traps, snares, and decoys involved perishable and sometimes bulky material, few reminders of the extent of these devices remain. Museums commonly pass them by or do not have them when arranging exhibits. The result is a somewhat distorted idea, or none at all, of their role in the pre-Columbian harvesting of game.

Some methods of this practice have left no artifacts at all, such as chasing or stampeding game into water to be speared, or over a cliff to be killed or crippled. Deer and other animals were also commonly herded and stampeded through narrow defiles along which hunters were stationed to take toll as the animals passed.

Akin to these techniques was the placing of traps, nets, nooses, pits, and deadfalls where animals were likely to pass. Creatures as large as elk and deer were taken by means of hidden pits and nooses set vertically between trees or stakes. Similar devices were used to harvest fish; basketry fish traps and scoops were as well known as nets.

Not only the artifacts themselves varied in form from place to place but also the methods of use differed. For example, the Yokuts, Indians of central California, made a carrying cage for a decoy pigeon. This bird was anchored to a shelf on which bait was scattered and next to which a blind was built. The wild birds, attracted and fooled by the presence of the decoy, came to feed within reach of the hidden hunter, who harvested them with the aid of a noose on a stick.

In addition to these visual decoys, there were auditory decoys that lulled or lured birds and animals to their culinary fates.

Atlatls, Slings, and Blowguns

Among the lesser known and used weapons are the atlatl, sling, and blowgun. The atlatl was almost completely obsolete in North America by 1492; the sling was considered by observers to be inconsequential; and the blowgun was limited to a comparatively small area in the South.

Although it had gone out of use in North America nearly altogether, the atlatl was still standard in the arsenals of the Aztec Indians of Mexico from whom it got its name. It is also called a "spear thrower." Its use had preceded that of the bow by a good many centuries. It has been identified as having been in use 20,000 years ago in the Old World, though not so identified for the New World until about 5000 B.C. In the Old World the bow is not identified for a period before 7000 B.C., and it is not evidenced in the New World until about A.D. 500.

Being quite perishable, the prehistoric atlatls of North America have nearly completely vanished. Only a few have been found in dry caves, but they have been in use in Alaska up to the adoption of guns by the Eskimos and have been seen and obtained from Mexican Indians just outside the political boundaries of North America.

One advantage of atlatls over other weapons is leverage. They provide an extra joint to the arm, hence an extra push, just as secondary explosions help our rockets. The range has been estimated at not more than three hundred feet, but would vary with the attributes of the spear or dart thrown and the strength and skill of the thrower. Judging by observation of "modern" Eskimos and Australian natives, spears could be thrown with considerable accuracy by experienced and skillful users of the atlatl.

In view of the obvious factors in the operation of a spear thrower, and, indeed, the ease with which a person could experiment for himself in their use, it is somewhat disconcerting to find the fashionable acceptance of their use in conjunction with all sorts of grooved and pierced objects popularly called "atlatl weights." In actuality, these weights would be hindrances if they

had any effect at all. (Where such "weights" have been found connected with atlatls, analogy would indicate them to be hunting fetishes or charms.)

Slings and sling stones have a less imposing stature in anthropology, although thanks to David and Goliath they are perhaps better known generally than atlatls. The use of slings and sling stones in North America has been reported from practically every area, but always as a minor weapon, mostly used for hunting. Inasmuch as the projectile was commonly an unworked stone and the sling was perishable in the extreme, not many examples survive. About the only case of possible identification for sling projectiles might be lemon-shaped pottery objects of a suitable size for sling use which are found in considerable numbers in northwestern California, where plenty of common sling stones are available. Their similarity to lemon-shaped projectiles used in slings in the South Seas points to similar use in North America, clay being easier to work to the desired shape than stone.

Blowguns, familiar as weapons in the arsenals of South American jungle Indians, apparently found their way across the Caribbean Sea into the South and have been made by Indians of the Southeast up to the present time. The North American blowgun did not use a poisoned dart, so it could have been used for small game only.

Fishing

Fishing, the chief form of harvesting food in the coastal areas, as already noted, involved the gathering of shellfish and the catching of bony fish in both salt and fresh waters. Fishing was also a minor form of harvesting in most other areas where there were streams and lakes.

Text continues on page 43.

Nets and Net Gear
1.199 Two large Yurok dip nets with different sizes of net spacing; foot rule indicates size of these nets
1.200 Model of Eskimo net with floats, weights, and anchor posts

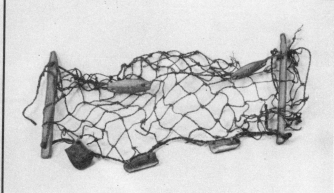

1.199

1.200

1.201

1.202

1.203

1.204

1.205

1.206

1.201 Net or fishline weights of various shapes; stone except bottom Eskimo whalebone weight of "charm stone" type

1.202 Wooden float carved to represent a larger size inflated sealskin float

1.203 Net and fishline weights. The "doughnut stone" was cut off an abandoned net by the finder, but the same form appears in an illustration in an old report on northwestern California Indians

as part of a bolas. The grooved-stone type has been found archaeologically as part of a surf-casting outfit. Both are Yurok.

1.204 Eskimo seal-shaped wooden float, and ivory float-valve necks

1.205 Various forms of stone net (or bolas?) weights from Deschutes River in Oregon

1.206 Typical flat pebble weights with line notches. This is a simple artifact found in various parts of the continent. (Used as bolas weight illustrated in picture of Pomo bolas.)

1.207

1.208

1.209

1.210

1.211

1.212

1.213

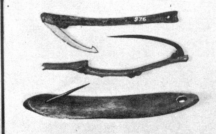

1.214

1.215

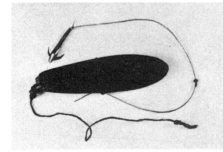

1.216

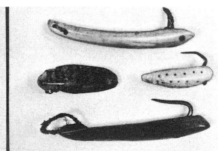

1.217

1.218

Fishhooks

1.207 J-shaped bone hooks; left, north-western California, right, Ohio Valley

1.208 Typical bone hooks from the Eastern Woodland areas

1.209 Bone hooks of somewhat unusual "V" shape from a cache found in Kansas

1.210 Three unusual bone hooks; left, Oregon coast; center, double hook, Arkansas; right, in-curled gorge hook with asphaltum "glue" and line marks on shank, Santa Barbara coast, California

1.211 Four typical copper hooks from Wisconsin

1.212 Four abalone-shell hooks of southern California coast type

1.213 Multipointed hooks, bone shanks, two with bone and two with copper points; largest one figured in E. W. Nelson's report on the Bering Eskimo as a tomcod hook

1.214 Top, composite bone hook, point with barb, Eskimo; center, locust tree twig with thorn, to show use of a natural form as a fishhook; bottom, ivory shank with copper point

1.215 Composite hooks with wooden shanks and bone points, a Nootka Indian style used for offshore salmon fishing

1.216 Fishhook weight and leader and one multibarbed hook and leader of a pair (one hook missing)

1.217 Four fish-effigy lure hooks, three with ivory shanks, one, stone; all with metal points; Eskimo

1.218 Bipointed-pin gorge hooks from central and southern California and (smallest one) from Wisconsin; two on left still have asphaltum "glue" and line marks in centers; top crescentic hook obsidian, two bottom ones shell; Wisconsin specimen copper; the others are bone.

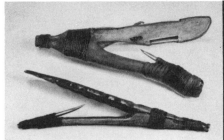
1.219

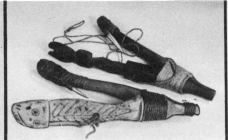
1.220

1.221

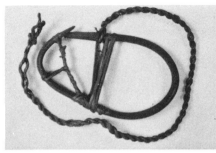
1.222

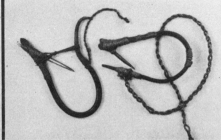
1.223

1.224

1.219 Tlingit-Haida Indian style halibut hooks in the position used. The halibut puts its upper lip over the barb, which holds the bait. The line is attached through a hole in the upper section of the hook. The top specimen is wood, the usual material, the lower of horn, unusual.

1.220 Two hooks of the same type as (1.219) with effigies, the bottom figure a carving of the halibut itself

1.221 Top view of horn hook in (1.219), showing Haida-type design, and (lower) effigy of a tribal "monster"

1.222 Haida-type black cod hook with lashing in place to keep it from opening when not in use

1.223 Kwakiutl-Nootka type halibut hooks in one U-shaped piece with bone barb

1.224 Steps of construction of shell hooks; one half-made bone hook and two abrasive reamers; the bone specimen Eastern Woodland, others southern California

Other Fishing and Hunting Gear

1.225 Bow case and quivers; left, buckskin, containing Plains-type bow; right, rawhide, with Apache-type painted decoration

1.226 A set of Eskimo fletcher's tools, feather setter for arrows, marlin spike and two sinew twisters for bow reinforcements

1.227 Eskimo ivory wristguards

1.228 Northwest Coast wooden quiver of Asiatic type hollowed from halves of a single piece of wood and rejoined, with lid or cap

1.229 Salish (Klikitat) wristguard made of bark

1.230 Southwest Indian (prehistoric) sighting and range-finding device with ornaments and tally marks, some of which may be a measuring scale

1.231 Line reels made of wood and bone, latter from northwestern California; provenience of other unknown

1.232 Set of Eskimo wound plugs. Concerning these, Nelson says they were used in the process of insuring that thin seals would float. Slits were cut in the skin, the blubber loosened with a long curved rod, air blown in through a tube, and the spot then "corked" with a wound plug. With several of these inflated spots a seal would float.

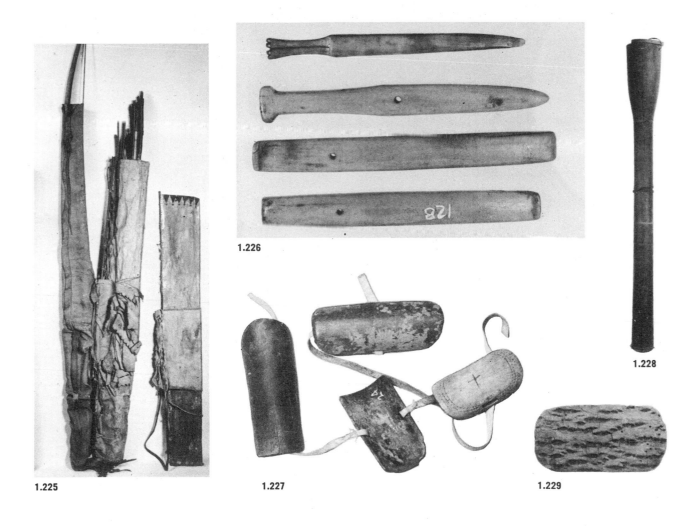

1.225

1.226

1.227

1.228

1.229

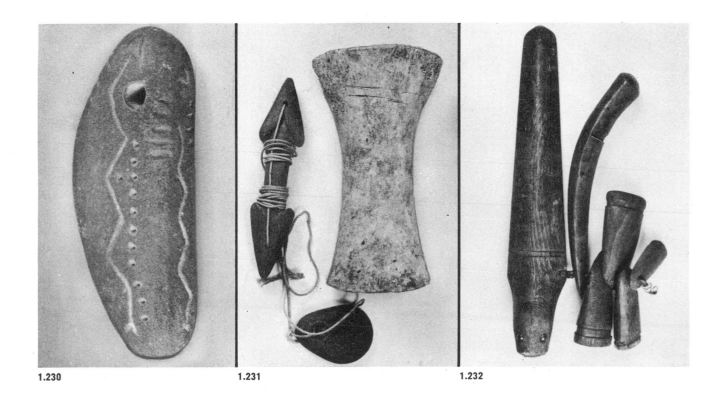

1.230

1.231

1.232

1.233

1.234

1.233 Eskimo tackle box hollowed out of a single billet of wood which has split and been repaired with an ivory patch at one end; the lid was fastened on by winding the thong around the box.

1.234 Northwest Coast Indian bait-and-tackle box constructed with a single piece for the sides, kerfed, bent, and sewed at the single join; the rippled surface of the lid is due to adze blade marks.

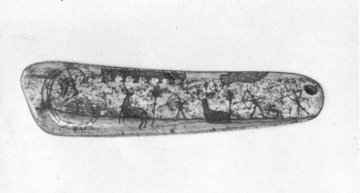

1.235

1.236

1.235 Full-size and toy ice scoops; used by Eskimos to dip out loose ice accumulated in fishing holes or seal holes; a bent bone laced with whale baleen on the full-size implement; spoon-shaped bone on small one

1.236 Eskimo hunting scene etched on a piece of fossil ivory; killing deer with bow, arrow, and spear; and a fenced corral trap with two animals in it

Being a means of subsistence, it was not thought of as a sport—as it is today—but as a business. Even in this, however, the Indian and Eskimo attitude differed from the present-day attitude. Whereas commercial fishermen have to be restrained from depleting natural resources and their sole aim is to make money by selling, the Indians and Eskimos took only what they needed for their own food supply, and occasionally for barter, leaving the rest to multiply under natural controls. Hence, there was no depletion of natural resources until the European conquest, when subsequent looting almost eliminated some species from many streams and even coastal waters.

Indians and Eskimos did not limit their methods of harvesting the fish from artificial ideas of sport or by necessary regulations of a police nature. They chose whatever means was easiest and surest to get the kinds of fish they were trying to catch.

Two methods that may seem odd to us left no traces in the form of artifacts. One was to catch fish with the hands; the other was to use narcotics. The former is not unknown to the Old World, being called "tickling" by the English. It involved what might be called stalking the fish as they rested in the water concealed under a ledge or rock, and gently easing the hands around (tickling) them until they were in position to catch and lift the fish from the water. The other method involved mashing the juices out of soapweed, turkey mullen, buckeye, or other plants with properties narcotic to fish, then dumping the juices into a suitable fish pool. In due time, the occupants would float to the surface, open to the fisherman's selection. The rejects recovered, left for another day.

Another popular method of fishing was to construct stone or wood fish weirs, mazes, or ponds. By building little stone-walled corrals with narrow entrances, the Indians could leave the fish to find their way in and be harvested with dip nets or the hands when they were due for the larder. Similarly, corrals were constructed of basketry fences—wicker woven on stakes—and dams were erected to hamper migratory fish. As mementos of these, we have found stone hand mauls that were used to pound the stakes.

The use of nets was nearly universal, as hosts of net weights and a few surviving nets themselves testify. These nets were of all forms and sizes; dip nets, casting nets, seines, and gill nets—merging into basketry nets and traps. Both Indians and Eskimos were expert net weavers, using many of the tools and techniques used by fishermen of the Old World. The operation of dip netting with large and heavy dip nets created one of the few instances of individual property rights. It was possible for individuals to own the sites of perches from which good dip fishing could be carried on. On the tribal level such rights were recognized only recently by the United States government in compensating Columbia River Indians for the submergence of their famous perches at Celilo Falls between Oregon and Washington.

Spearing and harpooning were other much-used methods, especially for larger fish that swam near the surface and to a lesser degree, shooting with bows and arrows. Archaeologically, it is sometimes uncertain as to how to identify an artifact as a barbed spear, arrow, or dart point, because if it were used with a line and fastened detachably, it would be a harpoon tip, but if it were not so used, it would be a spear. The Indians of central California, for instance, sometimes constructed little huts or blinds over a small stream and speared fish as they swam in the water below; some barbed points were for fish spears when so used. However, the same kind of points often have grooves or knobs for line attachment, which indicate harpoon use.

Finally we come to the method most familiar to us, or at least most popular: fishing with hook and line. Generally speaking, this method was used by Indians and Eskimos only when the other easier methods wouldn't work. Consequently, it is possible to find a great deal of fish garbage in an aboriginal site and yet find no fishhooks.

Where and when used, however, the pre-Columbian fishhooks were efficient, especially with the abundance of fish available. The fishhooks were of two types: the familiar J- or V-shaped hooks and the gorge hooks. The latter are unfamiliar to us. They were simply hooks intended to be swallowed so as to stick in the gorge or interior of the fish.

Gorge hooks, in turn, were of two kinds: bipointed pins with a line attached to the center, that turned and caught in the gorge or stomach of the fish, and a specialized kind of pin found on the southern California coast (and used by fishermen in the Orient) that resembles a conventional hook but has the point curled in far enough to prevent its catching in the fish at all. In the latter, the point is really for impaling the bait, not the fish, and the hook, again, operates on the gorge principle. Experiments indicate that the latter hooks were the only means, or at least the best, for catching desirable fish that swam rather deep in fast waters.

Conventional hooks seem mostly to have been shaped as "U's" for one-piece hooks and as "V's" for composite hooks. Once in a while they were barbed—the barb occasionally being on the outer side of the point—but generally they operated on the bent-pin principle. Among the larger of these hooks was a special type, again unfamiliar to us, developed by the Northwest Coast Indians for catching big, bottom-feeding halibut. These were in both "V" and "U" shapes, but the line, instead of being attached to the end of the shank, was attached in the middle, causing the hooks to hang in what would look to us a sidewise fashion. The pictures show their nature more clearly.

Hunting and Fishing Accessories

Besides the actual devices and weapons for fishing and hunting, Indians and Eskimos found a number of accessories necessary, including boxes and bags to carry bait, tackle, spare parts, tools, etc. Eskimo archers found special tools essential to keep the rigging on their bows tight, and both Indians and Eskimos used wrist guards to protect their wrists from the whip of the bowstring. When not in use, bows and arrows were commonly carried in quivers and bow cases, usually made of buckskin or rawhide.

Pre-Columbian Zuñi archers, and perhaps some others, discovered or copied sighting devices to determine range. Eskimo hunters of marine mammals used a lance into whose socketed pole-handle successive points could be inserted, and, as mentioned earlier, they made bags to carry such points. Doubtless many other specialized and/or localized accessories were invented because of necessity or convenience.

Preparing Food

Indian and Eskimo kitchens were largely of the picnic and barbecue type, but there were plenty of culinary utensils to choose from, and most of the foods gathered, hunted, fished, or grown underwent some alterations before arriving in the diner's mouth.

One tribe alone, the Kwakiutls, has furnished one hundred and fifty recipes for record. More than a thousand species of plants and nearly as many of animals (fish, birds, reptiles, insects, and shellfish) were consumed by one tribe or another over all of North America. While some were eaten raw, others were the subjects of several recipes. A complete aboriginal cookbook for North America would be a sizable volume indeed.

Two generalized processes were involved in food preparation, each requiring its own techniques and adjuncts. The first dealt with getting food into a form so that it could be cooked, the second process covered the actual cooking of it.

The best-known representatives of food-preparing utensils are pestles and mortars. Anyone at all acquainted with Indian artifacts is bound to be familiar with this pair and their use in grinding and pounding seeds, corn, dried fish, and so on. Somewhat less known, but older in time of use, are manos and metates; the mano being a hand stone used to rub and grind, and the metate a flat stone on which the grinding was done. Their Spanish names come from their major use in once-Spanish territories. Two other food pounders were handled hammers—often called "pemmican pounders" and standard among the buffalo Indians—and blubber pounders, used in the Arctic. The Eskimos also used a shallow wooden bowl and a short pestle to mash certain foods. The pestle had a rounded face exactly like that of the South Sea Island poi pounders.

Wood was used for both pestles and mortars in many areas to a much greater extent than surviving specimens seem to indicate. It was quite popular among the Eastern Indians and was used jointly with stone in most areas where pestle-and-mortar mills were in use.

The double-ended pestle in a mortar hollowed in the end of a log, sometimes seen in illustrations of Algonkian villages, is quite a remarkable artifact combination inasmuch as it is duplicated in general use in far-distant places in Asia and as far away as Africa. This fact has created quite a bone of contention between the enthusiasts of the diffusion and the separate-invention schools of thought.

Combinations of stone pestles with wooden mortars are indicated in California, where the former are found worn to a pointed face rather than a rounded face. A still more unusual California combination was a basketry hopper on a stone slab or in a bowl to replace the mortar.

Manos are commonly the shape of a cake of soap, but they do assume other forms, including two-handed examples. Metates are either suitable flat stones, usually oval in shape with depressions worn by rubbing, or they are grooved or troughed. The latter are more common in the Southwest than elsewhere. Big, oval boulder metates and soap-shaped manos coated with lime deposits from shell-saturated debris are the more conspicuous characteristics of the forms used by the ancient Oak Grove peoples of southern California. Basketry top and bowl mortars appear in more recent deposits.

Other artifacts, though less known because perishable and gone, are the bark, wood, and basketry mixing bowls, jars, colanders, trays, sifters, winnowers, and strainers needed for other forms of food preparation. Some of these are among the pottery artifacts so numerous in the East and Southwest.

Better known are knives, though less often thought of as kitchen utensils. The role of knives in cutting up game and fish is obvious. Meal brushes, meat hooks, and some other special tools were used by a limited number of tribes.

When it came to cooking, the Eskimos and Indians used the boiling method all over the continent, and Indians and Eskimos living within reach of wood used all the other methods to varying degrees. Boiling was done in two ways: directly over a fire, as is familiar to us; and with the use of hot stones dumped in the liquid and fished out until the stew, soup, or mush boiled.

Strange as stone boiling seems to us, it may have been the original method of cooking, aside from direct exposure of meat, fish, and vegetables to fire. Direct fire boiling came later with the discovery of pottery. The latter method is between three and five thousand years old in North America and the dates of its use here coincide roughly with those of the pottery-making areas. Stone boiling, however, did not die out completely in the areas that turned to boiling in pottery receptacles and stone pots over flame but was used on occasion. The two sometimes competed on the Plains and in the Great Basin.

Text continues on page 49.

44

1.237   1.238   1.239

1.240   1.241   1.242

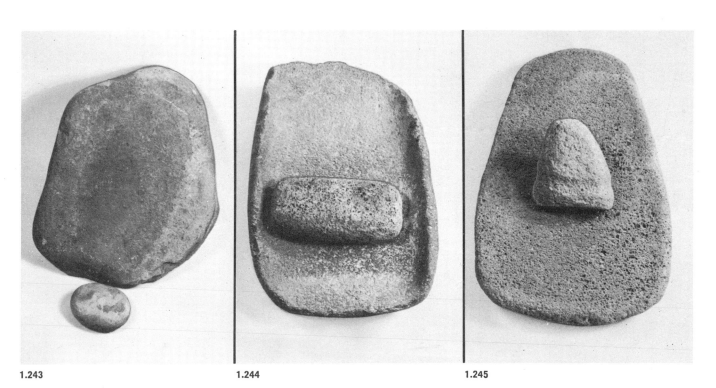

1.243   1.244   1.245

Manos and Metates

1.237-1.239 Three kinds of manos: (1.237) round, sometimes used in pairs; (1.238) oval; and (1.239) long, two-handed, upper used as both pestle and mano stone by northeastern California Indians; lower, a common form of rectangular mano used by Hohokam Indians of Arizona, both made of lava

1.240 Hoof-shaped mano, left, from Ohio Valley; others, northeastern California

1.241 Handled mullers, left from Arizona; right, Ohio Valley

1.242 Two-handled or "horned" mullers peculiar to northeastern California Indians and generally associated with grinding wokas seeds

1.243 Very old mano and metate "mill" from an Oak Grove site in southern California, mano coated with a heavy deposit of lime. Some of the Oak Grove manos are so old as to be partially disintegrated.

1.244 Troughed metate and rectangular mano from the Hohokam area in Arizona

1.245 Wokas-grinding outfit from northeastern California, both parts made of lava, mano hoof shaped with finger-grip groove

1.246

1.247

1.248

1.249

1.250

1.251

1.252

1.253

Pestles and Mortars

1.246 Three typical pestles and mortars of medium size

1.247 Four small mortars, size shown by ruler, possibly used to grind tobacco or pigments for paint

1.248 Three medium-size mortars made of sandstone and lava

1.249 Three tub-shaped mortars, left from central California, others, southern California

1.250 Mortar with bottom pointed to rest in sandy ground, decorated border

1.251-1.253 Large-size mortars: (1.251) Chumash Indian style, sandstone; (1.252) lava mortar, northeastern California; (1.253) boulder mortar, California

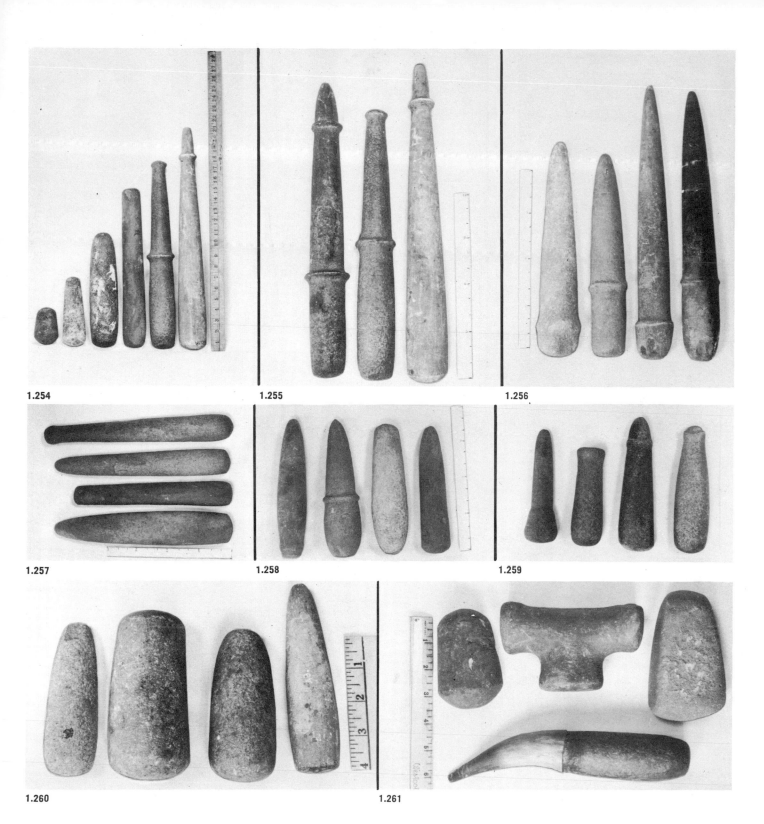

1.254 Various lengths of pestles: (a) smallest, 3 inches, and (b), southern California Canalino; (c) central California; (d) Alameda County, California; (e) northwestern California; (f) the longest, 21½ inches, southern California Canalino
1.255 Extra-long pestle, perhaps ceremonial, double-ringed Yurok, shown with two from (1.254)
1.256 Medium-size pestles, northwestern California
1.257 Four medium-length pestles (**average 15 inches**)

1.258 Four medium-length pestles (average 10 inches)
1.259 Small pestles (average 6 inches): (a) Pomo, (b) central California; (c) and (d) San Nicolas Island, southern California
1.260 Four short pestles (4 to 5 inches)
1.261 Four unusual pestles: upper, Canalino from southern California, Northwest Coast bar top, and mano-pestle, Canalino; lower, Yakima Indian, horn extension

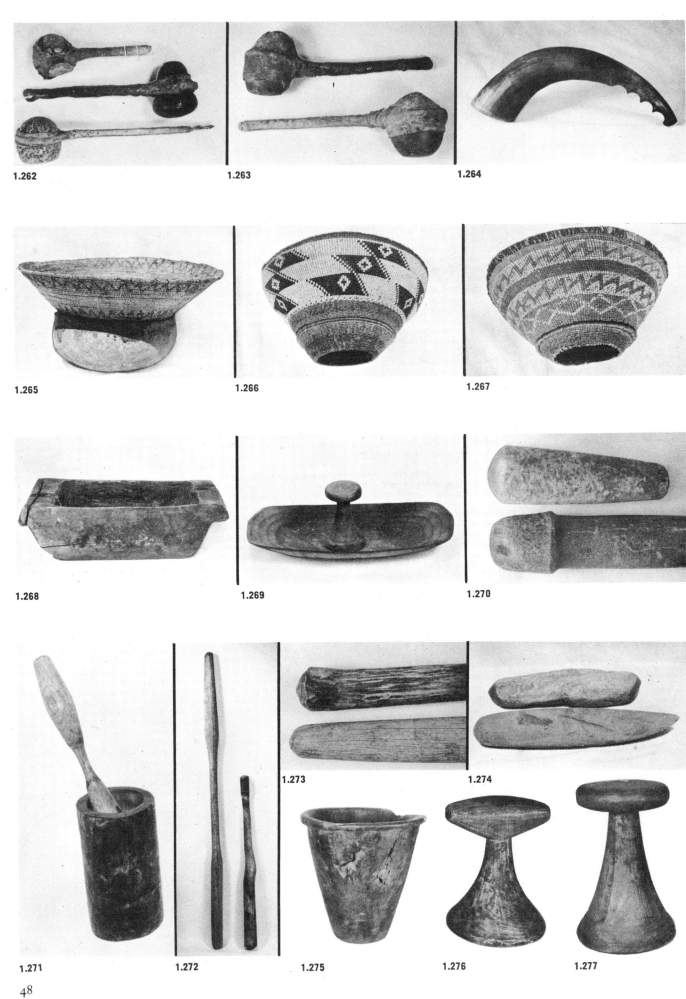

1.262

1.263

1.264

1.265

1.266

1.267

1.268

1.269

1.270

1.271

1.272

1.273

1.274

1.275

1.276

1.277

48

Food Hammers and "Mills"

1.262 Three Plains Indian food hammers with stone heads. Bottom one from the Cannon Ball Reservation still carries skins and stains from choke cherries.

1.263 Typical Plains Indian stone-headed utility mauls

1.264 Copper River Eskimo blubber pounder made of musk ox horn

1.265 Central California mortar hopper glued to bowl-type mortar

1.266 Northwestern California mortar hopper

1.267 Northwestern California style hopper

1.268 Wooden mortar cut in side of a billet of wood, Chippewa

1.269 Eskimo wooden food tray and pestle

1.270 Contrast pestles: upper, for bowl mortar; lower, for slab mortar, rounding face and chipped face, respectively

1.271 Typical Algonkin-style double end (dumbbell) pestle and end-of-log mortar

1.272 Long double end dumbbell-type pestle and single end pestle

1.273 Upper, pounding ends of wooden pestle in (1.272)

1.274 Central California stone pestles showing pointed ends from use in wooden mortars

1.275 Wooden (burl) mortar from middle Columbia River area

1.276-1.277 Two Eskimo wooden pestles (similar in form and rounded face to South Sea Island poi pounders)

As seen in the illustrations, the receptacles for stone boiling were various indeed. Even the styles of weave for cooking baskets differed from area to area on the Pacific Coast. Those used for direct fire boiling were pottery and, to lesser extent, stone.

Another style of cooking that left no definite artifacts except miscellaneous fire-tortured rocks was baking in an earth oven. This sort of oven, except in the Southwest, was simply a hole in the ground into which leaf-wrapped food and hot stones were placed and covered up with dirt—a device rediscovered in recent times as "a fireless cooker," and also a method introduced to lei-draped tourists in Hawaii.

Yet another method was roasting or broiling by direct exposure of the food to flame, familiar to all small boys and their friends as "weenie-roasting on a

Culinary Utensils

1.278 Yokuts Indian basketry sifter

1.279 Meal brushes of various forms of construction

1.280 Menomini Indian sugar sap strainer

1.281 Northwest California oil or grease strainer

1.282 Yokuts Indian parching and winnowing tray

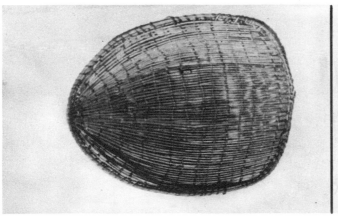

1.278

1.279

1.280

1.281

1.282

1.283

1.284

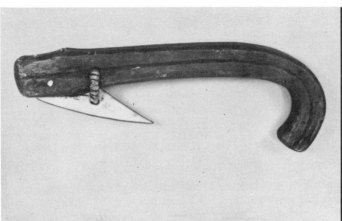

1.285

1.286

1.283 Northern California woven apaw huller, (rough, grater surface)
1.284 So-called "nutcracker stones," left, Ohio, others, central California (identity theoretical)
1.285 Eskimo meathook for handling slippery meat
1.286 Same, the upper hook for attachment to a pole handle

stick." Simple and easy as this system appears, it was manipulated by the Indians to produce a variety of very tasty results.

A number of aids accompanied cooking. Looped tongs served to lift out and deposit stones in liquids, and mush paddles stirred the foods. Sometimes it takes the burned spots on such paddles and on the insides of baskets to convince skeptical housewives that their Indian sisters really did a job with such an odd combination. Another utensil was allied to stone and pottery cooking vessels. This was a stone "frying pan," usually made of a flat or shallow piece of steatite (soapstone). Wooden skewers and a frame were, of course, adjuncts to roasting, but they are not commonly preserved as artifacts.

Manos and Metates

Manos are the hand stones and metates the slabs used together by Indians as grinding mills, largely in the corn-growing and seed-gathering areas. Older in use than pestles and mortars, they have, nevertheless, continued in use into modern times. Metates are, or have been until recently, for sale in stores catering to customers of Mexican extraction. Manos are one-handed and two-handed; are round and oval biscuit shapes; are bar or rectangular in two-handed sizes; are hoof-shaped; and occasionally have one or two handles. Metates are round, oval, and rectangular; are of thick or thin slabs; have shallow or deep depressions, which commonly take the form of troughs in the Southwest. Sometimes they have legs or supporting ridges.

Pestles and Mortars

Pestles and mortars were used to break up and mash as well as to grind. They were made of stone and wood and, in the case of mortars, were sometimes equipped with basketry or rawhide sides or hoppers, under which stone slabs were placed. Portable stone mortars hollowed out of boulders and bar or roller pestles are the most familiar combination found at sites, but both Indians and Eskimos often used wood. They developed numerous variations in both stone and wood. Mortar holes were also pecked and worn into rock outcroppings and large boulders. So-called "bell pestles" were hand mauls, at least in the West, and chips from the edges and cups in the faces indicate they were also so used in the East, although they could have been used as handled manos or mullers.

Cooking Pots

1.287 Much-used thin-walled Tlingit Indian (Alaska) basketry "pot." These are bolstered with earth or sand around them when in use, the colored bands of false embroidery are almost worn out.

1.288 Old Salish imbricated coil-woven "pot"

1.289 Salish wooden "pot," sides of one piece, kerfed, steamed, and bent; sewed at open corner

1.290 Northwestern California cooking basket; stone burns on interior

1.291 Central California cooking bowl

1.292 Yokuts Indian, central California, pottery pot

1.293 Large, perhaps ceremonial, Canalino Indian sandstone bowl, rim grooved for decoration with glued-on shell beads

1.294 Canalino olla-type cooking pots, soot-crusted bottoms

1.295 Diegueno (southern California desert Indian) pot

1.287

1.288

1.289

1.290

1.291

1.292

1.293

1.294

1.295

1.296

1.297

1.298

1.299

1.300

1.301

1.296 Hohokam (Arizona) olla-type pot, showing crack with holes bored for mending

1.297 Hohokam cooking jar and bowl, bowl of so-called "flame ware"

1.298 Southwest corrugated coil-constructed pot. This is an old form continued because of heat surface advantages in cooking.

1.299 Eastern Woodland area prehistoric cooking pot with lugs, Missouri

1.300 Northwoods Indian birch-bark pots; one on left with etched decoration

1.301 Eastern Eskimo steatite cooking and melting pot, holes for suspension, base soot caked

Other Cooking Utensils

1.302-1.303 Various mush paddles for stirring soups, mushes, and other liquids in basketry bowls, mostly from northwestern California

1.304 Loop tongs to extract stones from receptacles after their heat had been radiated

1.305 Ornamental steatite bowl, north-western California, carved in shape of the river canoes used in the area

1.306 Canalino steatite cooking "pans" with holes for pulling off fire

1.307-1.308 Two northern California steatite cooking or melting utensils of the type called "grease dishes," a form of dish common to the whole Northwest Coast culture belt. Steatite, or, as it is more commonly known, soapstone, is heat resistant.

Pestles and mortars,
made of stone or wood, were used to break up and mash
as well as to grind.

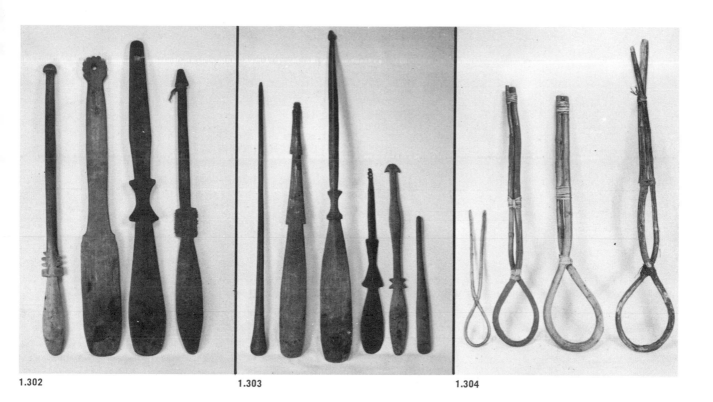

1.302   1.303   1.304

1.305   1.306

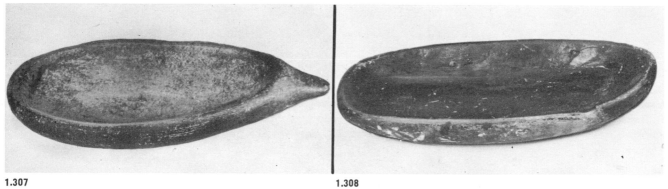

1.307   1.308

Food Hammers and Wooden Mills

Hammers called "pemmican pounders" were constant companions of Plains Indian cooks and housekeepers. As blubber pounders (to break up the fat pockets) they were likewise companions of Eskimo housewives. Of course, they could also have been used to pound or club things other than choke cherries and blubber—pegs, bones, and squirming fish, for example.

As already noted, mills made entirely of wood, or with one part wood and the other stone, or with addition of hoppers, were also widely used.

Culinary Utensils

Besides pounding and grinding, food needed other operations. One of these was simply cutting up with knives. Knives have been allotted to the section on tools, although it could be that they were used more by cooks than by craftsmen and warriors. Other utensils were used for sifting, straining, winnowing, and draining and were made mostly of pottery or basketry. Meal had to be brushed up or off; meat had to be handled; nuts and seeds had to be hulled; and so on. All these operations involved suitable utensils. Also in general use were numerous receptacles, particularly bowls and trays, many of which were lovingly decorated and today are regarded as objects of art rather than kitchen utensils.

Cooking Pots

The chief cooking pots were those used for boiling, although it must be kept in mind that other modes of applying heat existed but left few, if any, special artifacts behind. Boiling was accomplished by direct exposure of the receptacle to flame or by dropping hot stones into liquids. The former was possible only with pottery and stone pots; the latter could be used with basketry, bark, and wood, and was sometimes resorted to with the pottery and stone utensils from need or whim. Both methods were used by Indians and Eskimos, pottery favoring direct flame in the East and Southwest, basketry being used on the Pacific slope, and bark in the Northwoods area.

Other Cooking Utensils

Indians used sticks and paddles to stir the food and to keep the hot stones from too much concentration of heat. Burns on the faces of paddles attest to the fact that the stones were really hot. On the Northwest Coast, fish oils and greases were delicacies and could be served warm in steatite "grease dishes." Southern California Indians baked or fried on stone pans with holes for retrieving from fire. Southwest Indians made ovens, and other Indians dug holes and steamed or heat-cooked buried food. Skewers and racks were used for broiling.

Serving

The pre-Columbians' approach to eating was direct —when food was ready the hungry ones gathered and ate it. Perhaps this was varied by waiting for the "Mr. Bigs" to have first choice, if there was any point to it, and a few children, slaves, and prisoners might have had to wait their turns, if any. In the Arctic, the hunter was always Mr. Big, not for social reasons so much as because if he were not in good shape everybody else would suffer. On occasion, there were formal feasts and ceremonies involving food—potlatches and weddings, for example.

The artifacts used for eating varied from a minimum among the poor nomadic intermountain desert Indians to a maximum among the wealthy Northwest Coast Indians. For certain foods, especially liquids, bowls were necessary to serve and to eat from, so they might be termed the basic eating utensils. The bowls, as well as trays, saucers, cups, bottles, ladles, mugs, spoons, and jars, all might be more or less ornamented.

Food Receptacles
1.309 Northwest Coast carved wooden food bowl of box construction, sides sewed at one corner, kerfed and bent at others
1.310 Prehistoric Zuñi-type pottery bowl, New Mexico
1.311 Kwakiutl-type (canoe-shaped) dugout wooden food bowl or "grease dish," edges ornamented with brass-headed tacks

1.309   1.310   1.311

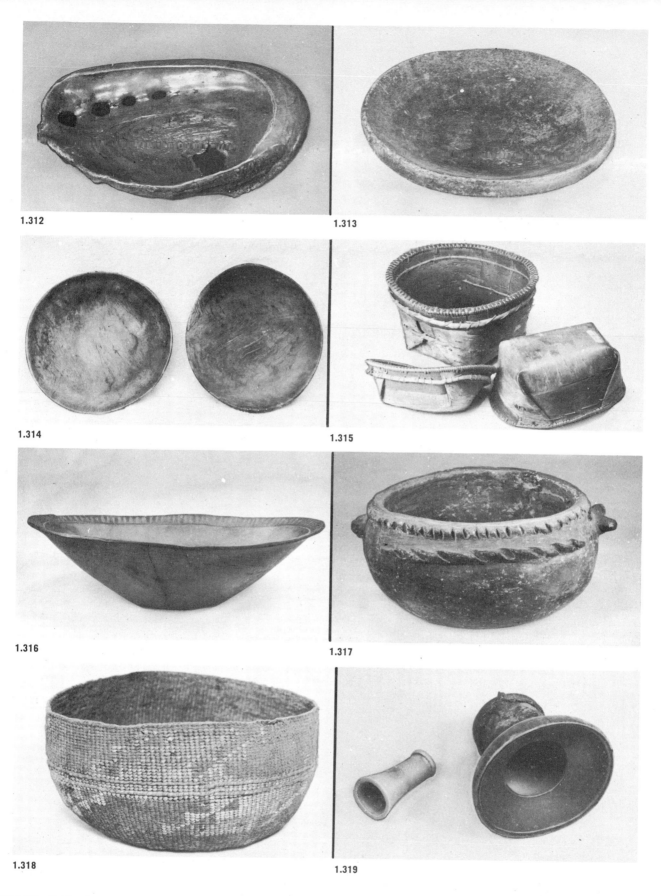

1.312

1.313

1.314

1.315

1.316

1.317

1.318

1.319

1.312-1.313 California south coast Indian dishes: (1.312) abalone shell with holes stopped up with asphaltum; (1.313) steatite with evidence of heating, line dug out around outside of rim for shell beads set in asphaltum

1.314 Plains Indian wooden dishes made of burl-like wood

1.315 Birch-bark bowls made by Northern Woodland Indians; folded, reinforced and sewed

1.316 Northwest Coast mountain sheep horn bowl with ornamented rim

1.317 Prehistoric "Mound Builder" bowl, Missouri; fish form

1.318 Northwest California Indian mush bowl, commonly used for native acorn porridge

1.319 Eskimo ivory bottle necks; fitted and lashed to bladder-skin bottles

1.320

1.321

1.322

1.323

1.324

1.325

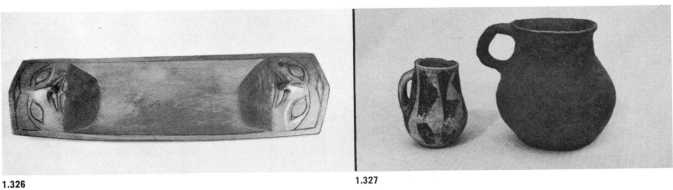

1.326

1.327

1.328

1.329

1.330

1.320 Arkansas black pottery bottle, incised decoration in the curving and curling fashion of the Eastern Woodland Indians (as contrasted to the angular geometrical designs fancied by Western Indians)

1.321 Navajo wedding basket with "spirit break" in the design

1.322 Pima basket with four-part radial design

1.323 Mimbres bowl, much worn by use, with typical precisely drawn lines and checkers

1.324 Hopi-type coiled basketry plaque, typical thick coils

1.325 Southwest coiled basket with area rather than tribal design; Pima, Havasupi, Apache? Note resemblance of checker-work in this basket and in the bowl in (1.323).

1.326 Northwest Coast wooden food tray with conventionalized hawk heads carved at ends

1.327 Southwest pitchers; thick-walled black on white and thin-walled corrugated red construction and design

1.328 Saucers made of horn, pottery, wood, and stone; Plains, Southwest, Eskimo, and California

1.329 Carved and painted box-construction wooden food bowl, Haida design

1.330 Prehistoric southern California cave find basketry and asphaltum bowl; upper part finely coiled basketry hopper, with coarsely woven bottom added

Spoons and Ladles

1.331 Shell and stone spoons; upper left, California, lower, Kentucky; two on right, Ohio Valley

1.332 Yurok-Hupa type carved elkhorn spoons for formal occasions

1.333 Eskimo ivory and wood spoons with painted and carved figures and designs

1.334 Yurok-Hupa carved wood and elk-horn spoons and a mussel shell spoon called a "woman's spoon"

1.331

1.332

1.333

1.334

Food Receptacles

Bowls for eating were often the same as those in which the cooking was done, the diners dipping out their mouthfuls by using their fingers as utensils. Much auxiliary use was made of natural objects, such as sheets of bark, vegetable shells, seashells, and leaves. Pottery makers and basketmakers could, of course, follow their notions in the matter of sizes and shapes. Ornamentation was usual, and many works of art (by today's standards) were just food receptacles.

Spoons and Ladles

The use of spoons and ladles was widespread among both Indians and Eskimos. Materials were mostly horn

1.335 Southwest pottery; black on white scoop, and red on buff Hohokam scoop; and black on white short-handled spoon
1.336 Eastern Woodland Indian hook handle wooden spoons; right one old Sauk-Fox, with dovetailed mend in bowl
1.337 Horn spoons, Yurok and Arctic Eskimo
1.338 Wooden spoons, Northwest Coast and Eskimo, with worn painted designs in bowls
1.339 Northwest Coast black horn spoons with totemic figures on handles

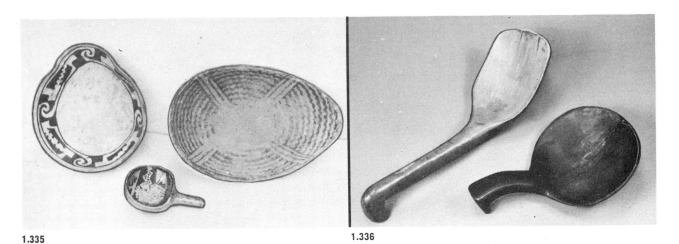

1.335

1.336

1.337

1.338

1.339

1.340 Paddle-like Northwest Coast berry spoons, right one with carved design on bowl
1.341 Wood and horn Northwest Coast spoons
1.342 Northwest Coast spoon with totemic carved handle and translucent bowl
1.343 Plains Indian horn spoons
1.344 Plains, left, and Northwest Coast horn spoons, latter with abalone-shell insets in handle
1.345 Braided quillwork and dangler decorated horn spoon (labeled Arapaho)

and wood, plus bone, ivory, shell, pottery, and bark; again with varying degrees of aesthetic manifestations. Horns, already partially shaped, could be rather easily worked further by heating and steaming, so they were chosen for spoons and ladles all over the continent— some of them meriting the title of "the great horn spoon." The potters among the Southwest Indians turned out various sizes of spoons, dippers, and ladles, with painted designs as a rule. Although some of these dining utensils look like their European counterparts, others among them are in distinctly Indian and Eskimo forms because of adaptation to use or to tribal fancy.

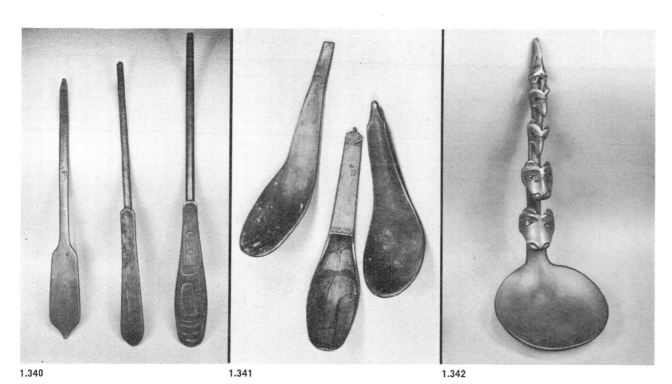

1.340   1.341   1.342

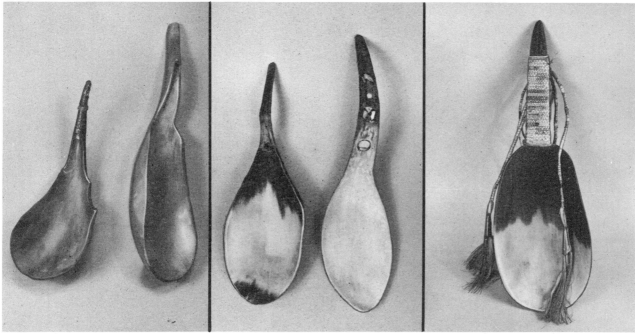

1.343   1.344   1.345

1.346 Wooden ladle, Olympic Peninsula Salish with effigy handle
1.347 Southwest pottery ladle with prehistoric Hopi-type design in red and black on light red
1.348 Shell inlaid and carved wooden Northwest Coast feast ladle
1.349 Eskimo whale baleen dipper
1.350-1.351 Large Eskimo and Nez Percé Indian ladles, apparently mountain sheep horn

Storage Receptacles
1.352 Pomo Indian storage basket
1.353 Pitt River (N.E. Calif.) Indian storage basket with typical black on white design of area
1.354 Yurok-Hupa storage basket with so-called "worm design"

Storage Receptacles

Overpopulation was a constant threat to most pre-Columbians in spite of the sparse population as compared to today and in spite of the teeming bounty of natural resources. This threat was due to shifts in climate which could cause cycles of plenty to be followed by cycles of famine; to liability to raids from hungry and, therefore, desperate and probably warlike neighbors; and to limitation of storage facilities. This is not to say that starvation was a universal danger frequently experienced, but that it was far more of a reality than it is in today's North America.

But the pre-Columbians were not helpless nor shiftless in the face of this discipline of nature. The Eskimos were well acquainted with frozen-food lockers before modern food purveyors "discovered" them. They also worked out schedules of who should die first if starvation came, and did it much more efficiently than we are working out preparation for the threat of atom bombs.

Both Eskimos and Indians built practical structures for storage of food out of reach of natural predators and pests. Coops atop stilts are familiar in native pictures of Eskimo villages, and it is said that the ubiquitous corncrib of eastern farmyards is a direct copy of Indian storage bins in Indian farmyards in the same areas.

1.352   1.353   1.354

1.355   1.356   1.357

1.358   1.359   1.360

Akin to these structures, but less permanent, were racks for drying, and dried, meat and fish that graced and scented the interiors and environs of Northwest Indian houses, Plains Indian tipis, and Eskimo igloos. Such structures are not customarily regarded as artifacts, and as they were quite perishable after desertion, they do not appear prominently in museums. Smaller storage receptacles, on the other hand, do survive as fairly common artifacts: boxes, baskets, jars, pans, and bottles, many of which were much larger than is commonly envisioned. The Pomos, for example, made some storage baskets large enough for adults to stand in, and the Apaches wove jars as large as small barrels.

1.355 Eskimo bucket, wood sheet sides, overlapped and sewed
1.356 Eastern pottery bottles, owl shape and long necked with pottery cap
1.357 Apache storage jar with typical Apache line-and-figure decoration
1.358 Eskimo fat-storage pan, overlapping wood sheet sides, crack in bottom sewed shut
1.359 Eskimo coiled basketry storage basket
1.360 Chippewa birch-bark sugar box, grass bundle sewed edges, and punch dent marks in floral design

2 Homes and Housekeeping

The First Americans had three versions of homes. One centered about a fixed dwelling in a fixed spot, as most of us understand home today. Another was a portable dwelling to be erected as home wherever a camp was established. The third was simply the family unit which moved from place to place and constructed a temporary dwelling in each place.

The oldest kinds of homes were the shelters and dens made by the first wanderers from Asia. Remnants of these are found in caves, in rock overhangs, and occasionally in spots exposed by weathering or excavation. Such homes are typically identified by remains of domestic fires which archaeologists call "hearths" and which have relics of ancient housekeeping scattered about them.

Those who continued nomadic life up to the European conquest had homes which were little, if any, improved from the ancient homes. Their shelters and dens were barely adequate to keep them alive through hostile weather. Also, their housekeeping gear was no more than could be easily carried or picked up around a camp site. The Plains Indians were the exception. Their adaptation of the travois and portable tent covering (after they had horses) gave them a quite comfortable home most of the year.

Many other Indians also constructed temporary homes, but they were what is called "seminomadic." That is, they lived in a permanent village during bad weather and went "on tour" in good weather, at which times they constructed temporary homes, usually based on frames covered with bark, hide, thatch, brush, or matting. Still other Indians did not roam about a great deal but did construct what might be considered temporary houses, in that they had to be repaired or rebuilt at rather short intervals. Most of the Eastern Woodland Indians and a good part of the southerly Western Indians lived in such dwellings.

In the East, the homes typically took the form of what has come to be called a "long house." This was a rectangular frame structure, relatively narrow and long, with a rounded roof, and the whole covered by sheets of bark. The houses of the Southeastern Woodland Indians were of a similar shape, though less known today. They had a gable roof, thatching, and mud-plastered wattle sides.

The typical form farther west was a hut made with a circle of poles bent over to join at a summit and then filled in, basketry fashion, with some sort of woofing finished off with thatching.

More permanent but still crude were earth-covered lodges, igloos, and huts constructed generally to combat severe weather. The permanent dwellings of the Eskimos were of this type, with timber or bone frames and tunnel entrances. In summer, the Eskimos put up conical tents with skin covering. The central and eastern Eskimos reversed the process and put up winter hunting structures of blocks of snow, which of course melted in summer. Indians dwelling in semipermanent villages along the banks of the more southerly tributaries of the Mississippi well out into the plains built large earth lodges over heavy frames. The ill-fated Mandans were typical users of such homes. Smaller huts on log frames constitute the earth hogans of the Navajos, which are still in use in the Southwest.

Proceeding to what we would call permanent homes, we come to the big plank houses of the Northwest Coast Indians. These were constructed of heavy frames sometimes including big logs, sheathed and roofed with planks generally split from cedar on the north Pacific Coast and of redwood in northwestern California. The largest of these houses were most impressive, being as much as a hundred feet long, and in the Alaskan and British Columbian villages, ornamented with paintings and totem poles. The entrances to these homes, including those of California in pre-Columbian times, or at least in the early days after European contact, were oval holes, called by the white pioneers "woodpecker holes." Sometimes such a hole was cut through the lower part of a totem pole.

Still more permanent, so permanent in fact that a few have been lived in since well before 1492, are the pueblos of the Southwest and the other masonry and adobe structures of that area, including the spectacular cliff dwellings. As is familiar to everyone, some of these constitute or used to constitute veritable apartment houses of several stories and many rooms. Their walls are as permanent as masonry or adobe can be, but roofs were made of wooden beams covered with a thatch of brush and earth that eventually collapsed after the structure was abandoned. The Southwest has many ruins of such structures and of smaller individual dwellings of similar construction.

None of these homes, from the simplest brush shelter to the big plank house and the masonry pueblo, was without its accompanying household artifacts. These were augmented by kitchen utensils, personal effects, and other tribal and individual possessions. However, the number of such artifacts that could be termed furniture or strictly housekeeping adjuncts was small. There were practically none in the poor desert Indian homes and they were limited even in the pueblos and plank houses. There were no tables and chairs as we know them, for example, although there were beds and benches which often were built in rather than separate. Fireplaces and chimneys were absent except in a rudimentary form in the Southwest, which meant that odor and often the presence of smoke were a bad feature of the pre-Columbian home, except, of course, in the Arctic, where there was no wood to burn.

Fire in the pre-Columbian open hearths and in the Eskimo oil stoves was vital to life itself, both for heating the home and for cooking. To make sure of it, every household kept or carried means of making fire either by striking sparks with suitable stones or by igniting dust created and heated by a fire drill. Fire so obtained was kept in the hearth which usually involved a pile of stones, and these in a way constitute the most significant of artifacts, marking as they do prehistoric American family homes by the thousands through ages long past. Their fire-tortured rock clusters are familiar to all archaeologists exploring ancient America. Yet a museum seldom, if ever, displays such an humble artifact. Perhaps it is because only *in situ* can its mute but eloquent voice remind the beholder that here once lived other Americans as alive and occupied with the day's affairs as he.

Fire-making Apparatus

In the development of man, the taming and use of fire rivaled the making and use of tools in setting his feet on the path to human civilization. How could he do without it? But he did do without it, just as the animals do, through many generations of his dawn days, and anthropologists have found people in modern times who are unable or unwilling to make fire. There are still primitive peoples who have fear and uncertainty about losing their fire and so use measures to keep fires going and to transport fire. The Eskimos hung on to their fire drill sets long after they could obtain matches.

The pre-Columbians, however, were adequately educated in this respect, presumably bringing their fire-making knowledge from the Old World, as indicated by evidences at the oldest archaeological sites which commonly involve charcoal and hearths. As already noted, they used two methods: strike-a-light and drill. The first was limited to places where they could pick up stones that would give off sparks when struck to-

gether, iron pyrites being the commonest. The second was accomplished on the general principles of friction heating, but the apparatus varied.

The simplest way was using the palms of the hands to twirl a stick (drill) in a pit in another stick (hearth). Sometimes, two persons could get faster action by teaming up so as to press and drill more steadily. The action produced a fine dust so hot that when blown on it would ignite. By augmenting the dust with tinder, a fire could be started rather quickly by a skilled operator. Other methods of whirling the stick are illustrated in the treatment of drills as tools to bore holes.

The use of fire so obtained differed between the Arctic Eskimos and the Indians, because the former had no wood in their ice- and snowbound homeland. The Eskimos burned oil in stone and pottery lamps or stoves, using moss along the edge as a wick. The Indians built their fires with sticks and billets as we do, except, as an Indian put it, "White man build big clumsy fire to cook; Indian build small, good fire." The Indian domestic fire was usually accompanied by a rock hearth for convenience and steadier heat, which was as near as he got to a cook stove, except for the earthen ovens constructed by the Pueblos.

Other Household Effects

Further utility artifacts of the pre-Columbian domicile were chiefly containers, mats, and bedding, with the addition of a few other articles of use in housekeeping, such as brushes, hooks, rakes, shovels, the fire-making apparatus just described, and, of course, food-preparing and serving utensils. Some articles are classifiable either as household or as personal effects.

There was none of the furniture familiar to us. For beds they used the ground or benches built in when constructing a house; the benches, naturally, could also serve as chairs. There were, however, some exceptions. The Plains Indians made a portable bed involving a sort of long mat of willow wands tied closely together with sinew, and the California Indians and some Indians in the Southeast made stools. Log and pole benches were sometimes suitable only to sit on. Tables were anything handy to use as such. The Yurok-Hupa cultures used wooden pillows.

Bedding was preponderantly of mats and furs and both were used as blankets or capes to keep warm or dry. Mats and hides were also used to cover temporary or summer house framework, to line interiors, and to partition for privacy and shelter from drafts. Like all other utility artifacts they were mediums for decoration by painted-on or woven-in designs, as their owners and makers fancied.

Containers included the storage baskets for food and similar boxes, baskets, rawhide envelopes, bags, etc. for holding personal goods and such tribal gear as masks, ceremonial costumes, and religious paraphernalia.

Brooms were usually handfuls of brush, but small meal brushes were both carefully made and much used.

2.1

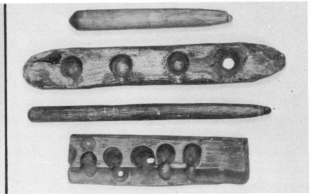

2.2

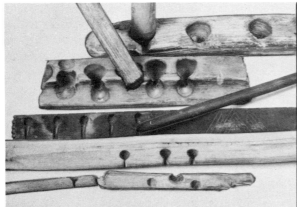

2.3

2.4

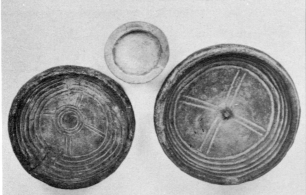

2.5

2.6

Antlers could double as rakes, and broad sections of horn or bone or wood served as shovels, which were of some importance for shoveling snow in the Arctic as well as for removing dirt.

Other household articles included house hooks and pegs, towels made of shredded ribbons of bark, slow "matches" made of the same material braided into a rope to carry fire, and other minor utensils to ease the lot of the pre-Columbian housewife and man of the house.

Household Effects

2.1 Indian fire drills and hearths, origins unknown; the drilled stick is called a "hearth" as is the open hearth in which the fire was kept, once it was started.

2.2 Eskmio fire-making sets, Point Hope, Alaska

2.3 Close-ups of hearths showing grooves burned from pits to tinder

2.4 Eskimo stone oil stoves, the larger 30 inches long

2.5 Eskimo pottery oil lamps

2.6 Eskimo stone oil lamp, scallop for wick at right

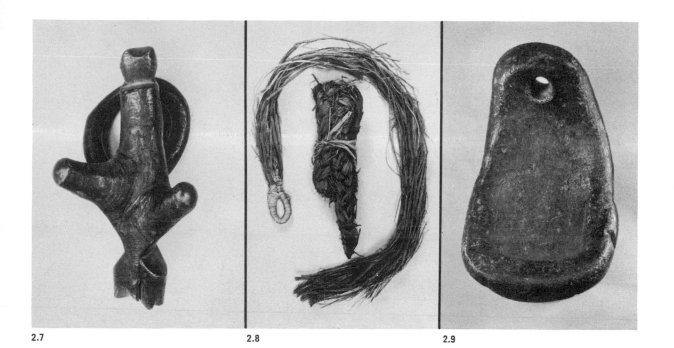

2.7   **2.8**   **2.9**

2.7   Northwest Coast movable house hook, loop created by bending a twig to be grown over by living tree
2.8   Salish bark strip towel and braided bark strip slow "match" to carry fire (Olympic Peninsula, Washington)
2.9   Shallow steatite bowl assumed to have been a Canalino (So. Calif.) lamp

Homes and Furniture
2.10   Miniature Plains Indian tipi with painted figures on sides
2.11   Totem pole with "woodpecker hole" door opening at base
2.12   Miniature Eskimo storage crib fastened together with wooden pegs; no nails

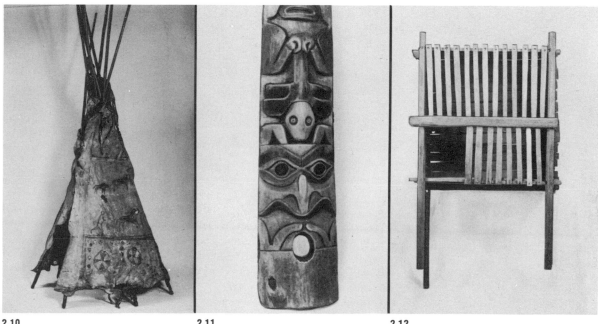

2.10   **2.11**   **2.12**

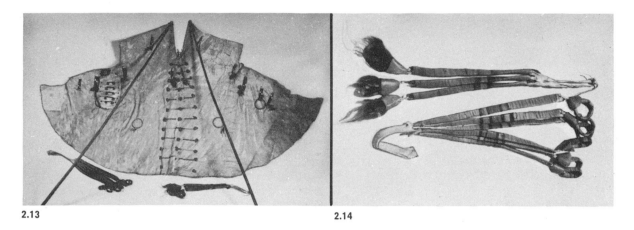

2.13   2.14

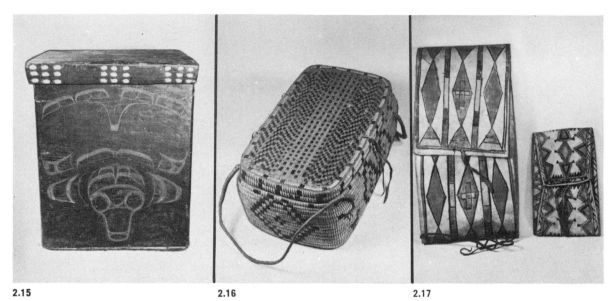

2.15   2.16   2.17

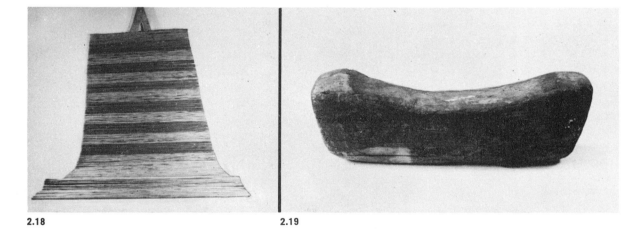

2.18   2.19

2.13 Miniature Plains tipi cover showing pattern used for these portable tents; oval at left is door cover; full-size tipi ornaments below to compare with those on right side of tipi cover.
2.14 Close-up of tipi ornaments: buckskin, sinew, horn, hair, and wrapped colored grass
2.15 Northwest Coast wooden house box or trunk, kerfed and bent sides; solid block lid, ornamented with shells and a painted design

2.16 British Columbia Salish coiled and imbricated basketry trunk
2.17 Plains Indian parfleche (rawhide) envelope trunks
2.18 Plains willow rod and sinew lashed bed, or back rest, loop for tipi tripod
2.19 Yurok-Hupa wooden pillow, commonly used by men in sweat houses

2.20-2.21 Northwest Coast house mats woven of ribbons of bark: (2.20) design created by different colors of bark strips: (2.21) design painted on checker-plaited mat

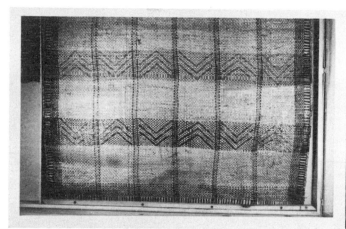

2.20

2.21

2.22 **2.23** **2.24**

2.25 **2.26** **2.27**

2.22-2.27 Eskimo etchings on ivory: top, (2.22) and (2.23) summer huts and drying racks, (2.24) storage crib with step ladder, men cutting and breaking wood, and smoking fish; (2.25) large earth-covered igloos, tunnel entrances; (2.26) earth-covered igloos, man skinning caribou or deer; (2.27) Eskimo family comes home from trip, one baby in sled, one in pocket of parka hood; boy runs ahead.

3 Manufacturing

anufacturing in the modern world is usually understood to mean making goods in factories with machinery. But in reference to pre-Columbian days it means making things with tools, or with the hands alone, the products being known as artifacts, or "relics."

Because nearly all things were made without metal tools and because the stone tools are most conspicuous in survival, the pre-Columbian period has been called the "Stone Age" in America. There were, however, numerous materials other than stone used for manufacturing, particularly in the objects made.

These tools are of two kinds: those used for general purposes and those used for special purposes.

General Tools

Many general-purpose tools were the same as those commonly in use in households today and were of types used for centuries all over the world: hammers, knives, axes, chisels, wedges, etc. Most were made of stone where we use metal, the chief exceptions being a very small percentage made of pounded copper from floats or shallow mines in the Great Lakes area and still fewer that occasionally show up in Alaska and the Southwest. Stone tools that needed cutting edges were usually flaked and chipped; others were pecked (struck with a quick, sharp stroke) to shape, ground, then polished.

Perhaps the oldest tools were sticks and stones, the latter coming to archaeological notice only when chipped or abraded in an obviously artificial manner; the sticks, of course, have not survived. These oldest tools were extremely crude, some being difficult to identify as artifacts. Crudity, however, is not in itself a proof of age or use confined to ancient times. In very recent sites, many crude artifacts have been found, some of which were, doubtless, rejects or abandoned attempts while others were put to use, crudeness being no drawback if they worked. Indians and Eskimos were realists and did not make their artifacts for cabinet and showcase display but for use in their daily lives.

On the other hand, fine quality and outstanding craftsmanship of an artifact do not necessarily mark it

as being recent in North American prehistoric chronology, as witness the work on some of the old Yuma and Folsom points.

Nor are forms of tools, of necessity, a total guide to age. A fist axe is characteristic of very old cultures in the Old World, but it is duplicated among artifacts of no great human age in Texas. This is also essentially true in the case of stone hand picks used by the Canalinos of the Santa Barbara coast.

Another fact sometimes forgotten or misunderstood is that a large proportion of stone artifacts were actually *pieces* of tools, the perishable parts having disintegrated, as in the case of sticks, mentioned above. Forgetting this has caused some assumptions which should not be taken too seriously. Certain agricultural tools are commonly called "hoes," but how can we know that they were not spades, or possibly axes? When we speak of a full-grooved axe, we are talking about what is actually only the blade of an axe.

Still other facts to keep in mind are that one artifact could have one use in one place and another in another and that some tools in constant use in one area were unknown in another: no stone adze handles in the East; no harpoons in the Southwest; no axes on the Pacific Coast.

Occasionally we run across tools that appear to have been made for some very definite use, but what the use was we do not, nor perhaps ever can, know.

Hammers and Mauls

A hammer was probably one of the earliest invented of man's tools and continues to be one of the commonest. All pre-Columbians used hammers in various forms to pound food, stakes, wedges, chisels, stones, and other pre-Columbians, though in the last form they are called "clubs."

The simplest hammer form was a hand-sized stone, distinguished as an artifact only by evidence of blows or abrasion. Because of their uninteresting simplicity and humble use, thousands of these have escaped notice or have been discarded. They are among the poor relations in collections. Beyond the simpler signs of wear, such hammers may have had two depressions or pits tapped into their sides (by another hammer). They may also, if fairly flat and round to begin with, be worn around their edges to a circular form and thus rise in the scale of importance by looking like discoidals. Their sizes run from that of walnuts to small boulders requiring two hands to use. Their shapes are all those which common stones have. Their materials vary as do the materials of stones in general, but they are usually of some tough, hard stone that can wear away softer stone.

Along with the thousands of such stones found lying in all pre-Columbian sites, there are also hundreds of single hammerstones much more elaborately shaped for their purposes. These are called "monolithic," and their shapes are seemingly not much recognized or not generally known.

The most widely distributed of monolithic hammers are those mistakenly called "bell pestles," but properly called "hand mauls." They are shaped with a handle and a face, the latter usually flaring out to give more striking surface and the former frequently having a knob or cap to better secure the grip. Those much used often evidence such use by having chips knocked off the edge of the face or by having a depression or cup in the face.

Eastern forms of hand mauls are comparatively simple, sometimes merging into pestle forms. But in the woodworking and carving area of the Northwest Coast Indians they were usually quite elaborately fashioned and, in addition, took forms identifiable with fairly definite parts of the Northwest Coast.

In the far north, such hammers flared out a great deal, sometimes at both ends, and occasionally they were reversible. The Salish tribes liked to have their hand mauls topped by a small knob or point above the top rim. The Columbia River tribes liked theirs to be bottle-shaped with a very heavy lower section usually convex toward a smaller face. Tribes on the southern Oregon and northern California coasts preferred two types: one rather squatty and bulging toward the face; the other longer and gently concave between top and face. Both kinds had typically mushroom-shaped caps at their tops.

In this same Northwest Coast area, some different forms of another monolithic hammer were in use from about Vancouver Island to the Klamath River. They were devised so as to project on a plane with the hand rather than from under it. Their commonest form was that of a broad paddle, somewhat on the lines of a ping-pong paddle, with a flat face and a rounded back. Occasionally, they had a ridge running from handle to tip. Three other forms were developed and used in a rather small area centering on the Olympic Peninsula. One resembled a baseball bat with four flat faces so as to be square in its striking section. A second had a large, circular "head," altogether resembling a frying pan. A third shape, reminiscent of a hairbrush, was devoted to pounding bark.

Besides their use as mauls to pound tools, these Pacific Coast monolithic hammers served to drive stakes for fish weirs that the Indians constructed at various points in all the sizable streams. From time to time, lost specimens have been found in the stream beds.

Another great division of hammers is in a form more familiar to us—a head, usually of stone, attached to a wooden, horn, or bone handle. This type varies in size from little tapping hammers to big mauls suitable for driving wedges or large stakes. Forms, methods of attachment, and shapes of heads differed within areas as well as between one area and another.

Two kinds of such hammers in particular stand out. One kind is a huge maul originating on the Northwest Coast, usually attached to a "T" at the end of a curved handle. The other is a short, heavy hammer, made by Plains Indians, generally with a rawhide-wrapped handle and often with the head itself encased in rawhide so that only the face is exposed. The mauls were used in woodworking, while the heavy Plains type were used to pound food, notably pemmican, to crack buffalo bones, to drive tipi pegs, and so on.

The specimens of this last division are complete hammers, of course, few occurring compared to the thousands of heads for hammers found almost everywhere except in California. Such heads are in all sorts of shapes and are hardly suited to classification. Those with one or more flat faces were evidently used as hammers, but many round or convex heads could have been either hammers or club heads, or both. Among the latter is a variety that has a groove around it with the addition at one point of a pit dug or reamed in as a socket for one end of a handle.

Besides possible use as clubs, many hammerheads of large size were actually anchor stones, the grooves being for the anchor ropes. Without data and without a handle, the only proof that a hammerhead was such is evidence of use in pounding.

Knives

Knives for cutting up food, skinning animals, and shaping other tools were among man's first tools, and they are still in general use in one of their first forms.

From the first flakes of stone used in the fingers, the Eskimos and Indians had developed three general forms of knives. One was a shape familiar to us—a blade set in the end of a handle. This the Eskimos called a "man's knife." Another, less familiar and now little used, often had as its handle just a pad for the palm over a broad blade. It still sees some use among us as a chopping, or "hash knife." Eskimos called it a "woman's knife." The third form approximated a farrier's knife. It had a small blade (perhaps just a flake) reminiscent of a safety razor blade, set in a slot on the side of the end of a bone. Because the bone was often a section of rib and therefore curved, it acquired the name "crooked knife."

At this point it is interesting to note that observers have often reported that both Indians and Eskimos draw their knives toward themselves when cutting.

Nearly all the thousands of knives surviving, or at least in displays or collections, are just blades, as the handles were perishable. Finger-held knives, which constitute a large part of all knives collected as well as of artifacts thrown away as too crude to keep, never had handles. However, enough specimens of the three kinds that did have handles have survived to tell us what they were like when complete.

In men's knives, there is an extensive overlap with spearheads—a one-way overlap, however, because while all spearheads could also have been knife blades, not all knife blades could have been spearheads. Spears, however, are more romantic than knives, so it is quite likely that were their true ancestry known, multitudes of artifacts labeled spears should be moved over to the knife displays.

It should be remembered that knives were used daily, by women as well as men, most families probably having several and wearing out numbers of them during a year. Certainly we may assume that the woman's knife was as much in use as the man's knife. In contrast, even among warlike tribes the warrior's spear spent considerable time in disuse. Even hunting spears were little used in comparison with arrows, harpoons, traps, clubs, and other artifacts involved in killing game or fish.

Among the Eskimos the commonest knife-blade shape was semilunar. Nor was this form unusual elsewhere, for, as among the Eskimos, the woman's-knife blade generally, because of its function of chopping, could be only vaguely semilunar and was sometimes rectangular or wide-leaf shaped.

Blades for crooked knives were so simple and slight that there is little doubt but that almost all of them escape the attention of those gathering or sorting artifacts. In fact, when they are noticed, the handles are much easier to identify, though probably many collectors have discarded some handles from assuming them to be merely bones with a split in one end.

As usual when classifying, we have to add a fourth or fifth class of knives, the miscellaneous. For, as with many of the forms of man's works, there are in-betweens: a woman's-knife blade set in its handle crooked-knife fashion, or a man's-knife blade set in woman's-knife fashion, and so on.

In all the forms of handled knives the blades were predominantly glued, cemented, and/or lashed in place—that is among surviving examples. In some Eskimo women's knives, a slot or hole was cut or pierced just below the handle so that the blade could be more securely lashed to the handle.

Just how long and large or how short and small a knife could be cannot be accurately measured, but there was a spread of a good many inches. Nevertheless, it can be assumed that all knives over about eight inches were impractical for utilitarian purposes and were ceremonial in character. While a few could have served as spears, they would probably have broken when first used. At the other extreme of size, some of the knives still combining handle and blade show that the latter could be ranked in the arrowhead or chip class.

Some persons assume that barbs could only have been used for spears. Actually, the probability is the other way. Anyone who has skinned game or opened fish knows that the initial opening made with a ripping cut is often more effective than a slicing cut, hence a barb hooked into a game animal could, with a ripping pull, quickly accomplish the task desired.

Adzes

The importance of the adze as a tool was soon forgotten when sawed and planed lumber came into use, but until then it had been a major item in woodworkers' kits in North America, even among the pioneers and carpenters of European Colonial days. It is or has been in use to the present time in various parts of the world where planing mills have not superseded handcraft. Its chief use in pre-Columbian times was in the Arctic and Northwest Coast areas, but it was also used elsewhere, appearing freely along with stone axes in the Eastern Woodland artifacts.

As with some other tools, its use extended beyond shaving and shaping wood. The Eskimos used adzes to cut up food, and they made special ones, as previously noted, for digging roots. The latter type was a close relative of the hoe and, also to recapitulate, some seeming adze blades may have been hoe blades. The Plains Indians also used an adze form made into a hide scraper with which they chopped off excess meat and hide.

Evidence of adze use marks many products of the Northwest Coast Indians—notably their totem poles and house planks, and sometimes their wooden boxes. Apparently, rippled surfaces of regular adze pocking were regarded as ornamental, just as adze-marked beams were considered decorative on ceilings at one time.

Complete adzes have survived in considerable numbers from Eskimo and Northwest Coast use and show quite a variety of forms. The commonest form, an elbow as on a hoe, was varied by setting the blade at all degrees of angles. These angles became so acute as to create a U-shaped adze found in artifacts of the Puget Sound area. Over most of the maritime part of the Northwest Coast from Alaska to the Olympic Peninsula, the "U" shape joined to form a "D" shape that looks much like a handsaw handle with the blade fastened vertically on the front.

Farther south, along the Oregon coast and in northwestern California, the adze handles assumed an upside-down "J" shape and were made of stone. Many continued in use after contact with European culture; some of these indicate the use of a leather apron in front of the knuckles. Blades for the later adzes in all these areas were mostly metal, but numerous stone blades are found among which are examples of shell and elkhorn blades.

The use of shell blades on the Pacific Coast—also in the South Sea Islands, where adzes are much used—indicates that the hollowed-stone blades called "gouges" could well have been adze blades and that they may have been modeled on shell blades used in the same areas.

Shapes of stone blades varied a great deal in all areas where adzes were used. Generally speaking, blades flat on one side and tending to a chisel edge were rather certainly adze blades. There are also examples of blades in handles which show that blades that look like celts and chisels, as well as gouges, could have been adze blades.

While the usual first assumption is that adzes cut out bits or shavings of wood directly, which many did, it must be remembered that pre-Columbians often used fire to burn out hollows, notably in dugout canoes. In that case, much adze work was simply to chop out charcoal.

Axes

Roughly speaking, the stone axe blade, although one of the most familiar artifacts among the collections of Eastern Woodland and Southwest representations, was confined to the corn-raising Indians who lived in those areas in pre-Columbian times. Only strays are found elsewhere, except on the Plains where the axe was used exclusively as a combat weapon. Might it be that the axe diffused northward from Mexico and the adze southward from a Bering Strait crossing?

There are a number of popular divisions of axe types. However, these classifications seem to have more significance for labeling cabinet displays than for defining their aboriginal uses. Most frequently applied are the classifications of axes as "full-grooved" and "three-quarter-grooved." There are also some that might be called "half-grooved." Fairly common examples have a rectangular cross section which gives them right-angle edges along the sides. Much prized because of their rarity are double-bitted axes; axes with marked ridges which in some cases closely resemble barbs; blades decorated with flutes, or, once in a while, with an effigy. There are also occasional examples of two-grooved axes. Further varieties such as pointed polls, flared bits, and other unusual features, challenge collectors of the rare and odd.

In addition to all these grooved axes, there are a great many without grooves. These are roughly in two forms: one quite similar to our household axes without a hole and the other with a somewhat pointed and diminishing poll, the latter being commonly dubbed "celts."

More examples of grooved axes set in wooden handles survive than do ungrooved axes attached to handles, but monolithic axes of ceremonial character indicate that the ungrooved axes were set in a hole or slot made for them in a billet of wood shaped into a handle. Sometimes there is a distinct difference in coloring and wear on a stone axe which indicates what part of it was set in a socket.

Handles were made for grooved axes by cutting away half of a round stave down part or all of its length. The stave was next presumably steamed or soaked, then bent around the groove. The handle was then secured by binding it with green rawhide that shrank tight to hold in the head. Such heads stayed in better if the handle was somewhat elastic so as to absorb the shock of blows.

The dull condition of many axe-blade edges indicates that they bruised their way through wood as much as they cut. That they were used for cutting logs is evident from the axe-marked logs found in prehistoric ruins in the Southwest. They were also used as weapons, being the original tomahawks. In one instance at least, they were employed as mining tools: two prehistoric casualties with their axes were found buried in a caved-in tunnel of an ancient salt mine in southeast Arizona.

Making axes into ceremonial adjuncts was a practice carried on in the South Seas, and, as adzes were used in place of axes on the Pacific Coast, the so-called "slave killers" found there may have been an idea borrowed from transoceanic visitors. The long flaring blades called "spuds" in the East may also have had a ceremonial use, as some of them are rather fragile for practical use.

Chisels, Wedges, Gouges, and Picks

The identification of chisel blades is somewhat muddled because, as already pointed out, they could also have been adze blades, picks, scrapers, or possibly wedges. It is almost certain, however, that if a blade is to be considered a complete chisel by itself, it must be capable of withstanding pounding, because stone blades could not reach the keen edge necessary to cut with just pushing. So we must regard the name as fanciful in many cases and not related to actual function.

Some chisels, however, can be so named accurately, because they are set in handles. Where such is the case, the blades are somewhat stubby and of shapes suited to use in a handle.

Horn and bone wedges are fairly easy to identify with certainty, though a few could have had other uses. When not too decayed or when "green," they often display obvious marks of pounding on the butts. The most complete range of wedges that have survived comes from the Yurok-Hupa cultures in northwestern California, where they were used into historic times. These run from short, stubby starting wedges to long splitting wedges. On the Northwest Coast, wedges were also made of wood, commonly with cordage lashing around the polls to prevent splitting. Wedges were in general use by all pre-Columbians who had occasion to split wood. Judging by battered polls, some stone axes were also used to split wood.

A gouge is a chisel with a curved or hollowed edge, and its identification among artifacts involves the same difficulty as that encountered with other chisels. As noted under adze blades, some gouges may have been stone versions of shell blades. One identifiable gouge is, or was, made by the Eskimos from a beaver tooth set in a handle. Certainly, the natural evidence was strong that it would make a good cutting tool.

Picks are usually associated with digging tools, but one type resembling the fist axe was used by stone masons for cutting steatite along the southern California coast. It was usually triangular like the drills of the area and bulged toward the top for a handgrip. The material used was, of course some hard, tough stone.

Drills, Reamers, Punches, and Gravers

Large numbers of pointed stones which do not look like conventional arrowheads are nevertheless clearly tool points of some kind. Many are judged to have been drills, or drill points. Some have such long, slender construction that they would not have stood up as drills. These may have been punches or, if with fine points, lancets or tattoo needles. When the point is very short and stubby, the guess is that they were gravers for scratching lines and grooves. When the point is rounded or widens at a relatively obtuse angle, the point is called a "reamer."

Use of certain of the long, choice specimens that are among the prides of some cabinet collections presents a puzzle, for they would have required a steady hand indeed to stand up as drills. Some persons, recognizing this fact, have assigned them the gratuitous function of hairpins.

Undoubtedly, much drilling was done with these bits of pointed stone by themselves, but a few drills with wooden shafts survive to show us, as might be expected, that the tips could be attached in the same way as arrows. Indeed, some such tips are "arrowheads," and once in a while an arrowhead is found with its edge worn smooth from drilling.

The numerous drill holes in stone, bone, and ivory that one sees show two kinds of drilling: "cone" drilling and "core" drilling. The cones were drilled by the tools just discussed. Core holes were drilled with a hollow tubular point that left a core when the material being worked was not drilled completely through. Core holes tend to keep the same diameter, whereas cone-drilled holes are widest where begun and diminish to a point.

On the subject of drilling itself, it should be noted that much drilling was done by fine abrasive sands or powders being continuously ground about in the bottom of an already started drill hole. As a soft drill rod would suffice for this purpose, it is likely that some core-drilled holes were made using hollow cane sticks or copper tubes with the abrasives.

While the more familiar forms of drill points and reamers have two edges, a possibly more efficient arrangement was devised by Indians of the Southwest and the California coast: points of slender pyramidal construction, hence with three cutting edges. The Eskimos varied this by using jade rods with points ground to three cutting edges.

All drills had to be rotated. The easiest way was to roll them between the palms of two hands or two pairs of hands, as noted in relation to fire drills. The problem of getting more pressure was solved by using a cap with a socket to hold the drill shaft. Many stone,

bone, and ivory tools were identified by such sockets as drill caps. The usual way to use them was to put a hand on the cap and press, but the Eskimos thought of another way and made caps with mouth grips as well as drill-shaft sockets, thus releasing both hands for work.

Another widely used device was a bow with a somewhat loose cord to wrap around the drill shaft. The shaft was kept whirling by moving the bow back and forth. Two operators could also twirl the stick looped in a cord held taut between two handles; one person holding the cap and the object to be drilled, while the other moved the handles back and forth rapidly. The Eskimos returned the job to one person by inventing a mouthpiece which could be used with a thong and handles as well as with the bow.

A further ingenious device was the pump drill. This consisted of a crossarm with a hole through which the shaft was run. By tying cords to the top of the shaft and ends of the crossarm, then twisting them around the shaft below the crossarm, a down pressure was caused which twirled the drill. As the whirl was insufficient to rewind the cord, a flywheel was affixed to the shaft. Because the wheel went on whirling after the end of a down push, it rewound the cordage ready for another down push.

These flywheels are similar to and even sometimes indistinguishable from spindle whorls, which performed a like function. Incidentally, these are the only forms of the wheel that crossed Bering Strait from the Old World.

Archaeologists differ as to native origin of the pump drill. Its use by Eskimos, Pomo Indians, Southwest Indians, and Iroquois in historic times is believed by some people to be due to diffusion by Europeans. But in view of its widespread use in Asia even at the present time, it seems unnecessary to suppose it could not have had similar dispersion in pre-Columbian North America. In fact, flywheels, or whorls, have been found on numerous occasions in prehistoric debris.

Miscellaneous Tools

As usual in listing objects of wide variety, there are a number of tools of less familiar character than those already described, or of restricted use. Some of these the author has assigned to a following section on special tools and crafts, but others remain in a miscellaneous category. There are also some tools which took quite a bit of trouble to make but which cannot be identified with certainty as to their use; the uses of some of them require unrestrained guessing.

One of the most practical of tools included under "miscellaneous" is the abrader in its many forms. Although chipped tools could be sharpened by rechipping, ground-edged tools had to be reground. These were two separate operations except in limited instances in the Southwest, where some clever Indians made an edge on a stone axe by chipping one side and then regrinding the other side to keep it sharp. Troughs worn by such a method are still to be seen. Similar troughs worn in stones that were evidently not saucers or the like may have had comparable use, including the sharpening of shell blades.

Grit stones with grooves in them are the best known forms of abraders. Some were for polishing arrow shafts; even more were most likely used as awl, punch, and needle polishers.

Not recognized by many amateurs are sandstone (or other abrasive) saws. These are thin slabs of sandstone which seldom if ever were given special shapes. They are recognizable as saws by the wear on an edge or edges.

When it is remembered that the polish on the bulk of pecked stone tools, and occasionally on chipped flint artifacts, was put there mostly by abrasive action, the importance of this element in aboriginal life can be better recognized.

Paintbrushes were another tool of wide usage. Although these were easily made by chewing out the fibers on the ends of suitable sticks and by the conventional method of tying bristles on a stick, the Plains Indians had a "brush" that is difficult to recognize until its use is explained. This was a scrap of porous bone ground to an edge or edges. Paint was absorbed in the bone pores and released on contact.

With paint also went palettes and palette knives or mixers. The most elaborate palettes were made by the prehistoric Southwest Indians and had sections of slate provided with rims which make them look like old-fashioned school slates. Similarly well-made circular disks in the Mound Builder areas could have had a like use. Elsewhere, simple slabs of wood, bark, or stone were used. An Indian informant once stated that the cupped discoidals of Mound Builder cultures were nothing more complicated than makeup palettes with a different color on each side, thus facilitating quick application of the makeup for ceremonials or the war-path.

In the pottery-making areas, many smooth-surfaced stones are picked up that saw use as smoothers for pottery in the "wet" stage. In the Eastern Woodland areas, such tools take a definite form as pottery toad-stool-shaped trowels. Very large trowels of this toad-stool type were possibly used to smooth the mud stucco on wattled hut walls.

A number of other tools of equal or less importance have doubtless been omitted, as the intelligence of the pre-Columbians combined with the rather frequent pressure of necessity struck many sparks of independent invention to meet situations both known and unknown in modern life. It should be emphasized again that much uncertainty must be retained as to the uses of even the most familiar of tool forms. When a woman uses a chisel to seat a screw it may make a man shudder, but if the chisel was no good as a chisel, the woman could be right. So, too, if an Indian chose to use a beautiful rose quartz discoidal as a makeup palette rather than the jewel of a cabinet collection, can we criticize him or pretend it was otherwise? (If such was its use, of course.)

Appended to this section of miscellany, besides such tools of unknown or highly uncertain use, are a few specimens of material recovered at various stages of transformation from natural to artifact form. It is surprising how much this construction side has been ignored. It could be made the aim of a most interesting specialized collection or display.

3.1

3.2

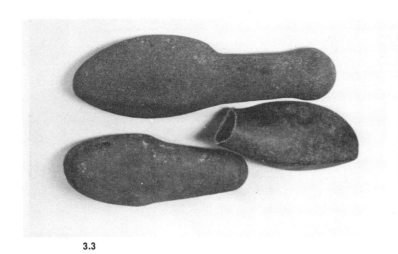

3.3

3.4

3.5

3.6

3.7

74

3.8   3.9   3.10

3.11   3.12   3.13

Monolithic Hammers and Mauls

3.1   Four hammerstones identified as such only by battered and abraded areas on sides and edges; these are usually dense, hard, and tough stones.

3.2   Three finger-pitted hammerstones; these are often in discoidal shapes with edges worn all around.

3.3-3.4   Paddle- and club-shaped hammers used by the central and southern coastal tribes of the Northwest Coast culture area: (3.3) upper hammer, Wiyot territory, northwest California; bottom, Olympic Peninsula, Washington; origin of central broken one unknown; these have flat faces, convex tops, and definite handles. (3.4) These are similar to the three preceding hammers; upper, Oregon coast; lower, Quinault Reservation; the latter has four flattened sides.

3.5-3.7   Northern Northwest Coast types of hand mauls: (3.5) spool type, Washington State and British Columbia; (3.6) and (3.7) hat-top types typical of coast Salish areas. The spool types sometimes have interchangeable ends, two faces.

3.8-3.10   Interior Columbia River types (3.8) and (3.9-3.10) four lava mauls from the southern intermountain plateau area. The bottle shape (3.8) left, is a distinct Columbia River type. The second smaller one (3.8) right, has ornamented "hat" rim and sides of face.

3.11-3.13   Five variations of the northwest California mauls (3.11-3.12), with cap tops, and (3.13) two Eastern "bell pestles." The California mauls were in use well into historic times for driving wedges and fishweir stakes. The fourth bell pestle in (3.11) has a polished and pounded cup or pit and the one to its left has one edge knocked off. The Eastern pestles have similar evidence of use as mauls, including worn cups.

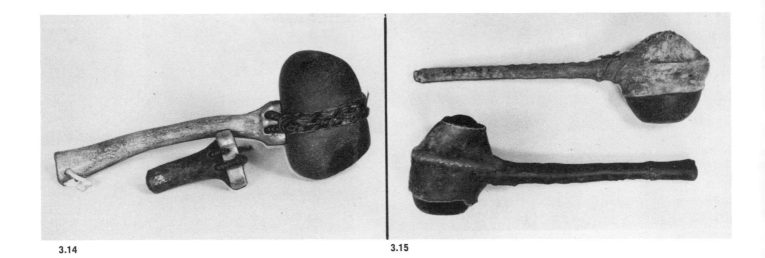

3.14

3.15

3.16

3.17

3.18

Handled Hammers and Hammerheads

3.14   Eskimo hammers, bone and ivory handles, stone and ivory heads

3.15   Plains Indian hammers or mauls, heads and handles encased in leather; these were used extensively by Plains tribes as utility hammers for all heavy pounding purposes, such as driving tent pegs, breaking bones, and mashing pemmican.

3.16   Five grooved hammerheads from various places

3.17   Heavy Plains-type maul head with pit for end of handle

3.18   Heavy Northwest Coast type maul head, vertical as well as horizontal grooving and flat face for T-shaped handle

3.19   Four grooved hammer (or club) heads

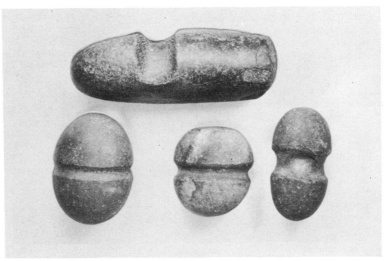

3.19

76

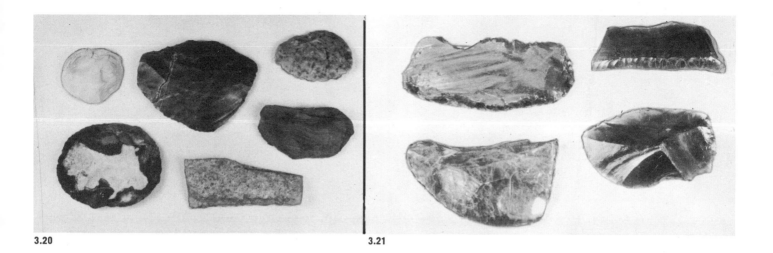

3.20   3.21

3.22   3.23

3.24   3.25

Knives
3.20-3.21 Monolithic chipped knives made from sharp-edged flakes of stone with or without secondary chipping. Pads may have been used with some of these and when attached to the blades created what the Eskimos call "women's knives."
3.22-3.23 Blades suited to handles, though not necessarily used with them; all edges with secondary chipping. A common practice in sharpening such knives was to rechip the edge, or edges.

3.24-3.25 Blades with notches, indicating attachment to handles: (3.24) northwest California types; (3.25) a "turkey tail" and a "corner tang" knife blade. The former is an upper Mississippi Valley type; the latter a Texas type. (Courtesy Willis Tilton.)

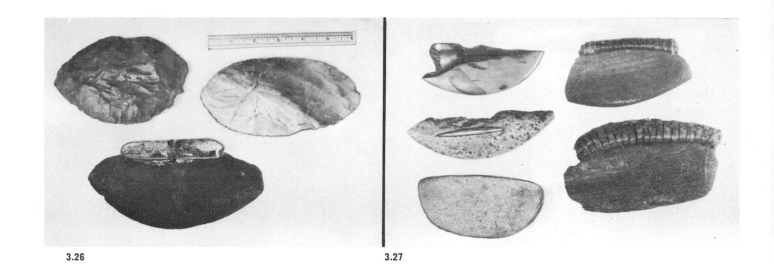

3.26

3.27

3.28

3.29

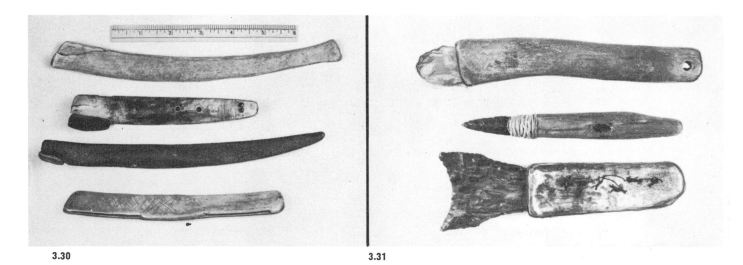

3.30

3.31

78

3.32

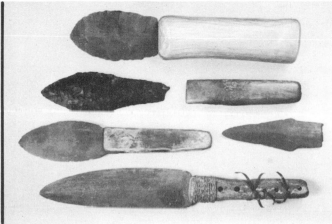

3.33

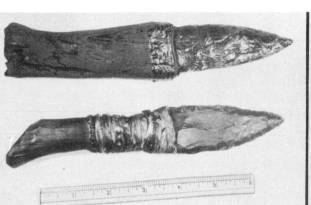

3.34

3.35

3.26 "Women's knife" blades, one with pad handles; top left, a Hopewell find blade, blue-gray flint with quartz core and tan shell; top right, chalcedony blade from a Columbia River island burial; bottom, Point Hope, Alaska, Eskimo knife with wooden handle secured by whale baleen threaded through a hole in the blade

3.27 Four Eskimo jade and slate "women's knife" blades, two with pads of baleen and leather, and a semilunar knife of ground stone (not slate) labeled from Tennessee; thickened flat top indicates use without handle.

3.28-3.29 Eskimo women's knives with wood, bone, and ivory handles showing varieties of forms in handles and attachments

3.30 Knives of the "crooked knife" type, similar to farrier's knives and held the same way; slotted for small flake-type blades; the two in the center with slate blades are Eskimo, others from Ree Indian sites in the Dakotas; the bottom one is slotted for two blades.

3.31 Unusual Eskimo knives: top, wood carver's knife, translucent green jade blade, ivory handle; center, doctor's lancet, black flint arrowhead-type blade set in wood; bottom, double-pointed blade (Dalton type?) set in an ivory handle with etched hunting scenes

3.32-3.33 Eskimo men's knives with flint and slate blades set in bone, ivory, and horn handles; four chipped flint, rest ground slate

3.34-3.35 Prehistoric knives in original handles: (3.34) upper, San Nicolas Island, California coast; lower, source unknown; (3.35) upper, northern Plains; lower, source unknown. The two of unknown origin were believed to have come from Ute territory.

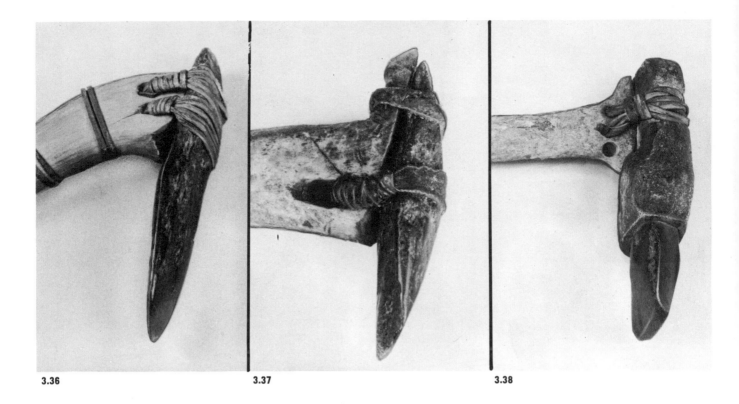

3.36   3.37   3.38

Adzes
3.36-3.38 Close-ups of Arctic Eskimo adzes with jade blades: (3.36) on a wooden handle; (3.37) on a bone handle; (3.38) socketed in bone on a bone handle

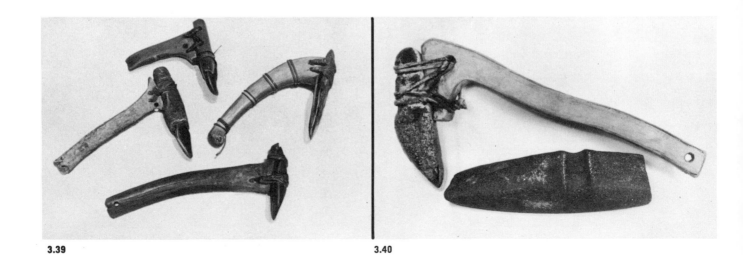

3.39   3.40

3.39 Four Eskimo adzes showing variation of relation between blades and handles
3.40 Heavy bladed Eskimo adze, and a Kotzebue Sound Eskimo adze blade

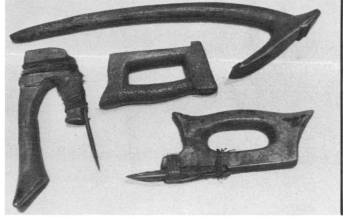

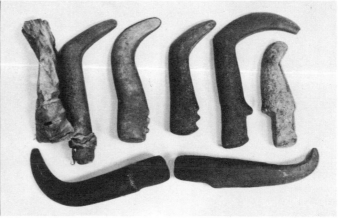

3.41

3.42

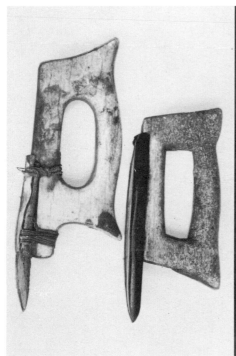

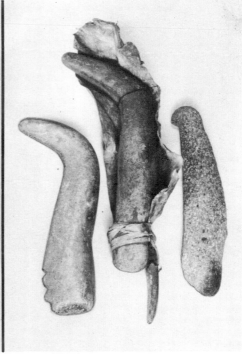

3.43

3.44

3.45

3.41 Northwest Coast Indian adze types: top, elbow-type handle; left, U-shaped Puget Sound type; D- or saw-handle shapes used all through the Northwest Coast from Alaska to the Olympic Peninsula in Washington

3.42 Northwest California Indian stone adze handles, one with leather knuckle guard

3.43-3.45 Close-ups of adze types: (3.43) "D" shapes and (3.44) "U" shape shown in (3.41); (3.45) stone adze handles, one with blade and knuckle guard

3.46

3.47

3.48

3.46-3.47 Eastern types of adze blades:
(3.46) from various localities, one a New
England gouge type; (3.47) two gouges,
New England and Tennessee, and two flint
blades (which could also be agricultural
hoes or picks)
3.48 Western and Eskimo adze blades,
thin type, as shown in pictures of complete
adzes

Axes
3.49 Four axes from various localities
3.50 Double-bitted axe with Northwest
Coast type of elbow handle and fastening
3.51 Methods of attaching axe heads;
left, with a blade of Southwest type; right,
with a Plains Indian type handle
3.52 Prehistoric axe found with its owner
buried in a collapsed salt mine tunnel in
southeastern Arizona; the lashing had
decayed or had been eaten by rodents.
3.53 Extremes in sizes in stone axe blades
3.54 Full-grooved axe blades, two center
ones hematite

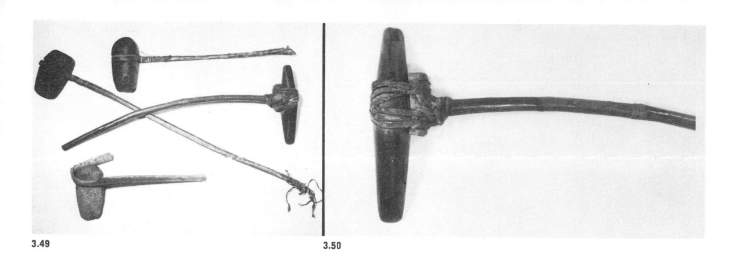

3.49   3.50

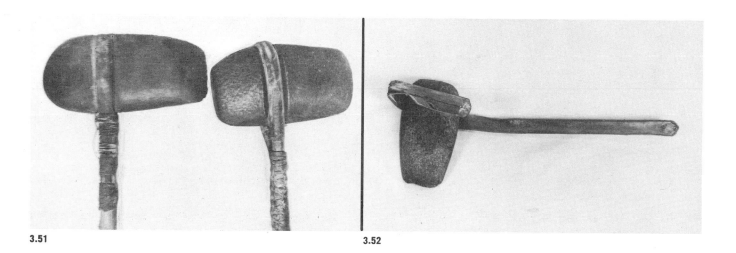

3.51   3.52

3.53   3.54

3.55

3.56

3.57

3.58

3.55 Four three-quarter-grooved blades; second one from Arizona
3.56 Axe blades with rectangular cross sections; right, half-grooved; left is like the complete Plains axe depicted in (3.51).
3.57 Ungrooved blades, celt type
3.58 Ungrooved blades with squared-off tops, third one showing division between open portion and portion buried in a handle

3.59

3.59 Flaring axe blades, lower one of chipped flint with considerable polish
3.60 Fist axe from Texas with crust of a flint nodule on its butt; an ancient type of artifact in the Old World

3.60

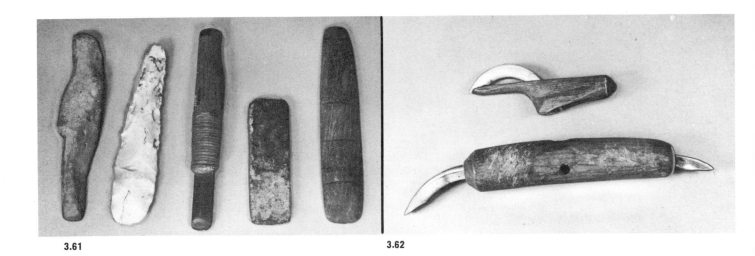

3.61

3.62

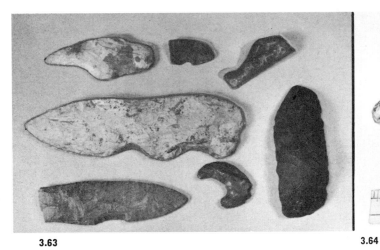

3.63

3.64

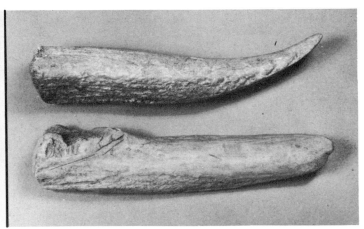

3.65

3.66

Chisels, Gouges, Wedges, and Picks
3.61 Chisels from Arizona, Kentucky, Northwest Coast, Wisconsin (copper), and Tennessee; all but the center one could also be adze or pick blades.
3.62 Eskimo beaver tooth gouges, one with two blades
3.63 Wood-working knives, five with semicircular cutting places
3.64 Three-cornered stone-working pick of quartz; Santa Barbara coast; point blunted and polished by use; akin to the fist axe
3.65 Crude stone scrapers or "plows," left one with edge worn blunt and smooth by use
3.66 Large northwest California elkhorn wedges; prehistoric; upper one curved type used to pry off planks

3.67

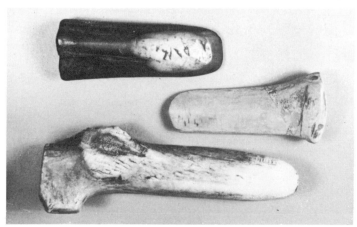

3.68

3.67 Short elkhorn and bone wedges; third, Pennsylvania, others California
3.68 "Green" horn (ethnological) wedges, center, Alaska, others, California

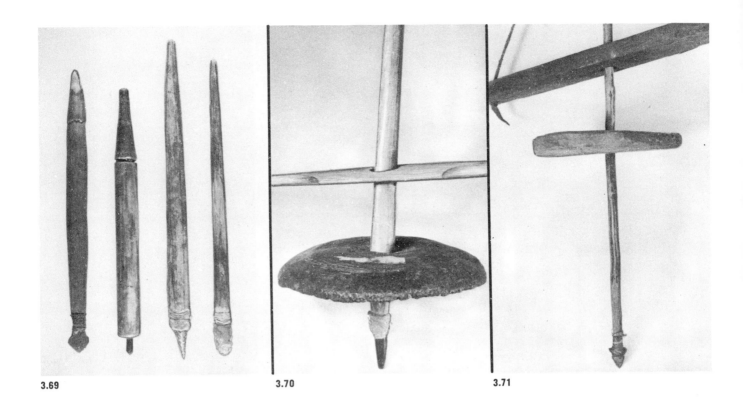

3.69

3.70

3.71

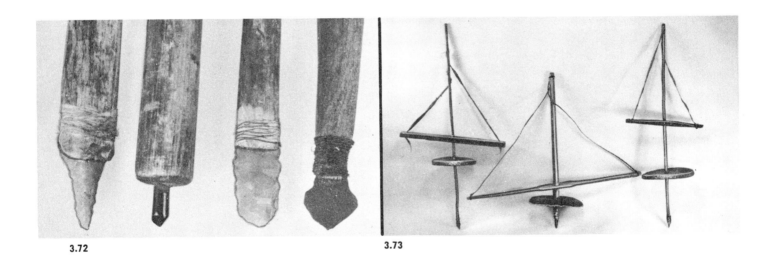

3.72

3.73

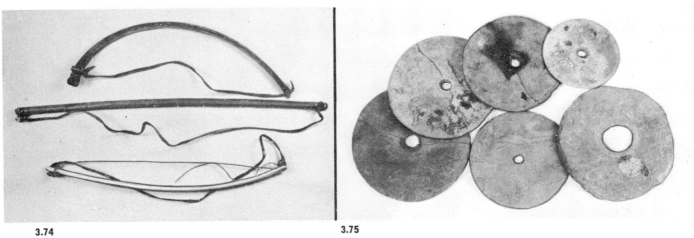

3.74

3.75

88

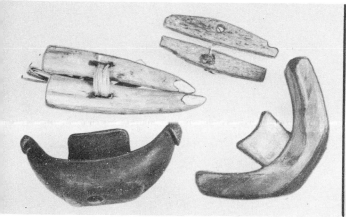

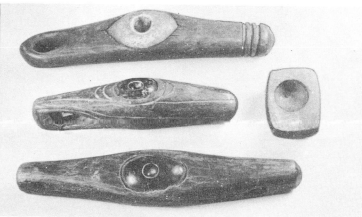

3.76 **3.77**

Drills
3.69 Four Eskimo drills
3.70 Close-up of Eskimo pump drill; jade tip; whale's patella flywheel
3.71 Close-up of Pueblo Indian drill; wooden flywheel; arrowpoint tip
3.72 Close-ups of Eskimo drill tips; (a) flint arrowpoint type; (b) jade rod tip; (c) flint reamer; (d) slate reamer
3.73 Pump drills; center, Eskimo, others Southwest Pueblo Indians
3.74 Three bows for drills; center Pomo, California, others Eskimo; bone, wood, ivory
3.75 Prehistoric drill flywheels from central California and the Southwest (could be spindle whorls)
3.76 Eskimo drill-thong handles and mouthpiece caps with stone sockets
3.77 Drill caps: wooden ones Eskimo with stone sockets; stone one Eastern Woodland; design on middle Eskimo cap is of ancient Bering culture type.

3.78

3.78 Typical drill-tip types from various localities; third "arrowhead" in lower row has edges worn to a squared surface by long use; second in the top row was used with fingers.
3.79 Slender pyramidal tips from Santa Barbara coast; also used in the Southwest

3.79

3.80

3.81

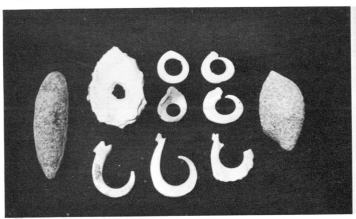

3.82

3.83

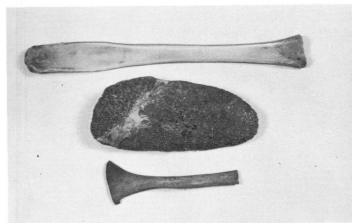

3.84

3.85

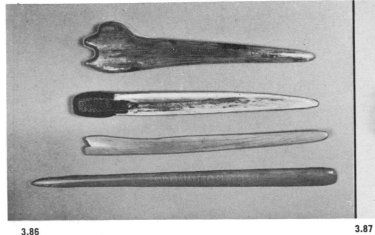

3.86

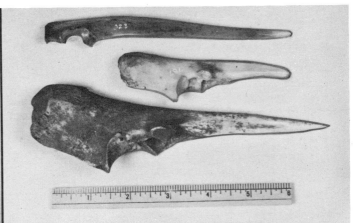

3.87

3.88

3.89

Miscellaneous Tools

3.80 Whetstone, possibly for shell blades; abrasive "chisel;" file made of abrasive fishskin on a bone tool base; caulking stones; and a pottery smoother

3.81 Sandstone saws, edges worn by use

3.82 Fishhook manufacture: various stages in construction, and abrasive reamers used to smooth centers

3.83 Trowels: left one for smoothing plaster on wattle walls, small one for pottery smoothing

3.84 Bone quill flattener, porous bone "paint brush," and bone palette knife or paint mixer

3.85 Stone palettes, Southwest Indians; similar flat stone disks with rims found in Mound Builder sites may also be palettes.

3.86 Knife-awl tools with various possible uses—arrow chippers, punches, basketry battens, etc.

3.87 Similar tools, top, identified as used for peeling off inner bark; bottom may have been an eel or fish splitter; center is a widely dispersed form suggested to be an arrow chipper.

3.88 Rectangular stones, always with two or more straight edges chipped and either ground dull or smoothed by use; they are found in numbers along the Columbia River and are suggested to be net spacers.

3.89 Edged blades of uncertain uses; perhaps scrapers or small hoes

3.90 Pointed artifacts possibly used as gravers, punches, lancets, drills, etc.

3.91 Slate ornaments in dummy shape: top, a butterfly stone blank; left, almost finished pendant; right, possibly a drilled unfinished banner stone

3.90

3.91

Some Special Tools and Crafts

As already noted, this is an artificial division, intended to combine the introduction of certain tools with a discussion of some of the major crafts of pre-Columbian days and to show the operations in some of the crafts. Among the more widely distributed crafts were weaving, skin dressing, sewing, and the making of bows and arrows, all of which were carried on practically all over prehistoric North America. Other important crafts were building—referred to in relation to housing; carving in all sorts of forms and manners; and pottery making, the latter also developed in detail elsewhere.

Bow and Arrow Making

By 1492, all the peoples of North America, with negligible exceptions, had learned to use the bow and arrow. This included the Eskimos, who continued—or possibly renewed—the use of the atlatl and spear which had preceded the bow and arrow. Therefore, they all had tools to manufacture these weapons.

The first Indian-manufactured items thought of in modern times are the arrowpoints that still dot the places where pre-Columbians once went about their daily affairs, fought one another, and were buried. Persons who have hunted these arrowheads, have, in many cases, come upon the chips left behind by their manufacture. In some locations where the wind has blown away lighter soil and particles, such chips may actually carpet the ground. How were they related to the making of arrows?

Some pretty silly answers have been bandied about, among them are "It's a lost art," and "They did it by dropping water on heated stone." The cure for belief of such answers is simple: Do it yourself. With no more than a nail and a little practice, anyone can make arrowheads. Some people have learned to make them so well that, as any experienced dealer can tell you, faking and its products have become a problem.

The Indians and Eskimos had no occasion for faking. What they made was for use and business. The basic tool was simple: a good chipping tool. This meant a tool with a hard, tough point, but one soft enough to get a grip on the edge of a flake and throw a good chip. An antler tip was ideal. A pad helped prevent cutting the hand. Perhaps a good tough hammerstone would be handy to knock off the initial flakes. Stone tools fashioned by skillful use of a hammer alone are said to be made with "primary flaking." Completing the formation of a flaked artifact by further chipping produced an artifact with "secondary chipping."

But making the arrowhead was the least of the operations required to make an arrow. In fact, a mere pointed chip of suitable size and shape could be a quite effective point. Making the shaft, notch, and feathering, and the lashing and gluing of the point were something else. Several tools other than chippers were involved, some general and some special.

One of the special tools was a gritty stone provided with a groove the size of half an arrow shaft. The typical form was a stone bar of some length, flat on one side and oval on the other, the groove being on the flat side. It is problematical whether these were to be used as mates with the groove of each coming together to round the shaft, but certainly quite a few have been found in pairs. Such stones are reported from all parts of the continent except the Eskimo country.

Often confused with such stones are grooved heat straighteners. Examination shows that these differ not only in their shapes, but especially in being made of smooth stone, commonly steatite, which withstands heat well. They do not have as wide a dispersal as the grooved polishers, nearly all being found in an arc from Texas through the Southwest and Pacific Coast to the Pacific Northwest. Their assumed use is the combination of heat and warping force. Experiment has shown them to be effective in reducing the joints of cane arrow shafts.

A special tool which also was widely used was an arrow wrench. Basically, this was a tool with a hole through which an arrow or dart shaft could be passed and gripped for local application of bending force. The tool could double as a gauge to obtain uniform diameter of a shaft, if such were desired. Most tools of this kind were of bone, a rib bone being typical material among the Plains Indians, although wrenches made of a sheep horn, of wood, of ivory, and of stone have been found. Ordinarily the hole or holes in Plains Indian wrenches were round or oval and about the size of shafts. Diamond-shaped holes were popular among the Eskimos.

Observant eyes have occasionally spotted semicircular notches in chipped knife blades which—because of their secondary chipping—were obviously created purposely. They have been called "shaft scrapers," but experiment shows a more extensive use; for if the notch is placed over a shaft the tool cuts more expeditiously than would a straight or curve-edged knife.

Other bow-and-arrow tools are pictured with the hunting gear; there are the Esikmos' sets consisting of marlin spikes and sinew twisters for cinching up the cordage on their bows and a feather setter to push the end of a feather vane into a slit—a method of fastening peculiar to the Eskimos.

Skin Dressing

One of the oldest crafts is skin dressing. This includes both preparation of hides with fur on and their preparation with fur off in the form of rawhide or leather. Even those tribes which used cloth or woven-bark products for clothing, or wore no clothing, did some skin dressing and used the tools that went with it.

Primary among these tools was a scraper to remove clinging meat, fat, and bulk from the inner surface of a hide. Its essential part was an edge of some kind that was not so sharp as to cut through the hide with a little pressure. The variety of ways in which such an edge was obtained and used is surprising.

The simplest and commonest identifiable scraper is a piece of stone with a half-round edge so that its cutting action was parallel to the skin rather than toward it, which meant that while it could cut away it did not cut through. Small scrapers of this type, of which thousands have been picked up, are called "thumbnail scrapers." Many were used between the thumb and fingers, and many more were fixed in some kind of handle.

A dull knife blade was also used as a scraper edge. There were many of these, of course. The Eskimos, for example, used their semilunar knives. Bone blades made satisfactory hide scrapers, and pieces of scapula were popular for this purpose in many areas. Ivory and horn took similar edges.

A rounded edge on a rough-surfaced stone was favored as a scraper among the Eskimos, as was a notched or serrated edge, particularly to clean off meaty fragments. Both tools are sometimes called "fleshers."

The Plains Indians were much given to the use of sharper blades set at a right angle in a handle adzewise. Lengths of elkhorn with a short right-angle bend which were used as handles for such tools are among the more familiar of Plains Indian artifacts. In modern times, the Indians used steel blades supplanting the chipped flint blades of older times—identified by the unwary as adze blades or celts.

One form of edged bone tool called a "beamer" was made in its simplest form of a length of rib. In a little more elaborate form it was made by scooping out the center of a long bone and using the two ends as handles. The hide was laid over a log to facilitate use of this tool.

Scraper handles took numerous shapes, from simple handles like knife handles, or the cutoff end of a spear, to pistol-grip forms and, in the Arctic where slippery, greasy fingers were a problem, to intricate grips with deep pits for the fingers.

Besides scrapers, there were smooth stones used as hide rubbers or softeners. Most of these cannot be identified, because ordinary water-worn stones could and did serve without artificial alteration. Perhaps a few "pestles" were so used.

Special strong, coarse combs were used by the Eskimos to clean out and smooth fur. Shells and bones with notches may have been used for scrapers or as fish scalers. The long bones cut diagonally across and provided with notches were fleshers. In later times, pieces of gun barrels treated the same way were certainly fleshers. A few are still being used in back country as efficient hide-working tools.

Cordage Making

Cordage includes rope, string, thongs, thread, and their equivalents.

Pre-Columbians found that nature offered much ready-made cordage. Halibut fishers in the Northwest Coast area, for instance, used long ropes of kelp as cordage. Strings and threads of sinew were in constant use, and vines, strips of bark, roots, and so on were effectively and broadly utilized.

The simplest type of manufactured cordage was a strip of leather or buckskin. The long fringes on some Indian clothing came in handy at times as short lengths of twine. The Northwoods Indians, of whom the Woods Cree were typical, made a style of string called "babiche" by cutting a strip of leather spiralwise so that it reached considerable length.

Cordage made with rolled and twisted fibers fashioned for use from thread to ropes was also known everywhere in great variety. A considerable display could be made of all the different ways, results, and materials involved in pre-Columbian manufacture of cordage.

Cordage was commonly started by rolling the material on the thigh, but spindles were well known in several areas, and the Eskimos developed a little whirling instrument made of ivory. Some objects with two holes might have been cordage twisters—gorgets, for example, when they were not worn as a decoration.

The variety of material made into cords is surprising: from fragile grass and hay to tough fibers of milkweed and nettles. Sometimes additional strength was gained by braiding—a common practice among the Eskimos and Plains Indians. Probably the strongest and thickest cordage was made by the Indians around Vancouver Island who hunted whales and made towropes of quantities of sinew that rivaled steel cables in strength. The other extreme was reached with the fine cordage used to string beads with unbelievably small holes.

Net Weaving

Among the direct uses of cordage was the making of nets. These are usually associated with fishing and marine cultures, but the pre-Columbians used nets a great deal for catching birds and animals—as is indicated in the section on traps and snares. A net forty feet long was a dry-cave find in the desert interior. It was used to catch rabbits and birds.

Netting also merged into cloth, being used for bags in decreasing mesh size till it was indistinguishable from cloth at first glance. It was made both with and without knotting.

All this called for special tools which took about the same essential shapes everywhere they were used: bobbins, needles, and net gauges or spacers made of wood, ivory, bone, baleen, and horn.

Cloth Weaving

Because buckskin garments are so picturesque and familiar in association with Indians, it is sometimes assumed that all cloth was brought to Indians by Europeans. This is not so. Cloth introduced by traders was, however, adopted early for imitation, decoration, comfort, and—in conformity to what were conceived of as white men's rules—more or less covering the person. Some cloth was put to peculiarly Indian usage, notably among the Seminoles and Navajos. It is also true that other materials were preferred in many areas, and for many a good reason, as witness the use of fur in the Arctic.

The most extensive use of cloth was in the Southwest, where it is still woven into garments on occasion, as well as into the well-known Navajo blankets. Weaving of textiles was practiced in the Northwest Coast area, also—for example, the Chilkat blankets prized by art connoisseurs—and in making lesser articles elsewhere in both historic and prehistoric times.

In the Southwest cloth was woven on regular looms, with all the "fixings" of batten sticks, needles, and combs; other forms of looms were used on the Northwest Coast. But much cloth was woven with the fingers, just as basketry is woven, and in some cases it merged with netting. Certain basketry-weaving methods are the same as some which produce cloth, and some basketry woven with soft ribbons of bark or with fine grass approximates a form of cloth in texture and appearance.

Among the minor oddities involved in weaving is what is believed to be a last. Made in the Southwest of flat stone, it had the exact shape of a prehistoric woven sandal. Another minor artifact connected with weaving is a loom weight.

Sewing

Sewing with needle and thread was practiced by both the Indians and the Eskimos. Some specimens from the Arctic rival the best European work in quality. However, just as much sewing was done with an awl—punching holes through which thread was passed—as awls were about the commonest and most widespread of bone and horn tools. All tailored garments involved sewing, as did a number of leather utensils and implements. Most of the thread used was made of fine strands of sinew.

Pre-Columbian needles differed in function and form as well as in length. Some long needles were used in thatching and in making mats. The Eskimos used a needle to thread a carrying cord through fowls' wings. Some needles were not needles at all but were awls with holes for cord loops. One artifact that appears to be a needle was neither a needle nor an awl, but a decoration. A California mound some few years ago yielded a necklace with forty such "beads." Things are not always what they seem.

One of the oddest forms of Indian needles was made by taking a cactus spine along with a length of the plant to which it was attached, shredding the length, and making it into a thread to be used by a needle that didn't need to be threaded. The holes were usually round and drilled, but in some cases they were slits sawed in the head of the needle. In one artifact, the eye of the needle is in the tip, as in our sewing-machine needles.

Along with needles went sewing kits and, in the Arctic, needlecases. In areas where the awl was used, the sewing kit involved an awl case—one of the most familiar of Plains Indian personal effects.

Use of needles among the Eskimos developed use of thimbles. The commonest kind of thimble in the Arctic was a leather patch with a loop to attach it to a bone or ivory hook called a "thimble guard." This was fastened to many needlecases, which were hollow holders of some kind made of bird bones or hollowed-out ivory or bone. Needles were put in and taken out of such a case stuck in a leather ribbon which passed through it. A common accessory of these needlecases and kits was a sharpener, usually a piece of jade on a thong. Sometimes the Eskimos made thimbles in finger-stall form.

An adjunct of sewing boots and moccasins in the Arctic was a small bone or ivory knife called a "moccasin creaser." It was used to make the creases for the wide, turned-up sections of Eskimo boot soles. Not so well authenticated are moccasin lasts—stones the shape of moccasin soles—which we see in some collections. Testimony as to their actual use in making moccasins is disputed, but it is possible they were used the same way our grandmothers used china and wooden "eggs" inside socks while darning.

A form of sewing not associated with cloth was practiced by basket weavers using the coil method; the fastening together of the coils is called "stitching." Some of the fibrous stitching thread was so fine and so closely placed that in the heyday of basket collecting, masterpieces were judged by how many threads or stitches were crammed into an inch.

Bark and Rush Weaving

As already pointed out, some materials woven with soft ribbons of bark and with grasses, including rushes, assumed the nature and uses of cloth. Most of these were mats, but in some cases were bags, such as the cornshuck bags familiar as products of the Nez Percé Indians and their neighbors.

Rush mats had widespread use for bedding, rugs, capes, and covers for temporary huts. Their construction involved fastening rushes together with cordage. This was done with successive ties by some tribes, but a Northwest Coast method involved passing a needle through the rushes. This needle was ridged, and while it was imbedded full length in the rushes being bound, a tool called a "mat creaser" was rocked on it. This tool had a groove which fitted over the ridge on the needle so that a crease in the rushes resulted from its use, making the mat more pliable and less likely to come apart by the rushes splitting.

Bark mats were nearly always made by simple checkerboard-pattern plaiting; decoration was effected by using bark ribbons of differing shades. Sometimes such mats were gaily painted with totemic designs.

Preparation of bark ribbons for the mats involved two kinds of tools. One was a chopper much like an old-fashioned hash knife in form but with a dull edge that crushed but did not cut. It was usually made of whalebone. The other was a pounder shaped somewhat like a hairbrush but with a solid block in place of the brush. Grooves were cut in the block. It is interesting to note that bark pounders in the South Sea Islands also have grooved faces.

Basketry

Basketry is commonly misunderstood, even by dictionary editors, as being confined to the making of baskets, meaning forms of basketry containers. This is probably due to the fact that of the products of basketry once numerous in olden times only the containers are still familiarly in use. The other products are forgotten. In pre-Columbian North America, basketry produced bedding, hats, cradles, sails, bags, moccasins, cages, etc. Otis Tufton Mason in his classic *Aboriginal American Basketry* states: "Before the coming of Europeans, basketry supplied nearly every domestic necessity of the Indians, from an infant's cradle to the richly decorated funerary jars burned with the dead." He lists more than a hundred uses.

Basketry is a branch of weaving, and it is somewhat confusing to distinguish some of its products from cloth and from netting in cases where the material is soft or where the purpose is to use meshes to catch things, as in fish traps. Generally speaking, however, its materials possess varying degrees of stiffness and elasticity as contrasted to the limp fibers or threads that compose cloth and cordage of nets.

Another difficulty that comes up in being precise about what basketry is, is the inclusion in its ranks of articles made by sewing. All basketry is either handwoven or sewed.

The other name for sewed basketry is "coiled basketry." This is basketry built on a foundation of rods, splints, or straws that coil as they create desired shapes and are fastened by welding the coils with over-and-around stitching that, in turn, coils around the coils. At least, that is the basic idea, though it is somewhat embarrassing to note that what Mason calls "coiled work without foundation" lacks the basic coils and, in fact, is cited by others as "knotless netting" (exemplified by the Northwoods Indian babiche bags and by Pima carrying baskets on frames made of agave twine). But, with due respect to Mason, these latter are more netting than basketry. Therefore, we may return to the stipulation that all coiled basketry has basic coils which correspond somewhat to the warp in straight weaving.

The chief, in fact the only essential, tool for coiled basketry was an awl. Of course, a needle with an eye would, and perhaps did, serve as well or better.

Coiled basketry has some ten varieties according to Mason's analysis. The differences are in the nature of the coils: single rod, splint foundation, grass coil foundation, and so on.

Woven basketry divides into five fairly distinct forms or methods: checkerwork, twilling, wickerwork, wrapped work, and twined weaving.

Checkerwork has no distinction of warp and **weft**, the structural elements having the same thickness and pliability. Characteristically, they have the appearance of ribbons. As they are plaited by passing alternately over and under, the resulting surface has a checkered appearance—hence the name. In modern industry, checkerwork often appears as the structure of clothes hampers woven with ribbons of wood, and it was once familiar on egg baskets. Similar use with ribbons of wood was popular among the Eastern Woodland Indians. Checkerwork with ribbons of soft bark, grass, or other pliable material has a quite different texture, though it has the same geometric appearance. It is the basis of nearly all bark matting and was a favorite weave for the bottoms of Salishan basketry. By using ribbons of different shades or colors, designs could be created to ornament the artifact.

Twilling was similar to checker plaiting in that in many examples there was no material distinction between warp and weft elements. However, twilling was basically a process of passing each element of a weft over two or more warp elements, thus producing a number of different geometric patterns other than checkering and usually involving a slant. It was also a favorite among the Eastern Woodland Indians. Much of the decorative basketry made by Indians of the Deep South is made in this way, using varied colors of ribbons as was done with checkerwork. Imprints of basketry on clay in Mound Builder areas indicate that the ancient inhabitants knew how to use substances of different widths for warp and weft elements, thus obtaining further ornamentation.

Wickerwork involves stiff, though elastic, elements. The warp is inflexible and comparatively thick; the weft is flexible and comparatively slender. Wickerwork is plaited like checkerwork, but its appearance is distinctly altered by the fact that one element is rigid and both elements are usually round instead of flat. It is the conventional weave for modern wastebaskets.

As a simple and utilitarian form, wickerwork had wide use, which extended to some constructions not customarily associated with basketry, such as fish weirs and house walls. It was popular for containers in the East, but was largely ignored for most basketry purposes among the Eskimos and Indians of the Pacific Coast.

Wrapped work is similar to wickerwork in that the warp elements are rigid and the weft elements flexible, but instead of the latter being simply plaited they take a turn around each warp rod in their progress. This means, of course, that they are much more flexible than most wicker wefts. As a representative technique in North America, wrapped work can be passed over as little used. It might be noted, however, that it was a form known to the Mound Builders.

Twined weaving, in five variations, shared with coiled or sewed weaving the major portion of popularity among the master weavers who flourished on the Pacific Coast, where basketry reached the peak of its use and beauty. It depends on relatively stiff warp strands on which flexible weft strands are twined and interlaced in various ways, producing a distinctly characteristic appearance.

Much basketry, especially on the Pacific Coast and in the Southwest, was ornamented. Structural ornament has already been referred to as the use of different colors of elements and the different appearance of surfaces resulting from modes of construction. In addition, there were other methods, among which were imbrication, false embroidery, and incorporation of feathers, beads, quills, yarn, and other additional materials believed to be decorative. Some examples are given in the illustrations.

Imbrication was effected by addition of colored ribbons or strips of colored bark or grass fastened to the surface of coiled basketry by being doubled over and caught by the stitching in such a way that the stitching is covered and only the imbricated surface shows.

Feather surfaces were created by catching the vanes of feathers in the stitching as it progressed. They were most freely produced by the Pomo Indians of California, who often covered entire surfaces with featherwork in brightly colored designs.

False embroidery was best exemplified in twined baskets made by the Tlingit Indians of Alaska. Like imbrication, the decorating material was caught as an extra strand outside the main body of the basket, and hence does not appear inside. It also created colored designs by the use of colored strands of grass.

Painting of basketry surfaces was another Northwest Indian practice, the designs usually being totemic and appearing on ceremonial hats and mats.

As an appendix to the discussion of basketry, there are a few comments about a modern aspect. The aesthetic character of Indian basketry was "discovered" around 1900 and burgeoned into a fad of the craze type, similar to later fashionable emoting over "primitive art," particularly Northwest Coast and Eskimo art. As its devotees became old ladies and gentlemen, however, the heat cooled off and their heirs came to wondering what to do with the accumulations. The result has been a plethora of baskets, a famine of collectors, and speculation as to whether desire to own baskets will "come back." A second result—good—has been the preservation of much basketry that otherwise would have been discarded and lost. But another result—not so good—has been a misinterpretation of the role of basketry in the life of the First Americans, emphasizing the pretty and ignoring the utilitarian. Museums have, to a large degree, followed the crowd in this misconception.

Arrow- and Bow-making Tools
3.92 Four major forms of arrow-working tools; shaft wrench of sheep horn, Southwest; heat straightener with what look like ownership marks engraved on it; antler arrow chipper; grooved shaft polisher
3.93 Various forms of possible chipping tools; a beveled point on an "awl" would seem to have no other purpose than to make it stouter for chipping.
3.94 Chipping tools and bone chipping points; top, Pomo; center, Northwest Coast or Eskimo; bottom, South Dakota and southern California
3.95 Eskimo pistol-grip chippers, point on top one made of copper.
3.96 Long-handled flakers designed to lie alongside the forearm for more leverage
3.97 Close-ups of tip ends of (3.96)
3.98-3.100 Arrow wrenches for concentrating bending on shafts, and in some cases possibly for measuring diameter: (3.98) Eskimo, with diamond-shaped openings; (3.99) lava stone, Nevada, traces of paint inside hole indicate use on a finished arrow; (3.100) left, two typical of Plains sites, these South Dakota; right, a Utah cave find, holes of different sizes

3.92

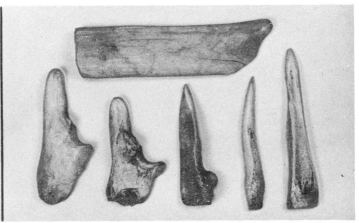

3.93

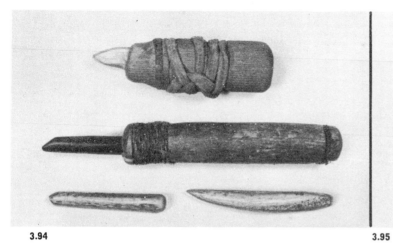

3.94

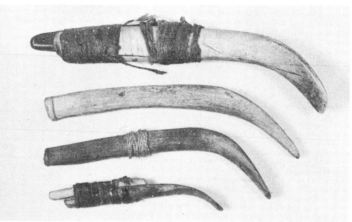

3.95

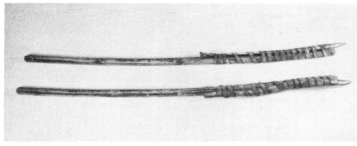

3.96

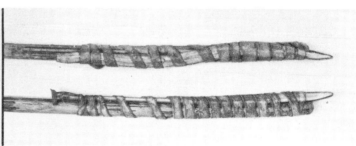

3.97

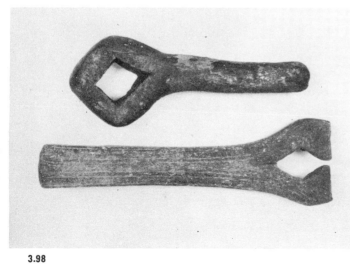

3.98

3.99

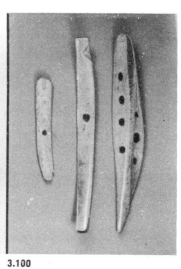

3.100

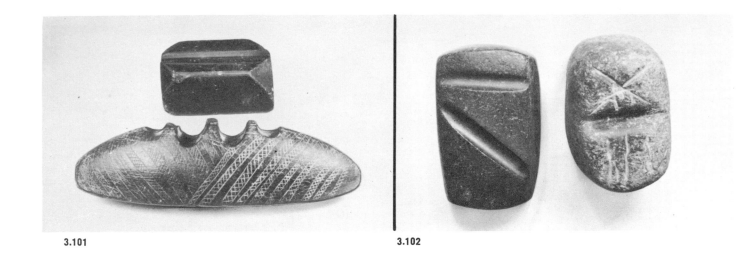

3.101

3.102

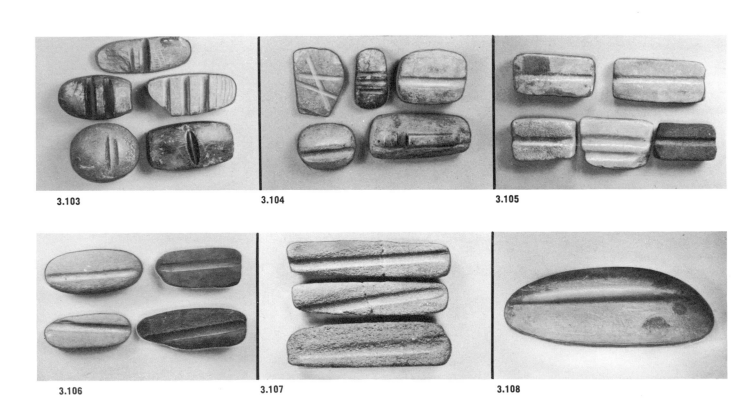

3.103

3.104

3.105

3.106

3.107

3.108

3.109

98

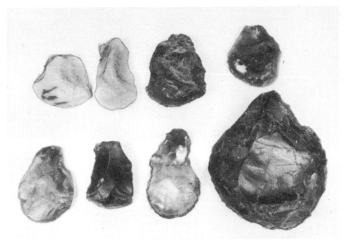

3.110

3.111

3.101 Unusually ornate steatite heat straighteners from Santa Barbara coastal sites, California
3.102 Straighteners with cross and diagonal grooves; with incised markings
3.103-3.104 Heat straighteners from Pacific Coast, Southwest, Kansas, and Texas
3.105 Abrasive shaft smoothers from various localities
3.106-3.108 Shaft polishers or smoothers, including three pairs from Columbia River, Washington, and California sites
3.109 Long Eastern Woodland shaft polishers; top, Butler County, Ohio; lower, provenience unknown, 8½ inches long

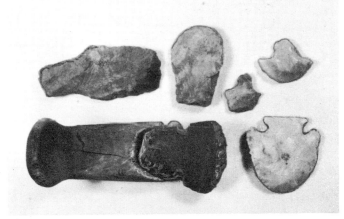

3.112

Skin-Dressing Tools
3.110-3.111 Skin scraper blades and tips, mostly snub-nosed of so-called "thumbnail" type. Some of these were fitted into handles like knives, others used with the fingers. Shell (3.111) may be a fish scaler.
3.112-3.113 Skin scraper tips or blades, one (3.112) set in Eskimo wooden pistol-grip handle to show seating (lashing lost); three in (3.113) for hoe-type handles

3.113

3.114

3.115

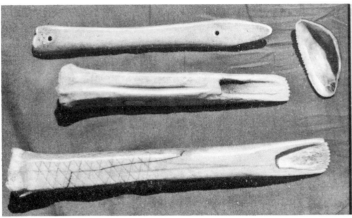

3.116

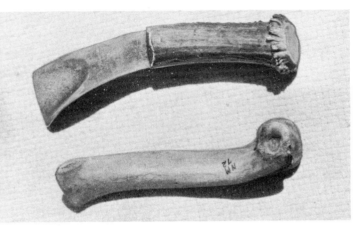

3.117

3.114 Edged bone scrapers, top for two hands, called a "beamer," used to scrape fur off a hide laid over a log

3.115 Eskimo bone and ivory tools; left top, fur comb; left lower, scapula bone scraper; right upper, edged bracelet or cookie-cutter-shaped scraper; the right lower scoop type with finger grooves was flipped in use to scrape forward and backward.

3.116 Serrated-edge fleshers; top, Southwest; center, Illinois; and bottom, Canadian Woods Cree; right, shell, central California

3.117 Horn and bone "fleshers," or scrapers, without teeth, Southwest origins

3.118-3.119 Eskimo finger pit scrapers, wood and ivory handles: two in (3.18) with round-edged abrasive stone blades; three in (3.119) with flaked snub-nose blades

3.120-3.122 Long-handled scrapers: (3.120) elkhorn handles; left, Blackfoot with flint blade; right, iron blade; (3.121) elkhorn handle and Arikara wooden handle with bone blade; (3.122) Eskimo and Northwest Coast pistol-grip scrapers, stone blades

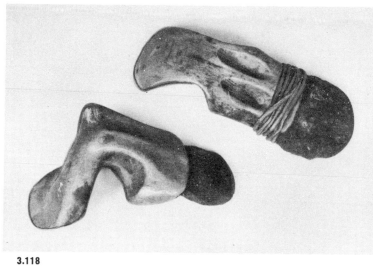

3.118

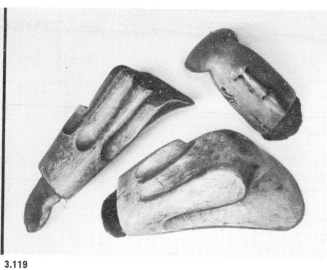

3.119

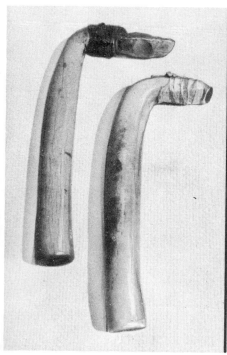

3.120

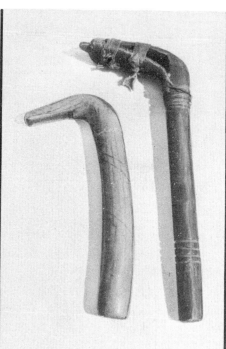

3.121

3.122

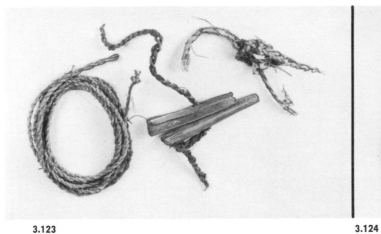

3.123

3.124

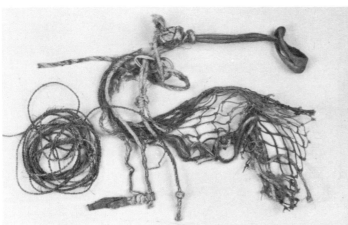

3.125

3.126

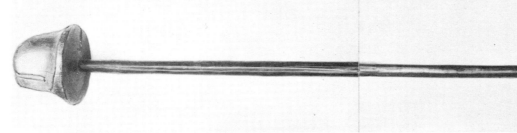

3.127

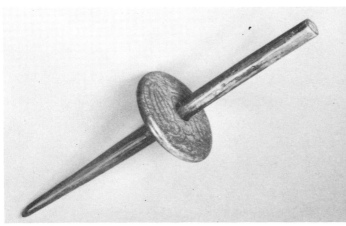

3.128

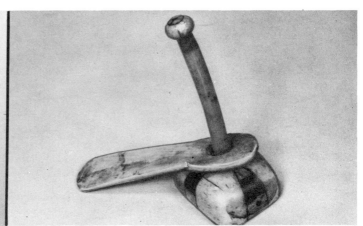

3.129

Cordage Making

3.123 Sioux cordage bowstring; sagebrush bark cordage through rushes, cave near Vantage on the Columbia River; and braided grass cordage from same area

3.124 Southern California sea grass cord, San Nicolas Island; hank of cordage fiber, northwest California; Plains Indian ribbons of sinew

3.125 Varieties of northwest California cordage; net specimen has four kinds.

3.126 Top, Paiute sagebrush bark rope; center, remnant of sinew fiber whale-towing rope, Makah Indians, Washington; bottom, section of braided rawhide picket or lasso rope, Sioux

3.127 Carved wood tool used by Makah Indians in making whale rope; cut from one piece of yew wood in effigy of a whale

3.128 Northwest Coast nettle fiber spindle with carved whalebone spindle whorl

3.129 Eskimo ivory sinew spinner. The sinew to be spun is attached to the flat arm next the hole and the arm is then whirled around on the rod.

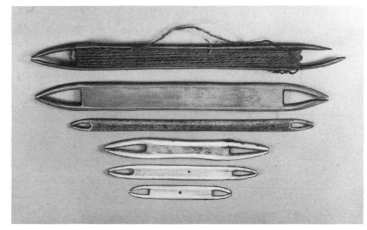

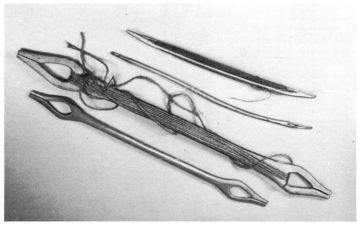

3.130

Net Making

3.130 Eskimo net bobbins; top two, wood, bottom four, ivory

3.131 Northwest California and Oregon coast net bobbins of bone and wood

3.132 Eskimo net needles, baleen and ivory

3.133 Net gauges or spacers, top to bottom center, four Eskimo; left, central California; right, Yurok, California

3.131

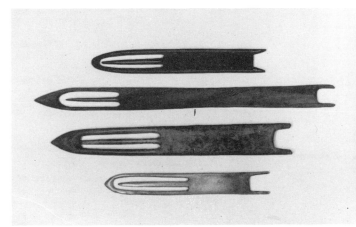

3.132

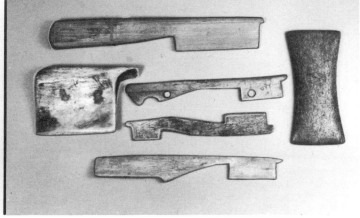

3.133

3.134

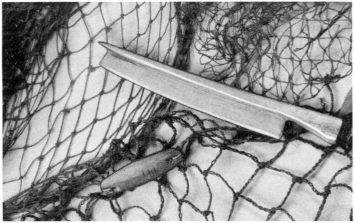

3.135

3.134 Northwest California net maker's
work bundle with wooden net spacers
3.135 Close-up of netting, and an Eskimo
ivory gauge with wide spacing; two upper
fine-meshed dip nets are from northwest
California; lower, a miniature Eskimo gill
net (note cordage twister); all nets are
knotted at joins.

Cloth Weaving
3.136 Woven strips of rabbit fur, a
favorite form of "cloth" for blankets and
winter wear
3.137 Prehistoric cloth fragments: Temple
Mound; cave, southern Arizona; burials,
central California
3.138 Native woven cloth, conventionally
woven (with fingers); (a) in Yurok-Hupa
dance snood, (b) in Pomo headband, (c) in
Klikitat headband
3.139 Net-type weaving: in bag, in Yurok-
Hupa snood, and in example of Canadian
Northwoods knotless netting with rawhide
strips (babiche)
3.140-3.141 . Model of Navajo loom showing
weaving tools, construction of loom and
method of using loom
3.142 Prehistoric batten stick, New
Mexico
3.143 Sandal last, Hovenweep Canyon,
Colorado

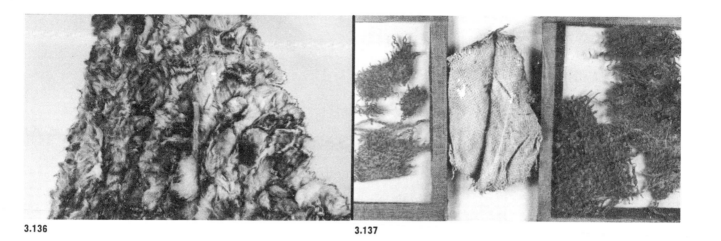

3.136   3.137

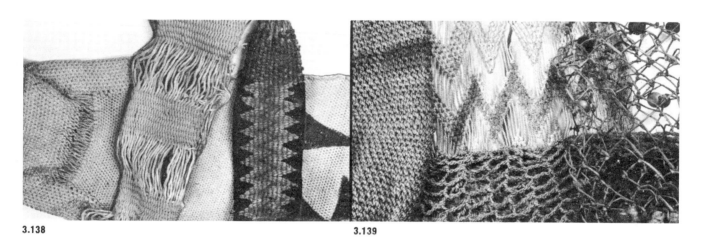

3.138   3.139

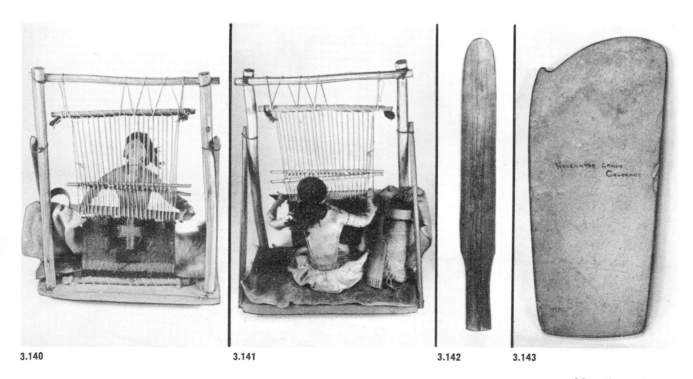

3.140   3.141   3.142   3.143

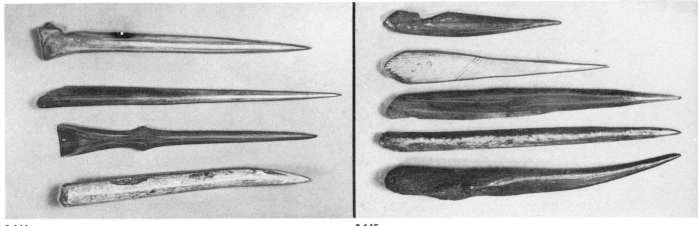

3.144

3.145

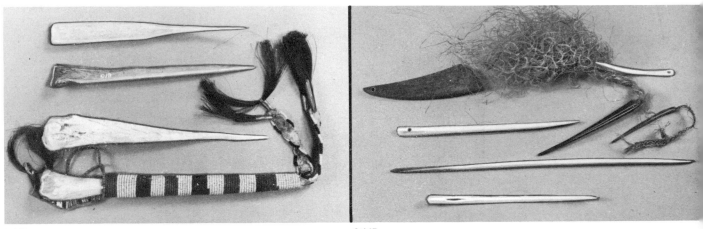

3.146

3.147

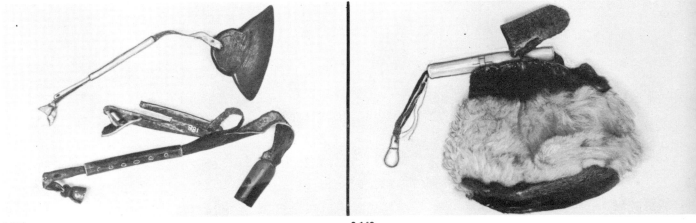

3.148

3.149

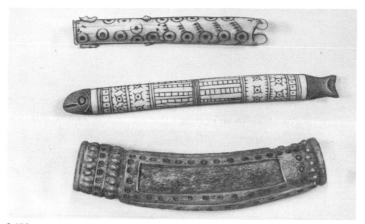

3.150

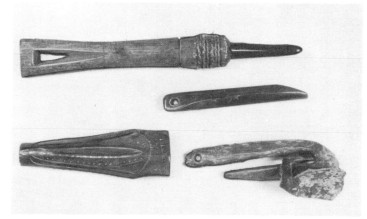

3.151

3.152

Sewing

3.144-3.145 Awls made of bone and ivory from various localities from New York to California and Alaska

3.146 Bone awls, bottom one in its beaded awl case used by Plains Indians

3.147 Needles; top group, bone with hole in tip, thorns with attached fiber loose and made into cordage, and shell needle; second row, bird bone with drilled eye; long mammal bone with slit eye, San Nicolas Island, California; and bird bone with slit eye, Oregon coast

3.148 Eskimo sewing sets with needlecases; top, with slate knife attached, needle in leather ribbon to be drawn in and out of bird bone, animal tooth ornaments on end of ribbon; bottom, similar arrangement, with whetstone, thimble guard, and patch-type thimble at one end of ribbon and ivory ornament at other

3.149 Eskimo fur sewing bag with ivory needlecase and finger-stall type thimble

3.150 Eskimo ivory needlecases; center, with fish effigy wooden stoppers

3.151 Needle sharpener in handle and another drilled for suspension; old Bering culture needlecase; and thimble guard or hook, with patch-type thimble

3.152 Awl or needle-sharpening stone with many grooves from early culture California site

3.153 Sharpening stones from New York, Ohio, Kansas, and California

3.153

3.154

3.155

3.156

3.157

3.158

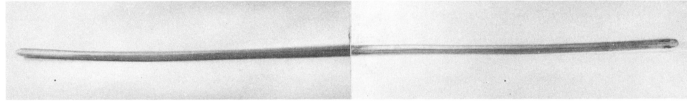

3.159

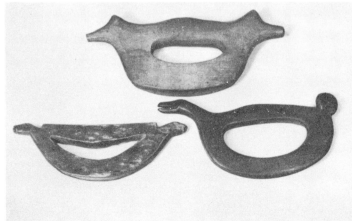

3.160

3.161

*Apache Indian basketry bowl; typical star
"snowflake" design with interspersed figures
in red and black*

Bark and Rush Textiles and Tools

3.154   Whalebone bark chopper for breaking bark fibers

3.155   Grooved bark pounder for shredding bark

3.156   Section of bark mat showing creation of design with different colors of bark ribbons

3.157   Plain checkerboard woven or plaited mat

3.158   Small rush mat; these, large and small, had widespread use among Indians as bedding, floor coverings, capes, and hut coverings.

3.159   A mat needle for rush mats; flat with a ridge to make a shallow triangular channel; run through rushes to sew them together.

3.160   Northwest Coast mat creasers, grooved and rolled over the ridge on the needle to create a crease, a succession of such creases along the sewed lines made the mat more secure from breaking and more pliable.

3.161   Close-up of rush mat, showing results of sewing with needle and creaser

Major Basketry Methods

3.162-3.163   Wickerwork, and Hopi tray woven by this method

3.164-3.165   Checkerwork, plaited bark ribbons, and Vancouver Island basket woven in same way

3.162

3.163

3.164

3.165

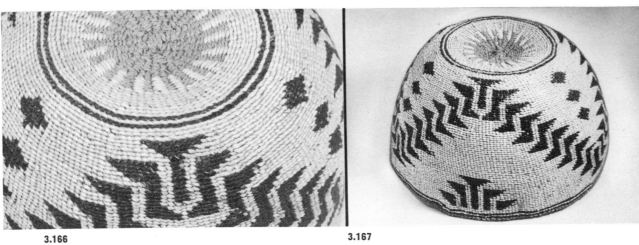

3.166   3.167

3.168

3.169

3.166-3.167 Twined weaving, and northern
California woman's cap so woven
3.168 Coiled (sewed) basketry, stitches
wound around coils in spiral formation
3.169 Maidu (?) bowl of coiled basketry

Basketry Ornamentation
3.170-3.171 Imbrication on a coiled
Thompson River (British Columbia) basket,
and the basket
3.172-3.173 False embroidery, colored
grass weft that does not go behind the
warp, so does not show inside, and Tlingit
basket so ornamented
3.174-3.175 Feather and shell decoration
on a Pomo coiled basket, a form of
ornamentation at which the Pomos are
experts
3.176-3.177 Painting on a twined
Northwest Coast hat; totemic design of
raven on the hat

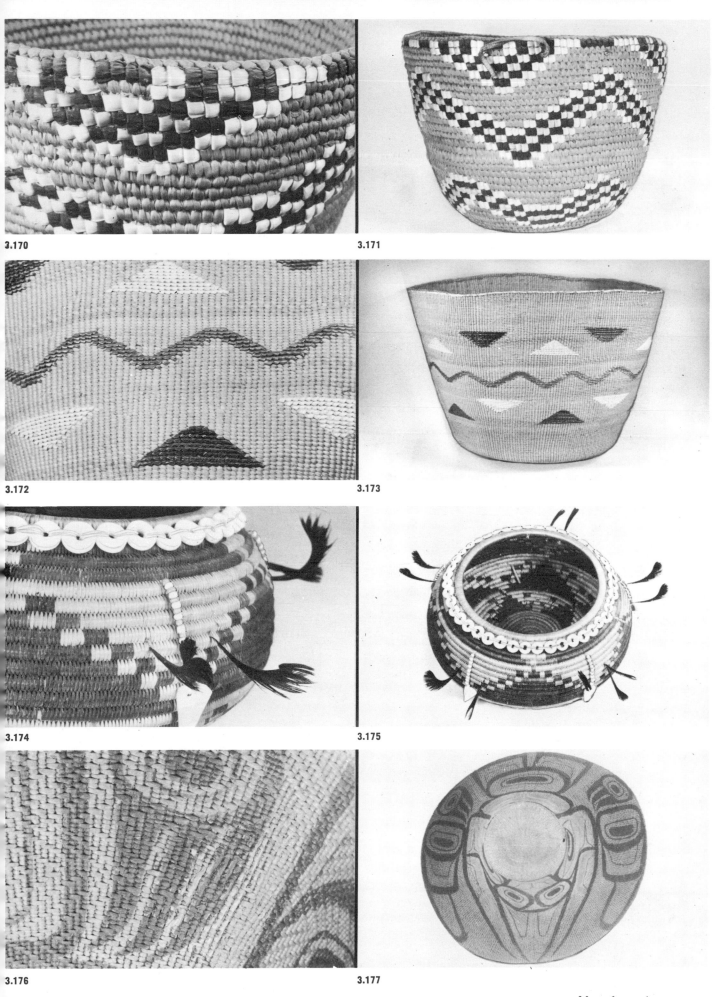

3.170

3.171

3.172

3.173

3.174

3.175

3.176

3.177

4 Pre-Columbian Clothing

The pre-Columbians were very casual, one might say natural, about wearing clothes. They wore them by compulsion from the elements rather than because of modesty; they shed them for numerous, though to us invalid, reasons. Even the Eskimos, among the most thoroughly covered up of earth's peoples, blandly went "back to nature" in the warmth of their igloos. The Indians' habits in respect to off and on of raiment were what a good Victorian would consider shocking; though the Indians didn't know this until missionaries and women from Europe converted them, or appeared to have done so.

Our impression that the pre-Columbians were as addicted to clothes as we are, besides our being protected by suppression of embarrassing facts, has been nurtured on the theatrical qualities of Plains Indian chiefs' regalia as seen in movie Westerns, old dime novels, Buffalo Bill shows, rodeos, and photos and picture postcards of the crowds at Southwest Indian snake dances. This sort of clothing was, however, somewhat of the nature of our displays of fraternal, military, and fanciful costumes in parades.

Nevertheless, pre-Columbians did have utility clothes and did wear them; albeit somewhat less seriously than we do. These clothes were of two styles: tailored and untailored.

The Eskimos wore tailored clothes (as we do). Their basic costume, consisting of a hooded coat or shirt called a "parka" and a pair of trousers, was, and is, fitted to their bodies and limbs by cutting to a pattern and sewing. Some of the northern Indians were in the first stages of beginning to tailor their garments. However, most of the rest of the First North Americans wore untailored clothing—or nothing or practically nothing.

The partly tailored clothing in use by the northern Indians included buckskin dresses and shirts with sewn sides and fitted leggings. The same Indians commonly made other dresses, shirts, and leggings that were not cut or sewn to fit. The two former garments were basically ponchos of two skins sewn at the shoulders, leaving a neck hole. The leggings were little more than leather tubes to protect the legs—a form of garment familiar today as cowboys' chaps.

Perhaps the most important item of untailored clothing was the blankets, made, as it had been for centuries of man's estate on earth, from the appropriated hides of departed animals. A variation of this simple hide type was a blanket woven with strips of rabbit fur. The reason the blanket was so important was that the regular clothing was not sufficient to keep even the hardiest Indian from freezing, or at least from acute discomfort, when quiescent. It was worn by simply draping and wrapping it about the person.

Along with blankets, the most universally worn article of attire was footgear in the form of moccasins, sandals, or boots. Next were breechclouts and aprons for men, and aprons, wraparound or belt-hung kilts, and dresses for women. Various other articles assumed importance in certain areas: rain capes and hats in the Northwest; a toga-style blouse and sash and kilts for men and women in the Southwest; and so on.

Most of these garments were made of leather with and without the fur on, which, in the latter case, was popularly spoken of as buckskin. Only in the Southwest were they made of cloth, which was woven there from native cotton and wool.

Women's Clothing

Although North America's pre-Columbian women could not enjoy distracting their pretty heads with fascinating worries about what was stylish in Paris, Hollywood, or among the hepcats, they managed to amuse themselves quite a bit, even with what little many of them had to wear. (Look what can be dreamed up to make one of our dwarf bikinis cost a day's income!)

One might think their Eskimo sisters were handicapped because they had to get along with the same pattern of clothing worn by men, assuredly styling that did little for a good figure. But it needs but a glance at a photograph of an Eskimo group to tell us that such handicaps did not at all interfere with telling which was the fair sex—and "What deliriously beautiful fur coats; and for everyday, too!"

Elsewhere to the south, Indian women's clothing was more specialized, and among the northern Indians nearly full-length buckskin dresses gave ample opportunities for decorative effects. Later, these dresses were tailored on the Mother Hubbard pattern, but the original versions were basically like ponchos—a hole for

Women's Clothing

4.1 Kilt or petticoat like a hula skirt, made of bark strands in locks, or tresses, looped at one end and strung on a belt cord; northwest California. This was the prevailing form of women's skirts on the Pacific Coast.

4.2-4.3 Buckskin apron (4.2) with pine nuts and braided straw on fringing. This, with a buckskin-fringed skirt (4.3) was another version of the kilt dress. Usually the fringed apron was in front with the leather behind, or both aprons might be of the same material.

4.4 Heavy buckskin "dress-up" apron, ornamented with fringing, abalone shells, and beads; northwest California

4.5 Indian and Eskimo belts; quilled and goat tooth decorations, and loom beaded on leather thongs

4.1   4.2   4.3

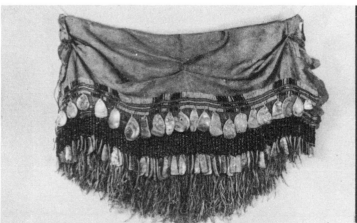

4.4   4.5

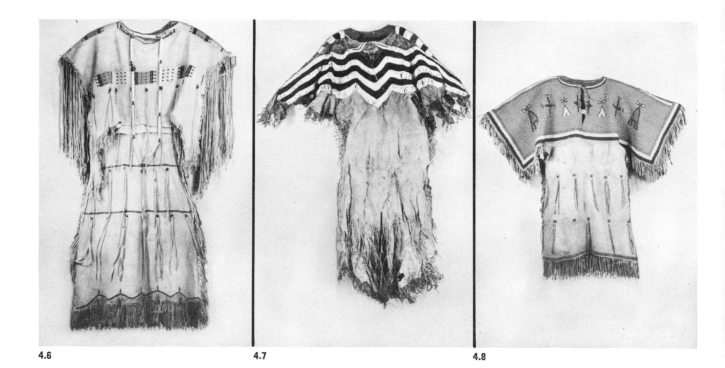

4.6 **4.7** **4.8**

4.6 Late period Plains Indian dress; beaded, fringed, and painted
4.7 Older form of dress, heavily beaded capelike top; pony beads; old design; deer tail tab under neck opening; same construction as typical man's shirt

4.8 Plains girl's dress, heavy solid beading; tipi and star design on a solid blue field

the neck with the back and front held around the body by a belt, leaving the sides unsewn.

Because the climate was milder to the south, the influence of the newer tailored clothing was less potent there, so dresses gave place to skirts or kilts. In prehistoric and early colonial times, most of the Indian women east of the Mississippi wore calf-length buckskin wraparound skirts with the edges barely meeting at one thigh to give freedom of movement. On the Pacific Coast, the basic costume was a kilt: sometimes a wraparound; sometimes suspended from a belt cord hula-skirt style; at times of leather or of ribbons, strings, strips of bark, grass, or native string, exactly like South Sea skirts. Another characteristic convenience on the Coast was to improve on the Eastern slit by dividing skirts into fore and aft sections.

Southwest Indian women wore a basic costume using a rectangle of native woven cotton or wool cloth folded in half across the width and wrapped around the body so that the fold was on one side from the armpit to below the knees. The upper corners were pinned over one shoulder as on a Roman toga, with the free end edges running down the same side of the body. The entire ensemble was held together with a sashlike belt. Colorful embroidery could enliven such costumes for dress-up occasions.

Another embellishment peculiar to the women of this area was the addition of bulky leg coverings created by puttee windings. One might wonder why

4.9-4.11 Plains Indians' dolls showing their own versions of how the well-dressed woman should appear; note earrings and nose ring of beads to liven up the (4.10) center doll's appearance.
4.12 Sioux woman's beaded leggings and moccasins
4.13 Plains woman's long leggings with extensions for fastening to a belt
4.14 Pueblo Indian doll, showing method of wearing toga with one arm free, a belt-sash, and typical fringe ornamentation; moccasins of local form topped with bulky wrap-around leggings; headdress unusual and worn for ceremonial purposes (Oakland Public Museum specimen). (Pueblo Indians wove their own cotton cloth and wore the poncho-kilt form of clothing.)
4.15 "Chorus line" of Eskimo beauties tripping an Arctic "light fantastic." This was an outdoor affair, as is indicated by the girls wearing full-hooded parkas, breeches, and boots; for indoor dancing see the anthropology books listed in the Bibliography.

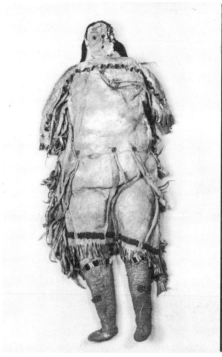
4.9

4.10

4.11

4.12

4.13

4.14

4.15

women would ever want to cover up these now popular evidences of allure and, above all, make them look fat. But if one considers that in the older American days the most triumphant catch a woman could attract was a good provider, and that a good provider might feed his light of love so well that her legs would get fat, a little figuring will show that vanity was served after all.

Similar leg coverings of gaily beaded buckskin tubes were also worn by Plains Indian women to ornament the areas between the bottoms of their dresses and their moccasins. Occasionally, they wore hip-length leggings with extensions fastened at the waist for the same purpose.

Men's Clothing

As already noted, except for the Eskimos, the pre-Columbian American man's basic costume was a pair of moccasins and a breechclout, or, if he preferred, nothing at all. Setting aside the matter of costume protocol, one wonders how those men who lived in the frigid weather of northern winter climates could stand it. To this there is an old answer concerning a hardy brave encountered in snowy surroundings so attired who answered this problem thus: "White man no cover face. Indian all face." Actually, if he was out in such weather and not running to keep his blood circulating, he wrapped himself in a blanket—in old days made of a furry hide, and in historic days of traders' wool. This practice resulted in the familiar term "blanket Indians."

The Indian man could dress in more extensive clothing on occasion. Perhaps most familiar along this line are the shirts and leggings of northern Indians, particularly those of the Plains. The shirts were worn for both comfort and ceremony, and their construction in olden times was the same as that of women's dresses in the area—sewn only at the shoulders—so that they were, in effect, a cape with a neck hole, or a poncho. The leggings ranged from tailored garments fitting the legs quite snuggly to skirt-like flapping affairs that have been adopted by white men as *chaparajos*, or, (abbreviated) chaps. It is possible that the transfer was in the opposite direction from the Spanish baggy leather riding overalls which the Indians may have adopted from the Spanish along with the horse. The main purposes of leggings seem to have been for protection from injury to the legs, particularly in thorny country, and for ceremony in dress rather than for warmth.

Southwest Indian men wore kilts topped off with belts and sashes, both made of native woven cloth, especially for ceremonials. They also wore elements of the neighboring Plains costumes and, in later years, adopted features of white men's garb—both Spanish and American. The Navajos, in particular, assembled a hybrid European costume that today identifies them. All in all, the men's clothing in this area became unusually varied and complicated, though the probability is that in pre-Columbian times it was consistent and

more in line with aboriginal men's clothing elsewhere in North America, though modified, of course, by the use of native cloth.

Just what was regular clothing for Indian men is not certain. This is partly due to the mixtures and confusions that resulted from Indian adoption of European elements and also some alien native elements. It is also due to the fact that most explainers of the Indian, including some professional ethnologists, fail to distinguish between what was worn for essential reasons—beyond the basic breechclout and moccasins and, to some extent, leggings—and what was worn to gratify peacock emotions or to conform to ritual in ceremony and religion.

Footgear

Footgear was clothing, of course, and was one of the commonly essential items. Though it has already been noted, it merits separate treatment because of its importance.

Pre-Columbian footwear was in three forms: sandals, boots, and low shoes commonly grouped as moccasins. There were also certain extensions up the legs that created either leggings or boot tops, the distinction depending upon the classifier.

Judging by their presence in the old cave dwellings and drier shelters where their essential frailty has been protected, sandals may have been the oldest form of footwear. They were made necessary wherever the presence of sharp stones and thorns would cut up even the most hardened feet. They have been worn until recently by some Indians of the Southwest and appear to have been standard in older times.

Moccasins and boots may be developments of the days when early man wrapped up his feet and legs to keep them from freezing and to protect them from bruises and cuts. The latter, however, may have been a minor consideration, because the Indians in regions of milder weather, notably those living on the Pacific Coast, went barefoot.

Moccasins were of two major kinds: soft soles and hard soles. The former were characteristic of the Eastern Woodland Indians, the latter of the Plains and Southwest Indians. The soft-sole kind were made by bringing the sole up around the foot and puckering and/or patching at the awkward spot on the instep. The word itself is Algonkian and applies to a low puckered and instep-patched shoe, often with an added flap that could be brought up to cover the ankles. This was the general plan of all Eastern Woodland moccasins.

The Plains Indian hard-sole moccasins could have been a compromise between a sandal and a tailored upper. Like the soft-sole footwear, they were made with all sorts of variations and additions and according to tribal styles. These styles were so distinctive that it was noted by early-day plainsmen and mountain men that the Indians, and in time they, themselves, could tell

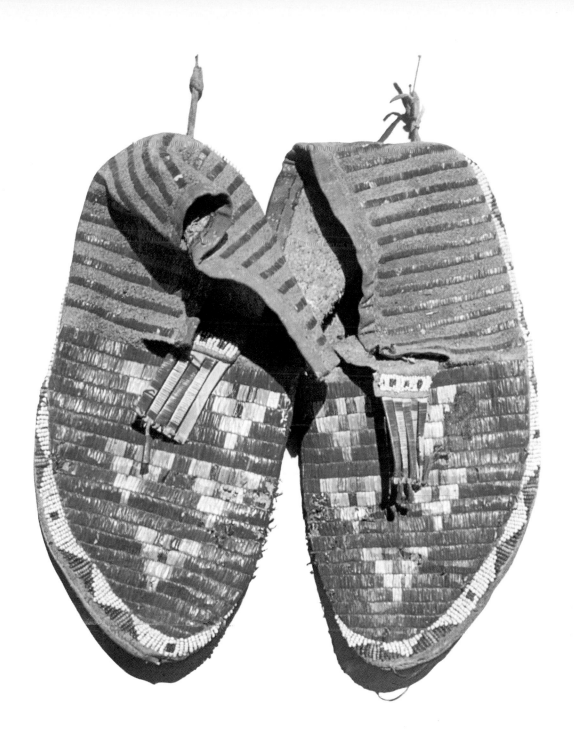

*Northern Plains Indian moccasins, full
quill work with beading in borders*

the tribe of a wearer by his footprints. Hard-sole moccasins were ornamented with beadwork and quillwork partially or all over. Some even had beadwork on the soles, and these sound a note of sadness, for many of them were burial moccasins. Occasionally, a pair is seen with long fringes attached to the heels. These are said, perhaps more romantically than factually, to have been designed so that the trailing fringe would obscure the footprint.

In the Southwest, where the dryness created thorny plants and there was a scarcity of running water to wear off the sharp edges of flakes and fragments of stone, the hard soles of the moccasins were curled up a bit to keep sharp things from running in between the seams. A Pueblo Indian described a clever way to fit these soles —place the foot in mud and after the print has dried, mold the rawhide in it, and let it dry. Incidentally, many of the Pueblo and other Southwest Indians departed from the usual moccasin-upper pattern to make what amounted to a flap-over-and-button shoe— perhaps another of their numerous borrowings from the clever white man. The Apaches, besides turning their shoes into boots, often brought the toes up to a point perkily curled up and topped off with a disk.

Speaking of boots, it has been noted that there is a little confusion as to when they are boots and when they are leggings joined to moccasin soles. The Eskimos were the major boot wearers. Sometimes their creations had moccasin soles which were puckered and turned up well, though not completely, around the foot. The uppers were of various materials and construction; some of stiff rawhide so as to resemble boot tops; others of soft fur-covered leather; and still others were just the bottoms of trousers sewed to the soles after being tailored to the insteps. Plains and Woodland leggings could be incorporated with moccasins in this same way, thus extending footgear upward so far that it was fastened to a waistband or belt.

A closing comment to offset this review of footwear and to justify the good sense of many Indians in going barefoot: It was not so long ago that European sailors were normally a barefoot lot; the poet's boy with cheek of tan was notably happy so attired or unattired; and we even wince to see, in these effeminate days, the dainty feet of our younger maidens padding bare about dance and supermarket floors.

Hats and Caps

The Eskimo parka had a hood attached to it, which was regularly worn over the head—a necessary ensemble for protection against the Arctic cold. Europeans have found this headwear difficult to improve on and have generally adopted it for Arctic wear. As well as the parka, Eskimo hunters wore a true hat, one made of thin wood bent around to form a cone and create a visor to protect the eyes from snow and ice glare.

Farther south, the Indians of the Northwest Coast were also true hat wearers, such a garment being practical because of the frequent pouring rains which prevail much of the year in their domain. Their hats, made of basketry, are so much like those of the Orient, similarly worn, that one is induced to suspect that they were copied from Oriental models. The originals could have been on the heads of mariners in transoceanic junks whose discovery of America lacked the press coverage and subsequent continuity of the Columbian voyagers.

Still farther south, caps appeared on the heads of womenfolk. Those worn by the Yakimas and their neighbors were, however, more like fezzes. Aside from these fez-like hats, the caps were all bowl shaped and are frequently mistaken by the uninformed to be bowls. There is more likelihood that they were more ornamental than practical, though it is said they helped prevent discomfort from the headbands of burden-basket tumplines, and they certainly kept the hair in some order.

Aside from these tribes, the wearing of hats and caps became increasingly associated with ornamental and ceremonial headgear. The basis of the flamboyant war bonnet was a cap, perhaps its original before it feathered, and the crowns of old felt hats are still found buried in some of the most pretentious of these headdresses. Cap wearing also is found among Indians here and there from the Iroquois to the Apaches. There were also larger and bulkier turbanlike affairs, akin to caps, which are envisioned most easily in connection with the Menomini and their neighbors and, linguistically, with the Flatheads—so named because their fur turbans were flat.

In somewhat similar roles to hats and caps were the bands wound around the heads of the Apaches and other Indians of the Southwest, and, in a way, the nets worn by some California Indian men.

Personal Effects

Review of pre-Columbian personal effects must err on the side of brevity, not for lack of material but because of the wealth and complexity of it. Although the pre-Columbians did not develop private ownership of real estate—even such things as canoes sometimes being public property—they had personal possessions aplenty. Many of these are described elsewhere: kitchen gear, weapons, tools, garments, etc. In addition to producing these communal and utilitarian objects, they expended personal efforts and attention on the creation and enjoyment of hairdressing articles and materials, other items for personal grooming and attire, snow goggles and visors, cradles, money, purses, wallets, fans, and all manner of bags, baskets, and boxes for trinkets and small gear. In post-Columbian times, they made gun and pistol cases, quirts, saddles, and martingales.

All these were carved, painted, and otherwise ornamented, usually in relation to how much they were likely to be seen and envied—a tendency not entirely absent from our enlightened times.

4.16

4.17

4.18

4.19

4.20

4.21

4.22

4.23

4.24

Men's Clothing

4.16 Buckskin apron, Plains style of quillwork and featherwork

4.17 Old trade cloth breechclout, ribbon, shell, and old trade beads decoration

4.18 Painted buckskin breechclout. Variations of aprons, breechclouts, and moccasins formed the basic items of most Indian men's clothing.

4.19 Trouser type of leggings, beaded strips in characteristic old Plains patterns

4.20 Chaparajo style of Plains leggings with metal bosses, beading, and fringing

4.21 Northwestern Woodland Indian wrap-around leggings with floral beading

4.22 Plains Indian buckskin shirt (so-called "war shirt") in two sections sewn at the shoulders and lightly attached at the sides, open half sleeves. Same construction as women's dresses

4.23 Long-sleeved buckskin shirt showing Eskimo influence, perhaps Kutenai; quilled and fringed

4.24 Heavy buckskin fringed and beaded coat with braided hair shoulder ornaments; long-skirted, split tail of white man's fashion of nineteenth century

4.25-4.26 Plains Indian dolls in buckskin dress and trimmings; left (4.25) with fringed leggings and beaded moccasins; the doll on the right (4.26) with a "beanie" cap with feather, carries a flint blade under his right arm.

4.27 Eskimo woven-grass mitten

4.28 Eskimo leather mitten

4.29 Eskimo waterproof parka made of ribbons of transparent fish skins or intestine walls, sewed together with a waterproofing stitch. The parka is for wear in boats rather than to fend off rain.

4.25　　　　　　　　　4.26

4.27　　　　　　4.28

4.29

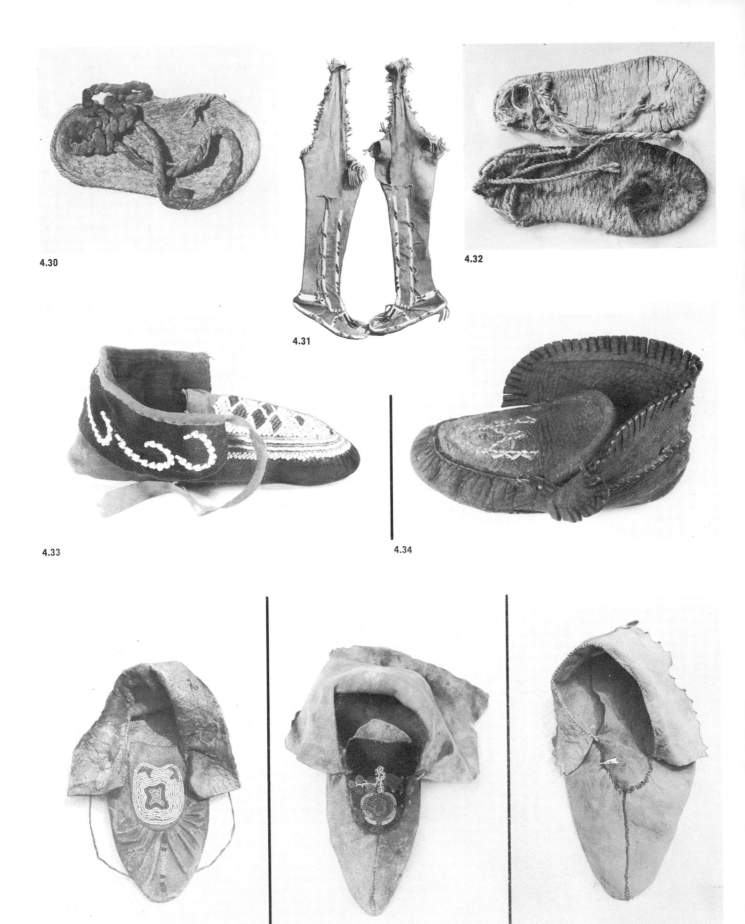

4.30

4.31

4.32

4.33

4.34

4.35

4.36

4.37

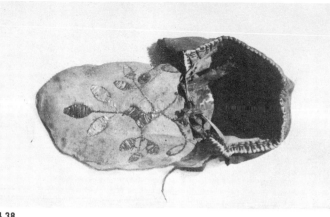

4.38

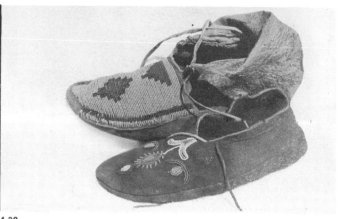

4.39

Sandals and Moccasins

4.30 Braided rope cliff dweller's sandal

4.31 Combination buckskin leggings and moccasins, with extensions for attachment to a belt

4.32 Woven plant-fiber sandals from a cave near Moab, Utah. Sandals were the original footwear of the Southwest and have been found in considerable numbers in cave and cliff dwellings. Semitight leggings were a typical Eastern Woodland Indian garment, and combination of leg and foot covering was a northern tailored clothing idea, but these are Plains Indian legwear.

4.33-4.34 Eastern Woodland Indian soft-sole moccasins in the form originally meant by moccasin (an Algonkian word), made in one piece with a puckered seam at the front bridged by an oval or U-shaped patch: (4.33) scroll-shaped white beading on ankle flap typical of Woodland design influence; (4.34) quilled; the ankle flap is a separate piece sewed on.

4.35-4.37 Variations of Eastern Woodland forms, with (4.35) and without gathering; beaded conventional floral designs on two; (4.36) shows sharply pointed toes created by puckerless construction.

4.38-4.39 Hybrid moccasin forms: (4.38) Eastern style of ankle flaps and floral quilling with Plains hard sole; (4.39) one-piece soft-sole construction, seam at one side of foot; upper with Plains design beading and lower with floral beading. The upper was provided with a furred innersole for winter wear.

Boot and Shoe-style Moccasins

4.40 Pueblo and Navajo style of Southwest Indian shoe-moccasins; semihard soles curved into uppers at edges; flap and button fastening; perhaps influenced by Spanish footwear

4.41 Eskimo boots with high-crimped waterproof hard soles

4.40

4.41

4.42

4.43

4.44

4.45

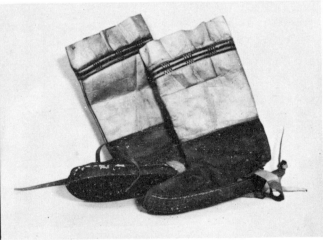

4.46

4.42 Waterproofed sealskin Eskimo boot; high sole gathered all around
4.43 Apache painted leather boots with fringed sides and curled up toes
4.44 Another form of Apache boots with typical southern band beading
4.45 Eskimo woven-grass socks
4.46 Eskimo waterproof sealskin boots, ornamented by use of different colors of leather

Plains Moccasins
4.47-4.48 Various shapes of hard-soled moccasins: (4.47) three typical beaded forms; left, Sioux; center, general Plains design; right, Crow design; (4.48) floral beaded designs: upper, pictorial; lower, conventionalized designs
4.49-4.51 Plains hard-soled: (4.49) typical northern Plains design, Indian star; (4.50) equipped with heel fringes, said to confuse footprints by trailing in dust; (4.51) child's burial moccasins, solidly beaded on soles as well as uppers
4.52 Quilled Plains moccasins with beaded edging
4.53 Southern Plains style beading in narrow bands; soles curled up to avoid taking thorns through the seams

4.47

4.48

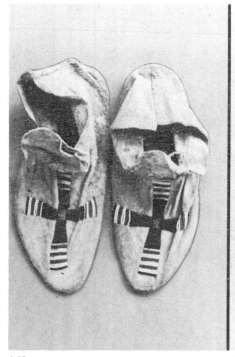

4.49

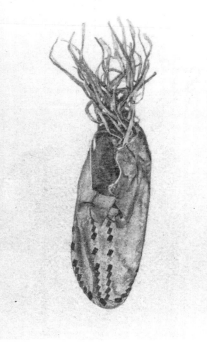

4.50

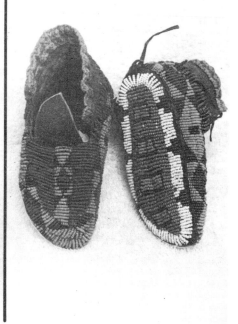

4.51

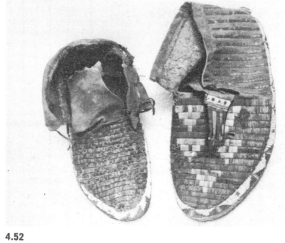

4.52

4.53

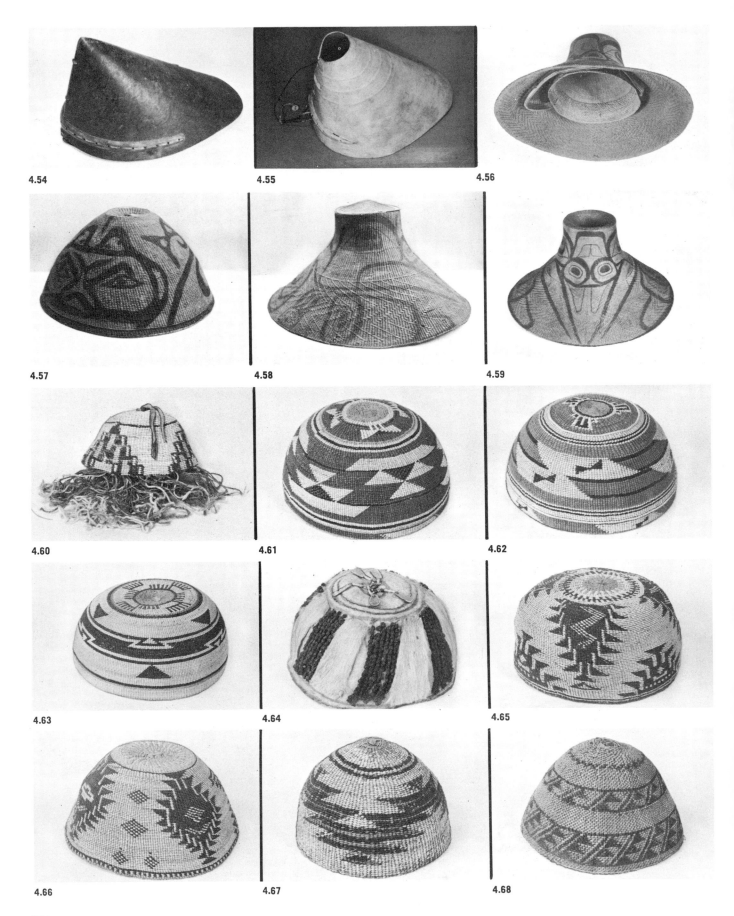

4.54

4.55

4.56

4.57

4.58

4.59

4.60

4.61

4.62

4.63

4.64

4.65

4.66

4.67

4.68

Hats and Caps

4.54-4.55 Eskimo dark brown (4.54) and (4.55) white painted Eskimo hunting hats made of bent sheets of wood with stiffening bows at back

4.56 Underside of (4.59) Northwest Coast woven hat showing inner crown

4.57-4.59 Northwest Coast painted basketry hats: (4.57) mushroom type; (4.58) and (4.59) broad-brim types; totemic designs and ornamental ridged weaving on brims

4.60 Partly woven middle Columbia River area fez-form squaw hat made of soft cornshuck material; buckskin thong tassel typical

4.61-4.62 Dark and light brown northwest California squaw caps

4.63 Black-and-white design northwest California squaw cap; outer design does not show through in caps made in this area.

4.64 Rawhide cap, northwest California; ornamented with viburnum seeds, paint, strips of white fur, and shell danglers; probably a woman shaman's cap

4.65 Northern California (Shasta) cap; design goes through.

4.66 Klamath and Modoc style of cap; fairly soft weave; design goes through.

4.67 Old Pitt River tribe cap, black-and-white overlay

4.68 Central California and Nevada (Paiute) cap

Personal Effects

4.69 Beaded and quilled Plains paint bag, containing vermillion paint powder

4.70 Attu (island) Aleutian Eskimo woven-grass wallet with colored silk woven in; the Attu Islanders are credited with some of the finest basketweaving known, this being comparable with linen cloth.

4.71 Plains beaded bladder bag

4.69

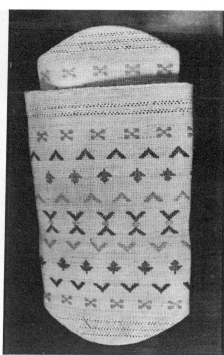

4.70

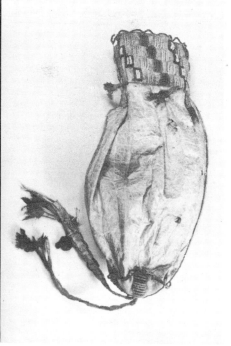

4.71

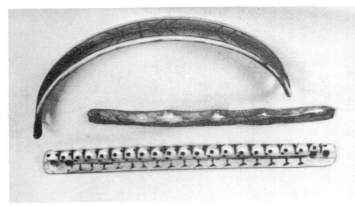

4.72

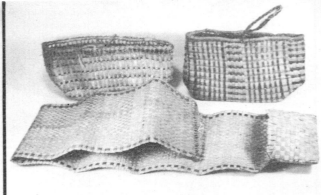

4.73

4.74

4.75

4.76

4.77

4.78

4.72 Eskimo ornamented ivory bag handles
4.73 Northwest Coast (Vancouver Island) checkerwork bark ribbon wallets and folding "housewife," the latter also used for fishing tackle
4.74 Women's small effects baskets from: left, northwest California; center, Eskimo; and right, Tlingit (Alaska), with rattle knob on the lid
4.75 British Columbia Salish coiled and imbricated basket with buckskin carrying straps and cover loops
4.76 Buckskin bags: larger ones quilled and beaded Eastern Woodland bags, left one, Ottawa; others, Plains Indian
4.77 Southern Plains Indian buckskin bag, with beadwork designs of that area
4.78 Plains parfleche envelope containers, painted rawhide

4.79 Rawhide and feather fan with painted decoration; Plains Indian
4.80 Wooden fan with colored drawings of ceremonial drum and dancers; Plains Indian
4.81 Buckskin and cordage bandoleer with "medicine" charms attached, from a cave in New Mexico
4.82 Thick, soft leather gun case with Eastern Woodland designs in quillwork
4.83 Beaded rawhide knife sheaths, right one with a Crow design
4.84 Pistol scabbard with quilled animals and insects
4.85 Cylindrical painted rawhide cases; Plains; a type used to carry and store war bonnets and other ceremonial gear.
4.86 Desert tribe water canteens; left, Paiute; right, Southwest; basketry, pitched
4.87 Plains Indian blanket strips, beaded buckskin; medallions in Indian star design

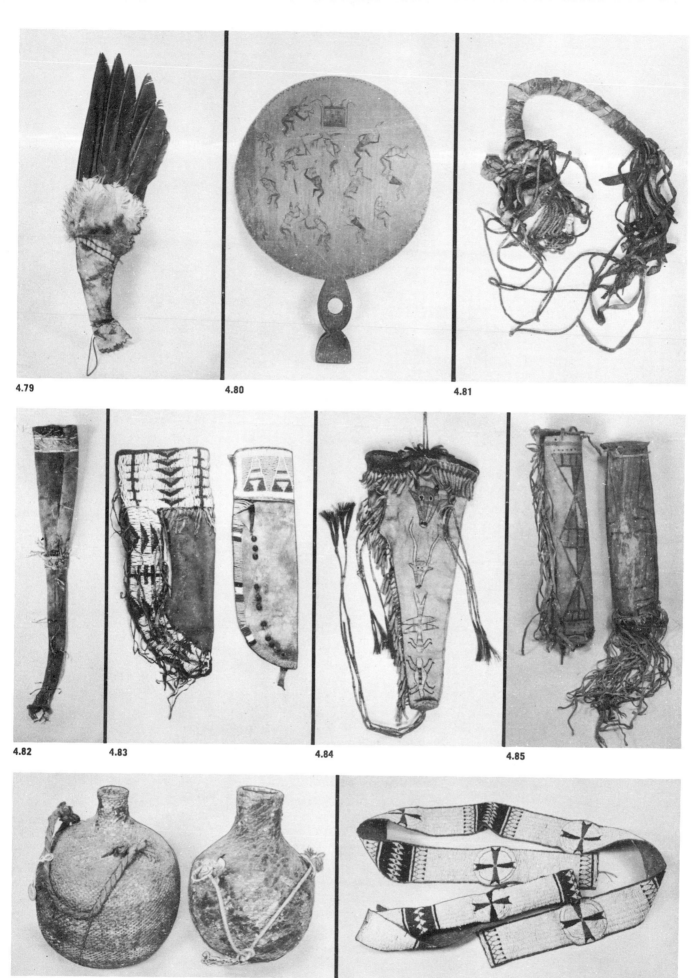

4.79

4.80

4.81

4.82

4.83

4.84

4.85

4.86

4.87

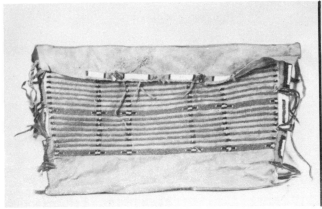

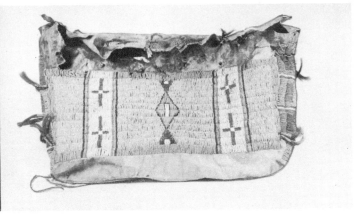

4.88

4.89

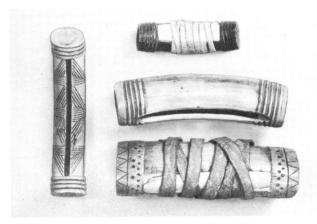

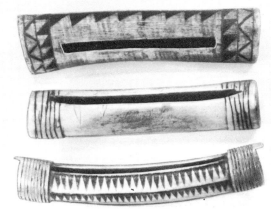

4.90

4.91

4.88-4.89 Plains Indian saddlebags, buckskin with heavy beading in general northern Plains designs on one side and on the edges

4.90-4.91 Northwest California elkhorn and deerhorn purses in which were kept the dentalia money strings used in that area: (4.90) two purses having their elkhorn wafer lids wrapped on with a buckskin thong: top one elkhorn; bottom one deerhorn; (4.91) elkhorn purses; bottom one with end tabs

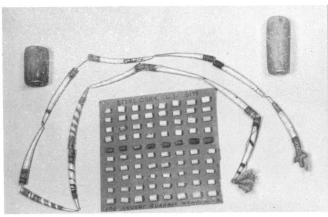

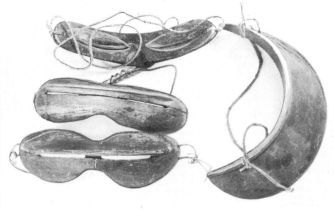

4.92

4.93

4.92 Varieties of Indian money; two large "beads" are magnesite, called by pioneers "Indian gold" and found in the Pomo territory on the north central coast of California; magnesite ($MgCO_3$) turns pinkish-brown and cream when heated; the dentalia "beads" on the string are valued according to length in northwest California; the ornamentation does not affect the value; white and purple quahaug-shell wampum (mounted) from Long Island, N.Y.; originally just valued shell beads, wampum was promoted into money with set value by the Dutch colonists and passed out of use after white artisans instituted "improvements" to produce it in quantity.

4.93 Eskimo wooden snow-goggles and eyeshade used to prevent snow-blindness from glare off the snow; an eyeshade ledge over the eye slits does not show well in the photograph.

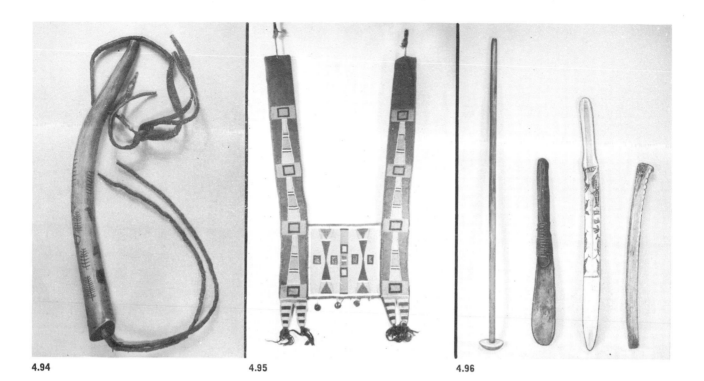

4.94

4.95

4.96

4.94 Plains Indian elkhorn quirt ornamented with pictures of elk, a buffalo, bear, and trees (?)

4.95 Crow Indian beaded martingale or apron for the chest of a horse

4.96 Eskimo back-scratcher and three versions of snow-beaters used to clean off snow from garments on entering the igloo

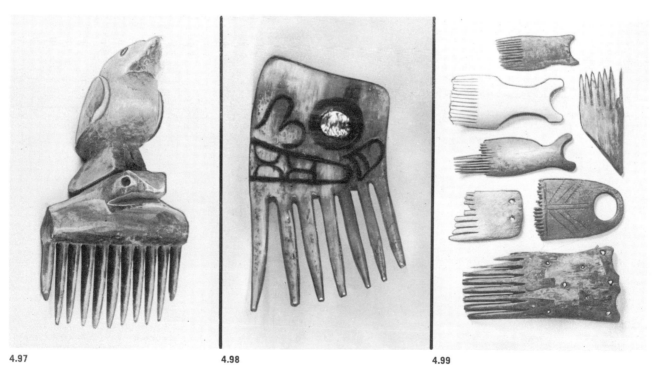

4.97

4.98

4.99

Combs and Hair Artifacts

4.97 Northwest Coast wooden comb with bird on frog-effigy handle

4.98 Northwest Coast horn comb with incised red lines and abalone-shell inlay

4.99 Eskimo combs; ivory and baleen

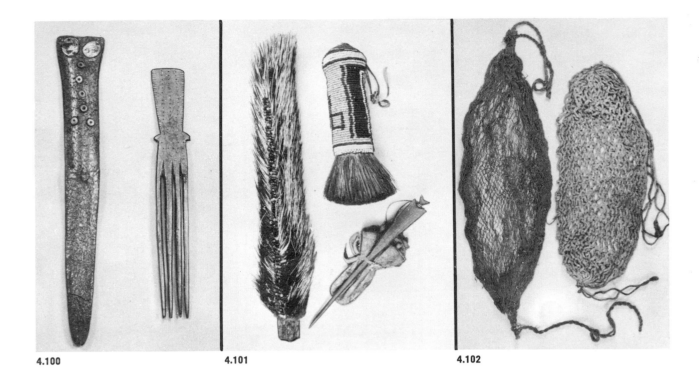

4.100   4.101   4.102

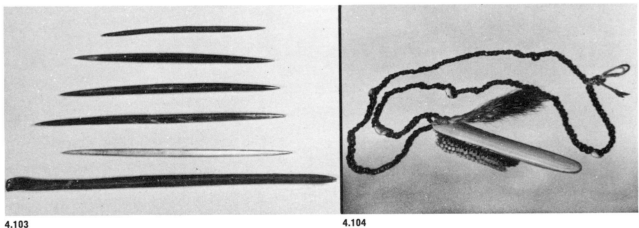

4.103   4.104

4.100   Abalone (and other shell) bead-decorated Canalino hairpin (possibly a strigil), and a dot and line ornamented bone comb from a prehistoric site in Umatilla territory, Orgeon

4.101   Plains Indian beaded hairbrushes, and a paint bag and paint stick for painting the hair parting

4.102   Hair nets worn by central California Indians

4.103   Central California bone hairpins used like hatpins as anchors for headdresses

4.104   Northwest California viburnum seed necklace carrying ornaments and an elkhorn louse crusher, a luxury toilet article among women of the area; the latter is also found in prehistoric sites.

Baby Carriers

4.105-4.106   Northwest Coast cradles: (4.105) coiled and imbricated basketry cradle; British Columbia Salish; carried on the back horizontally; (4.106) wooden, troughlike cradle; it was in cradles of this type that head flattening was carried on by some lower Columbia River tribes.

4.107-4.109   Northwest California sit-down type cradles: the three major types of this style cradle: (4.107) Northwest California, (Yurok-Hupa culture); (4.108) Pomo, north central coast; disk "wampum" shell beads attached to lashings; (4.109) Wintun, northwest interior valley Indians

4.110-4.112   Central California and Nevada cradles: buckskin covering (4.110-4.111) from eastern (Plains) influence, sun visors on all, California style; design on visors indicated sex of baby in cradle; left (4.110), girl; right (4.112), boy; center cradle is damaged beyond identification.

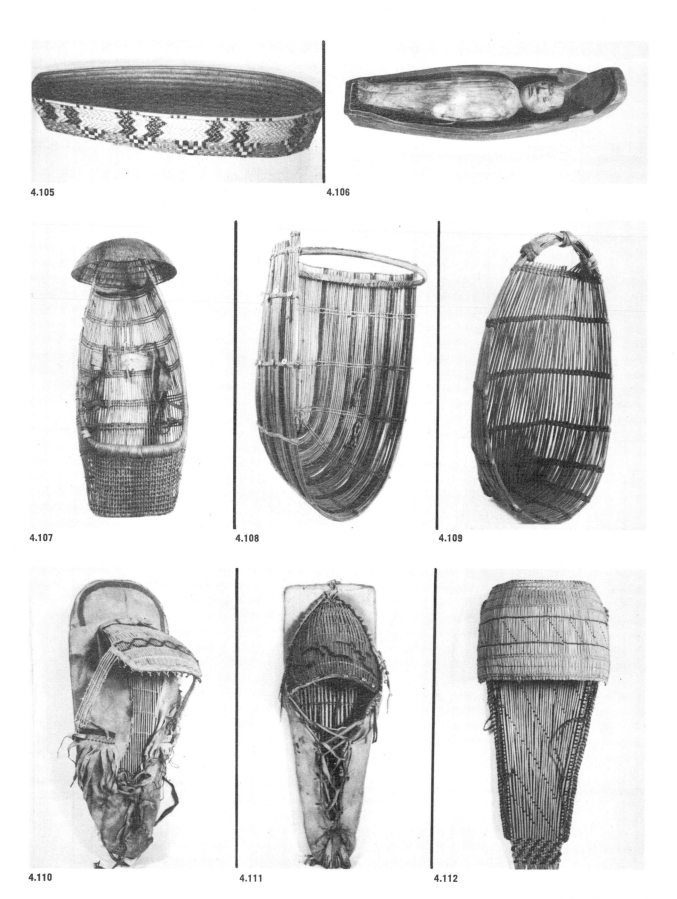

4.105

4.106

4.107

4.108

4.109

4.110

4.111

4.112

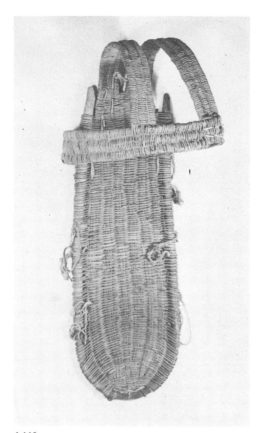

4.114

4.113

4.113 Hopi Indian baby carrier in wicker weaving
4.114 Western Apache cradleboard, wooden slat back and sun visor (photos courtesy Southwest Museum, Los Angeles, California)

Plains Cradleboards
4.115-4.117 Three typical kinds of Plains Indian cradleboards: (4.115) a buckskin and bead covered board shape popular from Colorado Utes to Blackfoot Indians; this one Blackfoot; (4.116) a Sioux to Comanche type with a bag attached to two narrow boards converging at the base and each projecting to a point above the bag; (4.117) heavy leather bag or hood form on a hard-leather back; Sioux style of bead design

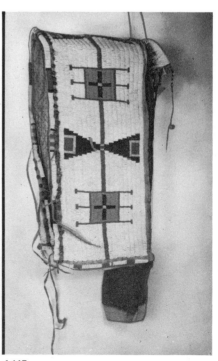

4.115   4.116   4.117

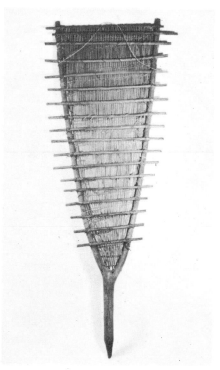

4.118 Yokuts (California) cradleboard designed to be set upright in the ground, hence the pointed bottom; wooden rods, basketry backing

4.119 Birchbark baby carrier, Athabascan Indians, northern Canada (photo courtesy Robert H. Lowie Museum of Anthropology, University of California; Cat. No. 2-2734)

4.120 Seneca, New York, version of a widely used Eastern Woodland Indian style of cradleboard (photo courtesy of Museum of the American Indian, Heye Foundation, New York)

4.118

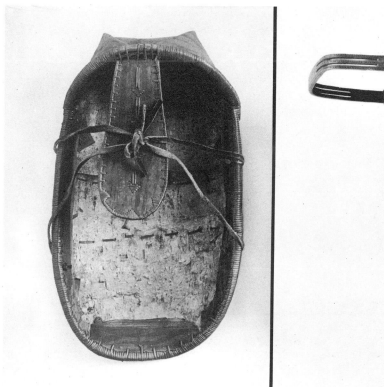

4.119

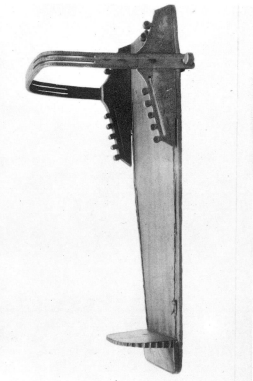

4.120

5 Personal Adornment

Personal vanity has always been of strong interest to women, and *they* say that it is much worse among men. The First Americans were no exceptions to this phenomenon, judging by their artifacts. It is a matter of record that their innocent enthusiasm for self-decoration led to much outrageous bamboozling by crafty white men. Such was the purchase of hunting (spelled p-r-o-p-e-r-t-y) rights to an island, at the time enjoyed by the Manhattans, for a string of beads—we hope as a gift to the chief's most faithful and ever-loving wife, but more likely for his own neck, since the aboriginal North American men were not too inhibited about emulating the peacock.

The first thing one thinks of in connection with primitive personal adornment is the necklace. It still shows no signs of abating in use among women, though its use by men is confined to lord mayors of London and other such dignitaries or, in America, to lodge officers and tourists to Hawaii. The Eskimos were somewhat hampered in displaying necklaces and other usual forms of dangling adornment, except facial. However, the North American Indians certainly went all out. Even the poorest affected gaudy displays of strings of nuts, seeds, bones, and other jewels strung on sinew, buckskin, or native string.

Although the neck was perhaps the choicest spot for gilding the pre-Columbian lilies with dangling ornamentation, other parts of the anatomy were not immune. Much of this was seen in the garments; but there remained noses, ears, lips, fingers, wrists, arms, legs, and even hair partings which were painted, tattooed, or bejeweled. They were all decorated in some way by some tribes and individuals.

Beads

The best known and perhaps the greatest number of pre-Columbian beads were made of shell, and a good part of these were small disks with holes bored through the centers. Although many carelessly call them "wampum," the real wampum was a small cylindrical bead made of the white and the purple parts of local clamshells by the Iroquois Indians and their neighbors. Wampum was later translated into European terms of money and thereby into enduring fame. Other shapes

of shell than these were, of course, devised, as well as shells being used whole.

Many easily destructible forms of material are known to have been popular—from analogy with post-Columbian beads and from a few of the fragile forms that have survived under favorable circumstances. We cannot, however, guess what other form was most popular, though we know that stone and bone beads are most numerous archaeologically after shell. Other common materials were mammal and bird claws, pine nuts and other nuts and seeds, parts of hoofs, fish vertebrae, even human finger bones, and, in post-Columbian times, the ubiquitous European glass and porcelain trade beads.

Necklaces

Necklaces were as diverse in material as the beads which formed their main part, and incorporated in them was a variety of pendants, gorgets, and other elements. Even after the traders' bewitching colored beads arrived, older native materials were often used in composition with the white man's offerings.

Among the handsomest and most generally valuable of necklaces are those still being made by the Indians of the Southwest using turquoise. Even today these may frequently be seen in combination with the ancient small alabasterlike and brownish-hued native creations from shell imported since time immemorial into that inland empire from both Pacific and Atlantic shores. Among the most numerous of ancient beads are those of California clam and olivella shell. They have been recovered in great quantities from sites all over California, but chiefly in the central great river valleys, where they were traded (we presume) up the streams from the coast far inland. Some even passed to the borders of Plains Indian influence.

Head and Limb Adornment

We still accept appendages for the ears as standard adornment for ladies and pirates, but are reluctant these days about putting plugs through lips and noses. The pre-Columbians had no such inhibitions. Besides devising earplugs, rings, and danglers without name that often did drastic things to the poor earlobes, they

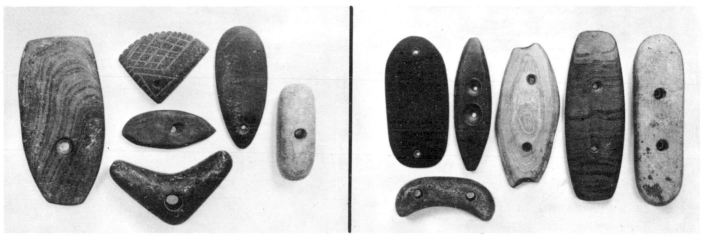

5.1   5.2

experimented with lip plugs (labrets) to a point where they sometimes weighed down the lower lip and with nose plugs that became like what one captive American sailor called "spars."

In addition, there were bracelets for the wrists and rings for the fingers, especially among the prehistoric Indians of the Southwest, where in some sites these broken, or occasionally whole, artifacts are fairly common in potsherd-littered debris. Other variations of these forms of adornment, as well as painting of faces and bodies and tattooing, are almost impossible to describe without going into a considerable amount of detail.

Jewelry

Much of the subject of jewelry has been covered in sketching beads, necklaces, and head and limb adornment, and jewelry was extensively incorporated in the decoration of garments and other objects, notably the feather baskets of the Pomos, which were frequently adorned with abalone-shell figures. But there are cer-

tain pendants, gorgets, and jewel-like objects that should be referred to at least. In the Mound Builder areas, for example, considerable numbers of stone, principally slate, artifacts have been recovered and would seem most certainly to have been in the class of aboriginal jewelry; perhaps some of the ceremonial stones were so used. In California, some of the showiest primitive jewelry artifacts occur in great numbers in varied and often quaint shapes made from iridescent abalone shells. In their pristine form, they must have been colorful in the extreme. Much fewer but equally artistic as jewelry are carved shells, some of which are found in the Southwest and some among the mounds of the East.

There is still talk among the uninformed about the use of gold and precious and semiprecious stones. Gold was used by the Indians south of the border, but, as bitterly disappointed Spanish explorers found out, was practically if not completely unknown to the North Americans. Turquoise was the most conspicuous gemstone in general use, and artifacts made of semiprecious stones, notably agate, turn up in varying numbers.

5.3

5.4

5.5

5.6

5.7

5.8

5.3 Large Eastern Woodland beads, slate and hard sandstone; size indicated by paper clip

5.4 Large southern California coast beads made of selected steatite with variegated colors and construction

5.5 Large black and gray steatite beads from the Chumash or Canalino area of California; left one retaining shell-bead decoration imbedded in asphaltum; size indicated by paper clip

5.6 Smaller size of black steatite beads from same area as (5.5). Nearly all came from Mescalatan Island, Goleta.

5.7 Bone, sandstone, quartz, magnesite, pottery, shell, and tooth beads; fourth from left on bottom is an ornamented finger bone from an Iroquois site; above and to the right is an elk's tooth; far left, drilled and grooved quartz

5.8 Copper, bone, steatite, slate, and sandstone beads; cordage preserved by long tubular copper beads; see also (5.13).

Typical Necklaces

5.9 Shell disk bead necklace and beads; probably the best known if not also the commonest of shell bead forms; sometimes called "wampum," but only vaguely resembling wampum in form, and seldom if ever used to fit a scale of values; these are from California.

5.10 Assorted shell beads gathered from Eastern prehistoric sites and showing a variety of forms; from a Wisconsin collection

5.11 Bird-bone and mammal hoof-bone necklace; Sioux Indian, Montana

5.12 Sea mammal tooth necklace of Eskimo manufacture

5.9

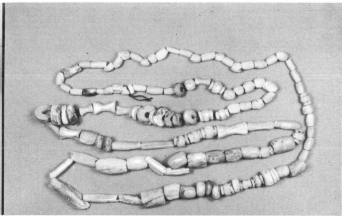
5.10

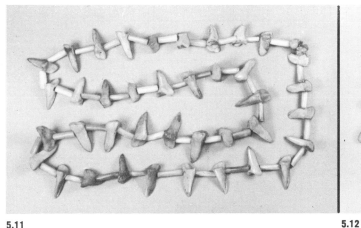
5.11

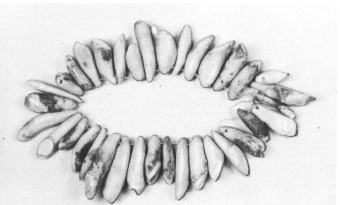
5.12

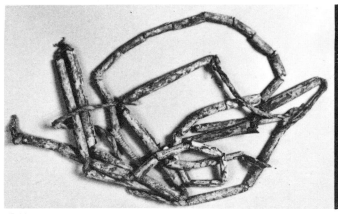

5.13

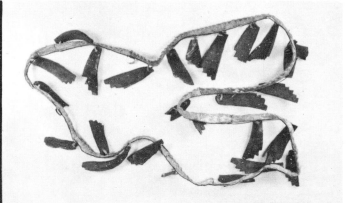

5.14

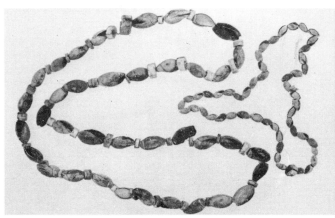

5.15

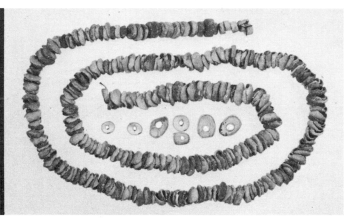

5.16

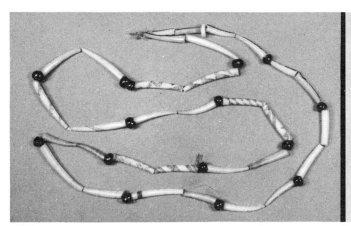

5.17

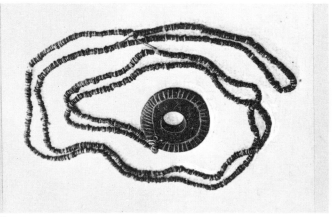

5.18

5.13 Copper necklace with string still intact; origin unknown, but may be from the Columbia River where rolled copper beads of both trade and prehistoric origin are found; Great Lakes copper was hammered and rolled in the same way.

5.14 Buckskin and cut horn or hoof pieces; Plains Indian

5.15-5.16 Two commonest types of olivella shell beads, found in enormous quantities in all prehistoric California sites: (5.15) whole shells made into beads by grinding off the tips; (5.16) cups of shells cut and drilled

5.17 Dentalia beads, some engraved, these from northwestern California, but a favorite shell for beads from the northern Pacific Coast far into the Plains

5.18 Tiny steatite beads with a pendant made from the mouthpiece of a pipe; Columbia River, near the mouth of the Deschutes in Oregon

Necklace Varieties

5.19 Southwest Indian shell bead and turquoise nugget necklace, with turquoise pendant

5.20 Seminole necklace with a mixture of "beads": pottery, shells, stones, and claws

5.21 Northwest Coast trade bead necklace with danglers of shell and horn rings (5.19-5.21 courtesy of Hugh M. Worcester; from the Joe Gest collection)

5.22-5.23 Northwest California beads: (5.22) pine nuts with braided straw and abalone pendant danglers; (5.23) viburnum seeds with limpet shells

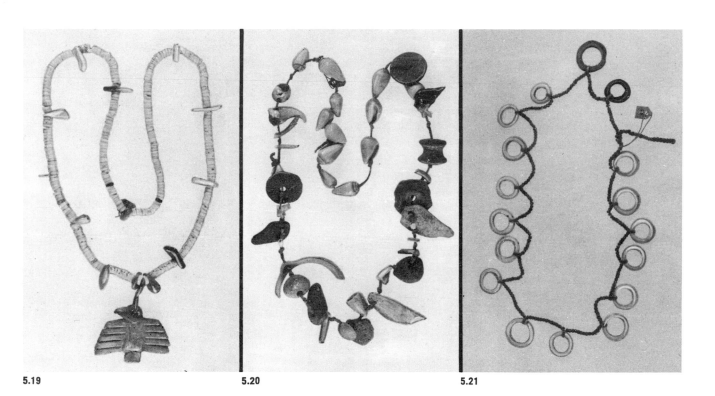

5.19   5.20   5.21

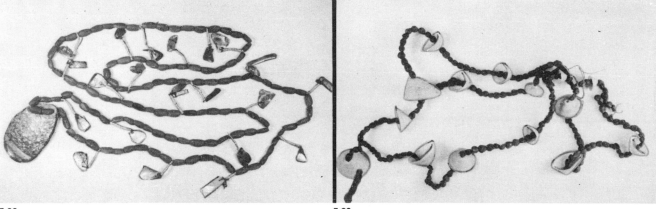

5.22   5.23

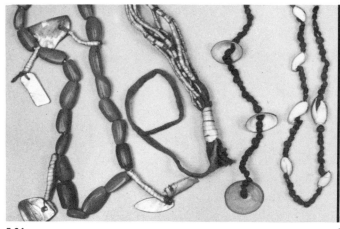

5.24

5.25

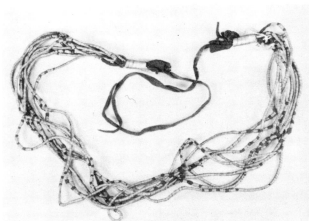

5.26

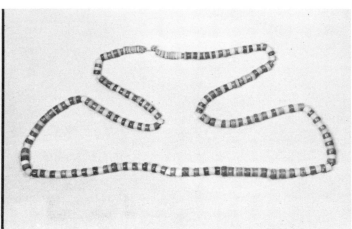

5.27

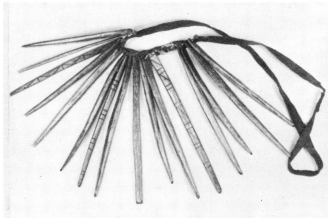

5.28

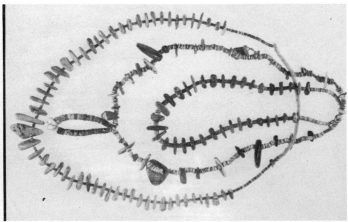

5.29

5.24 Close-up of pine nut, viburnum seed, and twisted and braided straw necklaces and shell attachments, from northern California

5.25 Heavy disk shell beads with a steatite bead pendant; shell identified as fossil oyster shell; south central California (courtesy Hugh M. Worcester, from the Joe Gest collection)

5.26 Bark or straw ribbons wound around leather, northwest California

5.27 Alternating turquoise and shell disk beads, prehistoric Southwest

5.28 Needle or awl-like "beads"; provenience unknown, but similar prehistoric examples have been found in California and historic examples from the Northwest Coast.

5.29 Three turquoise nugget and bead and shell necklaces of a style long popular among Southwest Indians (courtesy Hugh M. Worcester, Berkeley, California)

Head and Limb Jewelry

5.30 Earplugs or spools of steatite: two left, a pair, mound near Marysville, central California; upper center, Hohokam, central Arizona; two largest ones, a pair from a site near Oakley, California

5.31 Two pottery ear spools, central California; shell disk with copper coating, Mound Builders; pottery plugs, Ohio Valley

5.32 Ear ornaments: engraved bird bones worn through the ear lobes, central California mounds

5.33 Bone ring is Plains Indian hair lock holder; ear ornaments are, top, turquoise mosaic inlay on wood, Southwest; center, abalone danglers and trade beads, Western and Plains Indian type; bottom, Eskimo earrings, one in a wooden holder; right, Mound Builder shell ornaments, assumed to be earrings

5.34 Lip plugs (labrets), all Eskimo except center left, from Tennessee; materials shell, ivory, coal, sandstone, wood, and conglomerate

5.35 Nose plugs, upper, and finger rings; left, plug from northwestern California, other two from Hohokam sites; rings from Southwest, center one shell, others stone

5.30

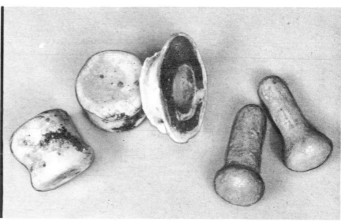

5.31

5.32

5.33

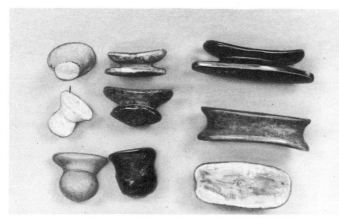

5.34

5.35

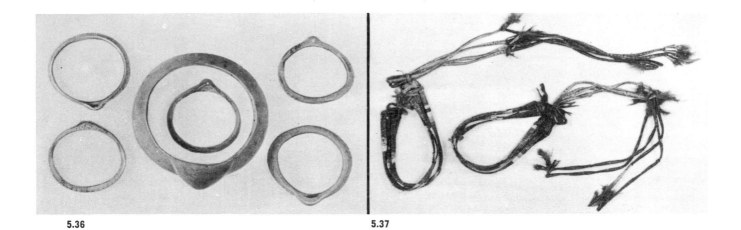

5.36

5.37

5.36 Shell bracelets made from rims of
clamshells; found in considerable numbers
in prehistoric Southwest sites
5.37 Buckskin arm bands wrapped with
colored quillwork, Plains Indians

Jewelry Forms
5.38-5.40 Plains Indian bone and buckskin
breast ornaments featuring the so-called
"hair-pipe" beads: (5.38) and (5.39) men's
breastplates; (5.40) woman's collar; these
are usually valued according to the number,
length, and quality of the "hair pipes"
(E. C. Counter collection).

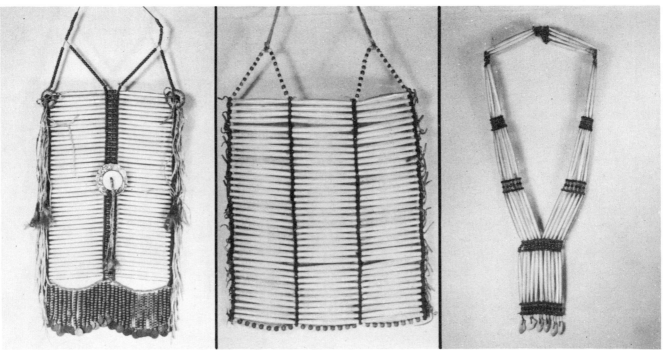

5.38

5.39

5.40

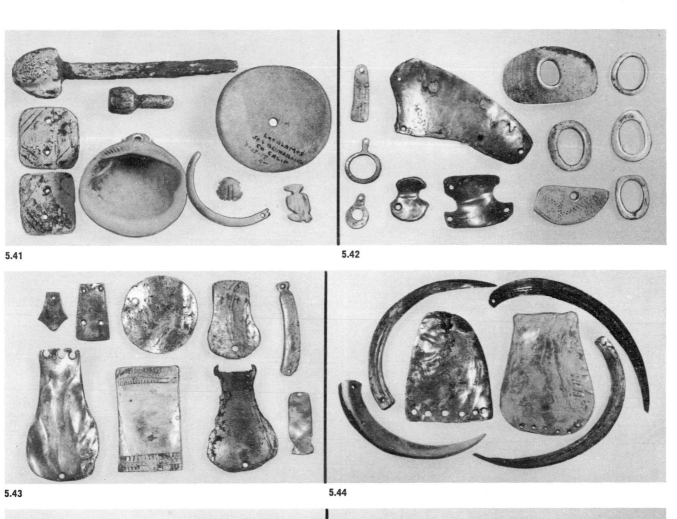

5.41

5.42

5.43

5.44

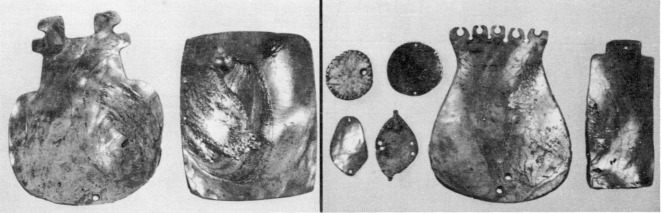

5.45

5.46

5.41 "Buttons" and "pins" Mound Builder shell ornaments; circular pierced shell, southern California; others prehistoric Southwest, tiny frog and bird assumed to be earring ornaments (though not pierced); the eyed semicircle might be a needle.
5.42 Southern California coastal types; dotted shells often pictorial; this has an animal; the circular ones are made from limpet shells.
5.43-5.44 Central California mound jewelry made of iridescent abalone shell; although there are many shapes from simple to complex, their number is limited and the craftsmen stuck to one or another quite faithfully; the crescents (5.44) are abalone shell rims.

5.45-5.46 Some larger abalone shell ornaments from central California; the big ones appear to have been worn on caps or headgear as they are commonly found at the sides or backs of heads in burials, though some are gorgets or breast ornaments; the one on the left in (5.45) is in the so-called "banjo shape" often regarded as the chief representative of this type of jewelry.

6 Ceremony and Religion

Important as ceremonies and religion are in the lives of modern Americans, their observance is but a pale shadow of the devotion to both that prevailed in the European world of yesterday—a devotion fully paralleled in the lives of the First Americans. The population of their spirit world was as dense as that of the mundane world. Their spirits' interest in the behavior of human beings was lively and constant, and an important part of that behavior concerned carrying out both tribal and personal ceremonies in exactly the prescribed fashion. Added to this serious aspect of religion was the same accompaniment of fables and legends that has grown up around our religions and ceremonies.

Anthropologists have devoted much effort to studying and recording the myriad details of all this, and the reports of their findings have explained why many of the often odd and puzzling artifacts came to be. But there were ceremonies and religious beliefs before any records were made. They are gone and lost for all time, and they, too, involved artifacts which now tantalize us with their evidence of much meaning but their complete silence as to what that meaning is. How, when, and why were they used? The carefully made birdstones, butterfly stones, and all the company of Eastern bannerstones, the stubby stone crosses in the Southwest, the zoomorphic monolithic axes of the Pacific Coast—we can only guess at their identities. On the other hand, there are some trappings and artifacts of ceremony and religion whose meanings are half revealed by similarity to known objects or through archaeological detective work. Notable among such known objects are charms and fetishes, whose meanings are explained in various ethnological reports.

Ceremonial Headdress

In the popular mind Indians are associated with feathers in the hair. There is reason for this idea, for everywhere feathers were involved in the garb they developed to wear in observance of religious and other ceremonies. Many of the costumes depicted in books or worn by imitators of their rituals are not typical in the sense of everyday wear. They are comparable to the plumed hats worn by Knights Templars in parades and the mitres worn by high-church dignitaries in the performance of their duties. The famous war bonnet of the Plains, shown in the group of combat artifacts, was originally reserved to warriors who had earned it, as are the campaign ribbons worn by military personnel.

Feathers surrounded the masks of the southern Alaskan Eskimos, topped off Kachina costumes in the Southwest, and assumed many strikingly imaginative roles atop the heads of California Indians. Quite likely they and the headgear that went with them were as ubiquitous in Mound Builder days in the Eastern Woodlands, but their fragile nature has left no trace.

Although the accent has been on feathers, it does not mean that they always dominated. On the Northwest Coast quantities of shredded bark strips were used instead, particularly on masks. Among the Yuroks and Hupas of California, crowns made of angled spikelike ornaments on leather bands were supplemented with cloth snoods. Miscellaneous ornaments were inserted into ensembles like flowers into wreaths.

Ceremonial Paraphernalia

As well as their often resplendent headgear, the pre-Columbians wore or carried all manner of objects that showed the most lively imagination. Most of the musical and noise-making instruments pictured elsewhere were among these, but equally prominent were articles carried to be held up and flourished: staffs, wands, coupsticks, obsidian blades, poles with deerskins or, among some tribes, scalps, mounted on them; ceremonial clubs to swing about, and other weapons often especially decorated for ceremonial purposes. This does not include articles of specific significance when added to a particular costume, or those which simply were suited to the occasion. Most tribes needed special storage facilities and guardians for all this paraphernalia.

In addition to these community objects, there were many personal possessions of religious or ceremonial significance grouped as charms and fetishes.

Masks

Because of their substitution of an inhuman for a human face, masks are the most spectacular of all articles used in ceremonies and religious observances.

Ceremonial Headdress
6.1-6.2 Front and back views of a Pueblo Indian crest, presumably for a corn dance ceremonial invoking or celebrating rain for the crops—ears of corn at the ends of the rainbow instead of the white man's pots of gold suggesting a difference in the hopes of the two peoples
6.3 Seminole Indian (Florida) turban decorated with feathers and a silver band (photo courtesy Museum of the American Indian, Heye Foundation)

6.1 6.2 6.3

Although mask wearing was popular in widely scattered places, it tended to be concentrated in certain groups. The Northwest Coast Indians are the most conspicuous of these because their masks were made of wood with, to us, many grotesque distortions and often considerably larger than one would associate with mask size. Their neighbors, the southern Alaskan Eskimos, were not far behind, but with their own distinctive styles and forms.

The Indians of the Southwest were equally active in this practice though their work is less familiar to us for two reasons: one, their masks blended into overall costumes to create a whole Kachina figure, of which there were many identifiable individual forms; two, they have always jealously guarded dispersion of their masks to collectors and tourists, so that museums have few or no examples displayed to the public, in contrast to the literally hundreds of Northwest Coast masks to be seen in nearly all museums.

As well known as the masks of these tribes are the fascinating false-face society wooden masks of the Iroquois, which are supposed to have been carved from the trunks of living trees. With their big, twisted mouths, piercing eyes, numerous wrinkles, and lank black or gray hair, the Iroquois masks have been traditional among this branch of Woodland Indians for hundreds of years. Less well known but much used are the odd and fairly pretentious but unique masks created by the Cherokees and their neighbors in the Southeast.

Certain Plains Indian masks are conspicuous in the paintings of Catlin, Bodmer, and other pictorial recorders of Plains life in the early nineteenth century. These are notably buffalo heads underneath which the bodies of wildly gesturing Indians cavorted. Other odd forms are recorded from the Sioux and other northern Plains Indians, which fact leads to the possibility that there was more mask wearing among them in the older times than in later years.

Ceremony and Religion 145

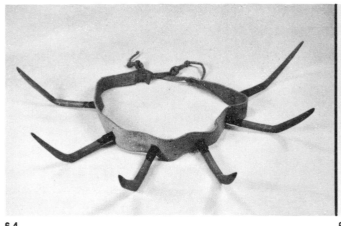

6.4

6.5

6.6

6.7

6.8

6.9

6.4 Yurok Indian crown; the spikes are usually sea lion's teeth, but in this case are wooden imitations.

6.5 Northern California Indian style of radiating feather crest, in this specimen mounted on a painted buckskin snood

6.6-6.7 Painted cloth (6.6) and netting (6.7) snoods worn by Yurok-Hupa ceremonial dancers to trail from the backs of their heads; left is finger-woven cloth resembling soft canvas and right, fine-meshed knotless netting; the bottoms are decorated with blue jay, hawk, and other bird feathers.

6.8 Menomini roach of red-dyed hair, equipped with a bone feather socket and feather spikes

6.9 Cree roach of natural color hair, with a single feather and a mink(?) skin trailer

6.10

6.11

6.10-6.11 Elaborate Indian headdress as shown in old photos of (6.10) an Omaha Indian and (6.11) a Paiute Indian; the latter being Chief Winnemucca after whom the Nevada town is named (courtesy Widel's Antiques, Berkeley, California)

Ceremonial Paraphernalia
6.12 Fawn skin with painted designs, Yurok-Hupa culture, northwestern California
6.13-6.14 Whalebone wands, Northwest Coast, carved and painted to represent real or imaginary figures, each with an auxiliary figure as shown in (6.14)
6.15 Three northwest California "puberty wands" made from one stick split into broomlike shape and carried in ceremonials
6.16 Northwest Coast shaman's staff or wand; top effigy a squid
6.17 A prehistoric and an historic obsidian blade, symbols of wealth flourished in Yurok-Hupa culture ceremonies

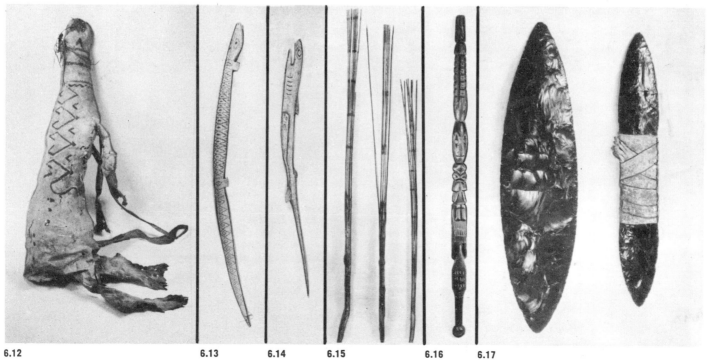

6.12 **6.13** **6.14** **6.15** **6.16** **6.17**

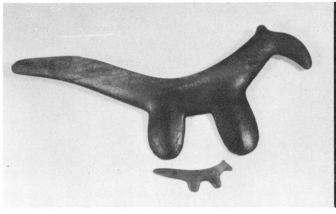

6.18

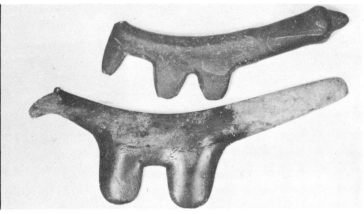

6.19

6.20

6.21

6.22

6.23

6.18 Black slate "slave killer" ceremonial club and its miniature mate; Gunther Island, Eureka, California (Dr. H. H. Stuart collection)

6.19 Upper, "slave killer" from western Washington, and, lower, from northwestern California; the handle of the latter is whitened by heat due to the burning of its wrapped handle in cremation.

6.20 Stone paddle clubs, western Washington; found in the same areas as "slave killers" and much like similar clubs of ceremonial character popular in the South Sea Islands, notably New Zealand

6.21 Flattened skull and normal skull; the former from western Washington and the latter, California

6.22 So-called "spuds" of Mound Builder origin; possibly from ceremonial axes similar to the "slave killers"; ceremonial axes and adzes were much used in the South Sea Islands.

6.23 Eskimo model of an indoor ceremony; center figures with effigy wands; four of the seated figures are tapping drums; the hole is the inner end of the entry tunnel into the igloo.

*Eskimo whalebone mask; note portrayal of
epicanthic fold*

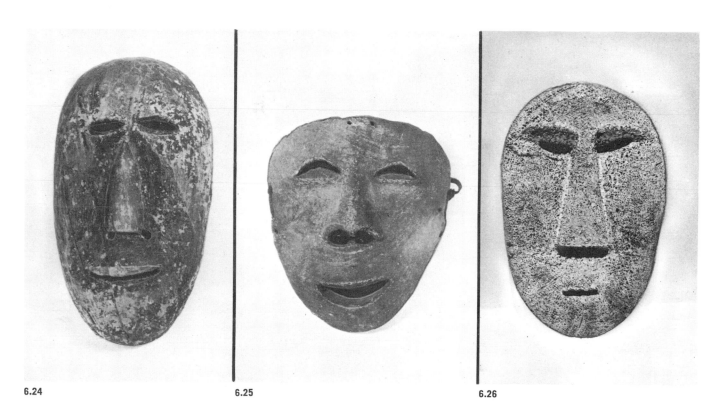

6.24

6.25

6.26

Masks
6.24-6.26 Northern Eskimo masks: (6.24)
and (6.25) old weathered masks of the type
associated with graves in the high Arctic;
(6.26) heavy whalebone mask, painted
tattoo stripes on the chin

6.27-6.29 Southern (Kuskokwim Valley) Eskimo masks made in an area with easier access to wood than the high Arctic; often surrounded by feathers when complete; (6.29) a typical "face" with a frame to help hold feathers

6.30-6.32 Two (6.30) and (6.32) animal masks, approaching the "face" form among the Northwest Coast Indians just to the south of the Kuskokwim Valley; (6.31) one of a pair of finger masks; these were worn on the fore and middle fingers and carried on conversations Punch and Judy fashion; the halo of feathers is gone.

6.27

6.28

6.29

6.30

6.31

6.32

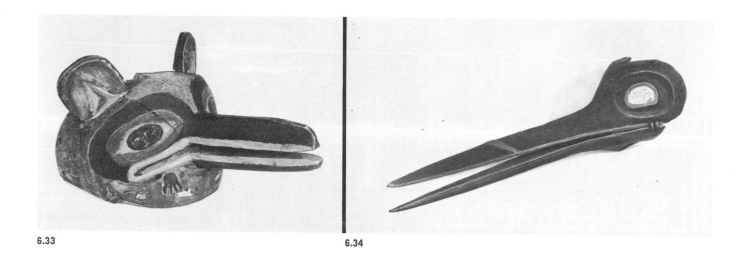

6.33

6.34

6.35

6.36

6.37

6.33-6.34 Northwest Coast Indian carved and painted wooden masks: (6.33) animal figure painted black, red, green, and blue; part of a headdress crest; (6.34) bird mask with movable bill, abalone eyes; this type was usually worn with a mop of shredded bark like a wig.

6.35 Brown, stained cedar wood mask; protruding tongue a popular element in Northwest Coast carving

6.36 Mask painted in alternations of black, red, and blue

6.37 Whalebone, with copper eyes; a rather rare use of this material. This and (6.36) are also Northwest Coast.

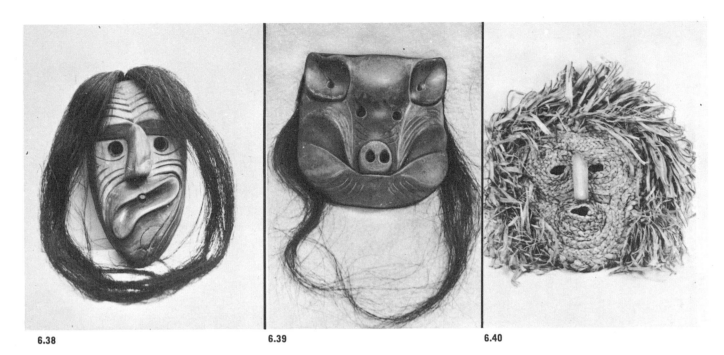

6.38   6.39   6.40

6.41

6.38-6.40 Three Iroquois false-face society masks: (6.38) showing the typical features of such masks, distorted, huge, twisted mouth and nose, deep wrinkles, and long, lank hair; this particular one supplied with a hole in the mouth through which a pipe was smoked by the wearer (the pipe accompanying the mask shown in the pipe group); (6.39) pig mask; in former times a bear was part of a ceremonial feast, but as civilization took over New York State it became necessary to substitute a pig; (6.40) Seneca mask fashioned of cornhusks, braided, sewn, and molded to shape

6.41 Two of a number of painted wooden masks in the F. H. Cushing find at Key Marco, Florida, 1896; around twenty were found, some fifteen of which were pretty well preserved; full-sized face masks, equipped with string holes and holes for feathers, they indicated well-developed prehistoric use of such objects by Southern Indians (photo Florida 21, B.A.E. collection, Smithsonian Institution).

6.42 Zuñi Kachina (Sekya) mask, 17 inches to top of feathers
6.43 Hopi Kachina (representing Hehea Kachina) mask (photos (6.42) and (6.43) courtesy Museum of the American Indian, Heye Foundation)
6.44 Bust of Kachina doll showing the use of masks to right, on a caped figure, with the typical bulging eyes, bill, and extended ears illustrated in (6.42) and (6.43); many Kachina dolls are rather faithfully executed statuettes of living Kachina dancers.
6.45-6.46 Paintings on hide—reputed to have been made by an Iroquois Indian in the seventies—showing two forms of Plains Indian masks: (6.45) a buffalo head (illustrated in Catlin and Bodmer paintings in the first half of the nineteenth century) and (6.46) a keystone-shaped mask with real or simulated deer horns and some sort of crest
6.47 Shell mask, possibly a large pendant, of a type found in prehistoric sites throughout the Southeast, clearly imitating faces, with eyes, nose in relief, and mouth; ceremonial use assumed

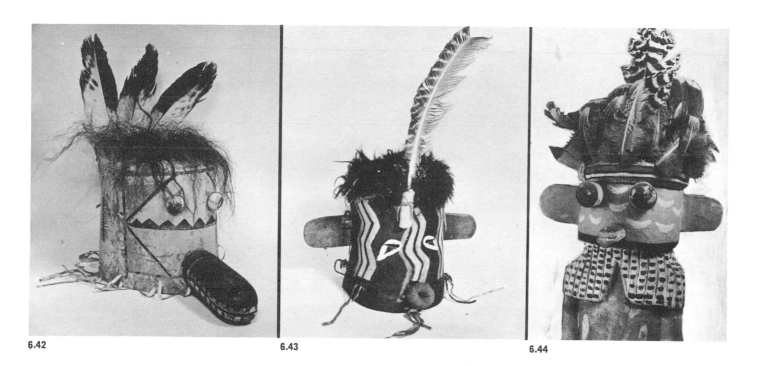

6.42   6.43   6.44

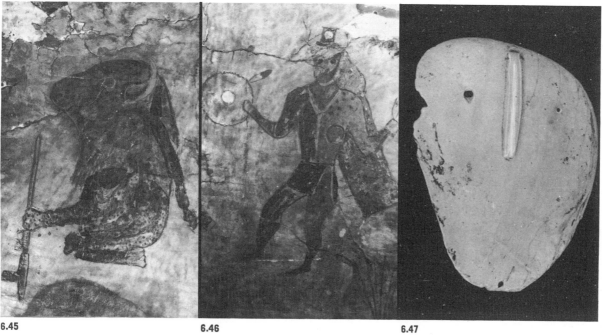

6.45   6.46   6.47

6.48

6.49

6.48 Cherokee mask, booger type, 12 inches high
6.49 Cherokee mask with rattlesnake on brow, booger type, 12½ inches high (both photos courtesy Museum of the American Indian, Heye Foundation)

Fetishes and Charms
6.50-6.51 Pueblo Indian (Zuñi) fetishes; lower in (6.50), a gambling fetish and (6.51) two hunting fetishes; odd-shaped pebbles and horn touched up to look like creatures and decorated with feathers, beads, and shells. These are the type that are "fed" by their guardians.
6.52-6.53 Eskimo fetishes, more like charms than Southwest Indian fetishes: (6.52) ivory whales; (6.53) sea mammals, one with human legs
6.54 Chipped stone fetishes used by the Eskimos in connection with fishing and hunting; top right, a California form assumed to be of fetish nature, usually having rudimentary legs
6.55 Northwest Coast fetishes (seen here mounted on explanatory cards) tied to cradles to guard the occupants; a practice also noted in northwest California
6.56 Southwest Indian fetishes of a more modern nature and a leather bottle for sacred meal; alabaster bear, New Mexico; small brown bear ornamented with turquoise
6.57 Plains Indian medicine objects and an Arizona fetish (lower left) made of a nut with copper tacks; the Eastern Indians' medicine objects were as varied as individual experience and fancy could make them, being something like school children's souvenirs combined with luck-bringing qualities; these, a half buffalo hoof with a beaded edge containing a stone, and a little buckskin bag with a shriveled claw attached.

6.50

6.51

6.52

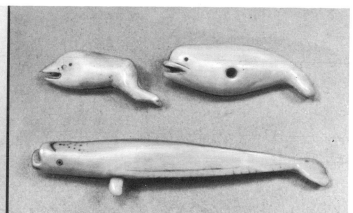

6.53

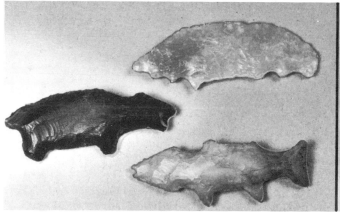

6.54

6.55

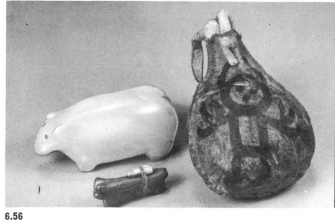

6.56

6.57

6.58   6.59   6.60

6.58   Baked-clay figures found in northwest California burials which apparently have the same purpose as similar figures occasionally found down as far as the Southwest, where they are associated with fertility rites or superstitions.

6.59   A flat pebble with "tree" markings similar to those on the California pottery charms, found from time to time along the Columbia River in Washington; and a "hub" stone which Dr. David Banks Rogers identified as a medicine man's center stone for a mystic sunburst arrangement of charm stones.

6.60   Beaded pads said to contain umbilical cords and to be kept from birth to death by Plains Indians; the pads are usually shaped like lizards.

6.61   Knob- and bar-type charm stones, California

6.62   Another form of California charm stone, notched at both ends; bottom one has the beginning of a core-drilled hole in the side.

6.63   Charm stones found in considerable numbers in the southern (Yokuts) part of central California

6.64   California charm stones of wider distribution and provided with suspension holes

6.65   Plummet-shaped California charm stones, two with black asphaltum to "glue" attached cord still in evidence

6.66   Variations of south central California charm stones

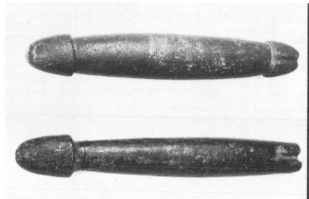

6.61

6.62

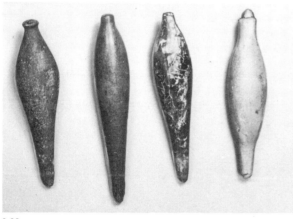

6.63

6.64

6.65

6.66

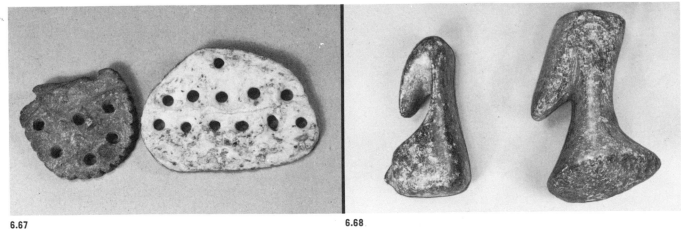

6.67   6.68

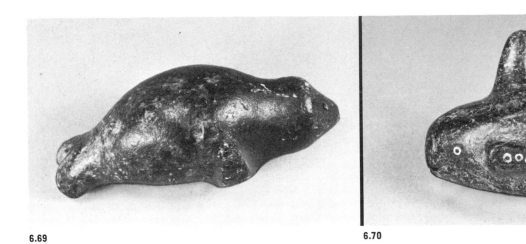

6.69   6.70

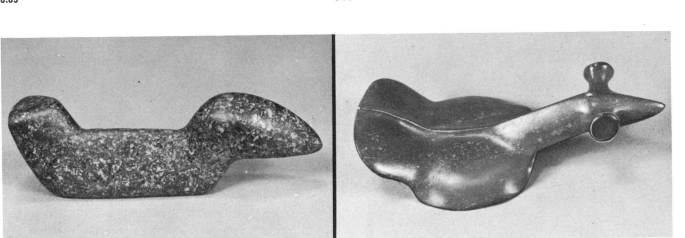

6.71   6.72

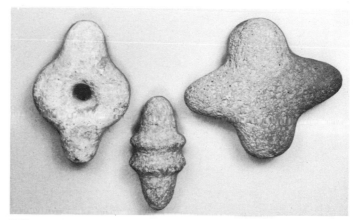

6.73

6.74

6.75

6.67 "Grandmother stones," so called because they are said to be an Indian grandmother's tally of her grandchildren; left from central Oregon, right from San Nicholas Island, California

6.68 "Pelican stones," charm stones popular among the southern California maritime tribes, named from a fancied resemblance to pelican heads; possibly a fishermen's fetish; made in a wide variation of sizes

6.69-6.70 A steatite seal (6.69), and (6.70) whale, the latter with beads inlaid with asphaltum; nearly as numerous as pelican stones, these, too, may be hunting or fishing fetishes; some charm stones are as realistically made as these, others are mere token shapes.

6.71-6.72 Eastern "Mound Builders'" birdstones, pictured here as possible fetishes: (6.71) speckled granite, Michigan, and (6.72) a "pop-eye," very unusual both because of material and of origin, being made of catlinite (pipestone) and having been found in a site near Chamberlain, South Dakota, far west for such stones

6.73 Three problematic stones from the Southwest, significance unknown; several of the cross type were found in one instance disposed around a burial.

6.74 A banded slate butterfly stone from Ohio, commonly provided, as in this case, with a transverse hole through the junction, indicating possible use on a wand or peg

6.75 Eastern Woodland boatstone, from resemblance to a canoe; significance still a matter of conjecture; this one from Arkansas

6.76 A token Northwest Coast Indian copper in the shape of one of that culture's prized shieldlike slabs of copper representing great wealth and sometimes being objects of central importance at potlatches; this one is possibly a souvenir of some such occasion, or possibly a symbol of possession of one of the full-sized coppers.

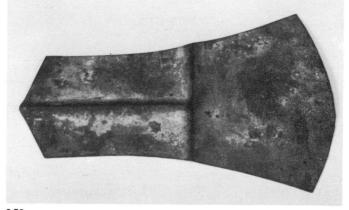

6.76

7 Indian and Eskimo Art

The happy and natural exuberance of artistic enjoyment and execution shown throughout all Eskimo and Indian art, particularly as applied to the creation of the most commonplace objects, is in somewhat humiliating contrast to the plodding drabness of the bulk of our artifacts and the often pinched and painful distortions that appear in semiprofessional efforts to produce art with a capital and modern "A." It is always evident that the uncivilized Americans enjoyed their art, whereas the dominant notes of modern polyglot American art are false and sour. This, of course, hammers one point of view, but it is an appropriate thought in directing attention to Indian and Eskimo art expression without the usual condescension that accompanies many of the sophisticates' recent interest in "primitive art."

This happy use and appreciation of art is not only indigenous to North America, but it has proved strong enough since 1492 to produce some purely native expression in mediums of European origin or in European-inspired ways. Among these is the use of black slate among the Northwest Coast Indians using their masterful wood-carving techniques. The origin of this has been traced to imitation of the scrimshaw work which they saw going on among the whalers and ships' crews of trading vessels. Another expression that is more recent, but in a way similar, has been the activity of certain Eskimos who have used their ivory-carving skills on soapstone (steatite). And, of course, there is the extension of native Indian quillwork to creation of Indian beadwork with which we are so familiar.

Basketry

The meaning of basketry and the methods of construction have been discussed from a utilitarian standpoint. As an art, it also presents structural and surface beauties of great variety and merit. Some of the weaving is, in itself, so skillfully and lovingly done that it excites pleasure and admiration, and the surface treatment has a valid place in a worldwide consideration of man's aesthetic efforts in design and color. Most such designs were woven into the fabric of the basket with various colors of warp and woof and of stitches around the coils. However, a number of tribes developed other surface-design methods: the Pomos added feathers and beads; the Salish tribes used imbrication; the Tlingits varied theirs with false embroidery and, sometimes, painting.

Basketry Designs and Design Areas

Although not infallible, the design on a basket will usually tell tribal origin, because most groups developed their own traditional patterns within which they delighted to weave countless variations and combinations.

The Aleuts incorporated little spots of colored wool and silk into their grass basketry, usually in squares and rectangles. The Tlingits luxuriated in brightly colored bands of false embroidery around their cylindrical baskets, using rectangular elements, often with conventional representation. Their Salish neighbors worked with imbrication, also in bright colors, and favored all-over designs of chevron or zigzag construction. The Nez Percés put painted or yarn patterns on cornshuck baskets in designs showing admiration of Plains Indian art.

In California, the northern Indians wove geometric designs that emphasized black and brown parallelograms, trapezoids, and triangles running in bands and chevrons. In central California, the Pomos created a basketry art "kingdom" of their own, using less rigid geometric designs and numerous less angular elements, all softened by the curved shapes of the baskets. The Pomo style influenced all north-central California tribes, but it was departed from in the territory occupied by the Washos and other tribes in western Nevada and the eastern slope of the Sierras, where a thin wedge-like triangle, sometimes reminiscent of a flame, recurred in their weaving of some of the finest coil-work basketry made.

In the south-central valley, a group of tribes made baskets grouped as "Tulares." These feature bands, both horizontal and vertical, frequently using a favorite band of reddish diamonds and half diamonds said to be patterned from the backs of rattlesnakes. South of them, in turn, the so-called "Mission Indians" in southern California developed their particular designs that featured two intertwining star forms of differing colors. These star forms were based on a coiled groundwork of flecked white through brown (which often reminds

Pictorial Basketry
7.1 Attu (Island) unfinished basket woven of grass as fine as linen, trimmed in straight and eyelet embroidery and using, in this case, European silk to make tiny flowers
7.2 Tlingit, with a false embroidery rendering, in color, of a salmon
7.3-7.4 Two sides of an Upper Chehalis (western Washington) basket picturing animals and Chinese laborers who fascinated the Indians during the building of the Northern Pacific Railroad tracks, circa 1873

7.1   7.2   7.3

7.4

one of gold) to black, thus creating a background that is distinctive to this area.

The Southwest was also rich in design areas which differed individually to create many subareas. The general structural scheme was radial on the many bowls and trays woven, and twining on jars; all, except some Pueblo wickerwork, in coiled basketry. The Apaches' designs are often reminiscent of snowflakes, and the Pima Indians created a characteristic swirl using black lines that alternate from ribbon wideness to line thinness. The Pueblo Indians distinguished their work not only by the use of wicker weaving, but by making their coils very thick, fat, and comparatively soft. They also used colors, whereas the nomadic tribes rather stuck with black designs on straw color or white coiling.

Much of the Eastern Woodland Indian weaving activity died in the distant past, perhaps even before Columbus, and only remnants and imprints are found now and again in the mounds. That which survived tends to the utilitarian and was constructed of thin ribbons of wood or cane, or was made with coils of grass. There was one distinctive form of decoration developed, however, which used designs created by manipulation of the plaiting so as to create patterns made of squares

and parallelograms in yellows, reds, browns, and blacks against the basic straw colors of cane ribbons.

Pictorial Basketry

Most of the western and southwestern tribes frequently resorted to graphic presentations on basketry, ranging from conventional figures to outright pictures. The Apaches delighted in including little figures of men and animals in their designs; the Pueblo Indians portrayed Kachina dancers on their trays; the Tulare tribes created baskets with figures of men and women holding hands all around the basket, sometimes called "friendship baskets"; the Mission Indians and the Pomos resorted to presentations of the natural world around them: snakes, butterflies, palm trees, etc.; the Makahs liked spirited marine scenes with whales, boats, and sea gulls; a rim border of little birds is characteristic of some coast Salishan baskets; the Wasco Indians decorated their cornshuck "sally bags" with their own ideas of sturgeons, butterflies, antelopes, and men with feathers on their heads; and the northern Northwest Coast Indians painted totemic figures on mats and hats and sometimes wove in textile "paintings" of creatures in place of their usual colored bands.

7.5   7.6   7.7

7.8   7.9

7.10   7.11

7.5 Makah Indian, northern Washington coast, showing a sea gull perched on a whale, with a common disregard for relative sizes

7.6-7.7 Wasco Indian (Oregon) "sally bags" with figures resembling those found in pictographs and petroglyphs along the Columbia River; shown are antelopes, butterflies, sturgeon, and men.

7.8 A Yokuts (California) "friendship basket," so called because of encirclement by figures holding hands; center band of "rattlesnake design"

7.9 Mission Indian (southern California) basket depicting native American palm trees that flourish in their area

7.10 A Pueblo Indian Kachina basket depicting one of the Kachina dancers, emphasizing headdress and sash

7.11 Apache picture basket with more than seventy-five figures of men, animals, and butterflies

Area Designs in Basketry
7.12-7.13 Tlingit baskets (southern Alaska) with colored bands in geometric figures, often having conventional symbolism of hills, strawberries, snakes' noses, butterflies, flies, etc.; finely twined weaving with thin walls
7.14 Vancouver Island checkerwork woven wallet, using different colored ribbons of bark to create the designs
7.15 Coiled, left, and twined, right, Salishan basketry; coiled favored by British Columbia and interior Salish and twined by coast Salish; zigzag angular designs typical; rim border of twined Quinault basket typical of coast Salish

7.12

7.13

7.14

7.15

7.16 Interior (British Columbia and Washington) Salishan baskets: a cornshuck bag, Nez Percé, with Plains-type design painted on it; a loop-rimmed Yakima, or Klikitat, basket, with typical chevron design in colored imbrication; Thompson River imbricated basket; checkered diamonds in variations represent a root of wild rice, a cluster of flies, a heart, and a big bead; and, containing the others, a British Columbia Salish baby carrier; upper half decorated with a form of imbrication called "beading"

7.17-7.18 Obverse and reverse of a Nez Percé cornshuck wallet, decorated with colored yarn designs showing affinity with Plains Indian ornamentation

7.19-7.20 Yurok-Hupa culture designs; lids an older feature of basketry in this area; use of parallelograms, trapezoids, and triangles in designs in diagonals and chevrons illustrated

7.21-7.22 Northeastern California designs in (7.21) a Pitt River area carrying basket and (7.22) a Klamath gambling tray, illustrating likenesses and differences in comparison with northwestern California (Klamath) designs; Pitt River designs characteristically in bold black on white

7.16

7.17

7.18

7.19

7.20

7.21

7.22

7.23-7.24 Twined and coiled Pomo basketry: (7.23) diagonally twined design emphasizing geometrical and zigzag motifs given curve by the shape of the basket; decorated with scattered beads; (7.24) single stick coiling, giving a flatter surface effect than usual coiling

7.25-7.26 Two forms of Pomo feather basketry: (7.25) with individual tufts of red feathers and quail feather tufts on the rim; (7.26) solid feathering creating design with different colored feathers, and a fully beaded and feathered collar

7.27 Maidu coiled basket; designs similar to Pomo

7.28 Washo (Nevada) basket with rather attenuated black or red triangles somewhat resembling flames as characteristic elements; fine and regular stitching

7.23

7.24

7.25

7.26

7.27

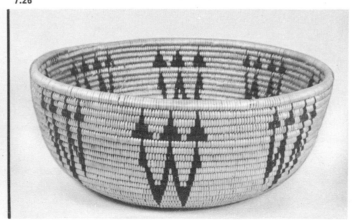

7.28

7.29

7.30

7.31

7.32

7.33

7.29-7.30 Two common applications of Tulare (central California) Indian basketry: (7.29) band around the basket in red and black; (7.30) bands from base to rim in red and black; frequent use of triangles and diamonds

7.31-7.32 Two expressions (7.31) and (7.32) of Mission Indian (southern California) designs: black and cream on a flecked brown base radiating from the center in intricate, often interlocking figures

7.33 A Chemehuevi jar; this small group, which created basketry distinguished by clean white regular coiling with simple black designs and well-proportioned shapes, is classified between California and Southwest culture areas.

7.34-7.36 Pueblo Indian basketry: (7.34) and (7.35) thick, soft coils with colored designs; left with end of coil open and right with end closed, indicating respectively a maiden and a married weaver; (7.36) a wickerwork tray, also with colored design

7.37-7.38 Pima basketry illustrating two characteristics, spiral motion and alternating thin and thick lines breaking into each other in angular fashion; designs in black

7.39 Apache star or snowflake design in red and black; sprinkling of little figures typical

7.40 Western Apache jar showing netting effect of design common in these utensils; has scattered figures as in (7.39)

7.41 Eastern Mescalero Apache, using a distinctive flattened coil and designs in sage green and reddish hues

7.42 Eastern Woodland coiled basket with coils made of soft scented grass, hence called "sweet grass baskets"

7.43 Southeastern, Gulf coast (Chitimacha) Indian basketry using black and yellow ribbons of cane on a straw-colored field with twilled weaving to produce herringbone designs; use of ribbons of wood or cane a common practice among Eastern Indians

7.44 A Mandan Indian gambling basket showing design influence from the East and a Plains device of weaving in wood ribs for stiffening

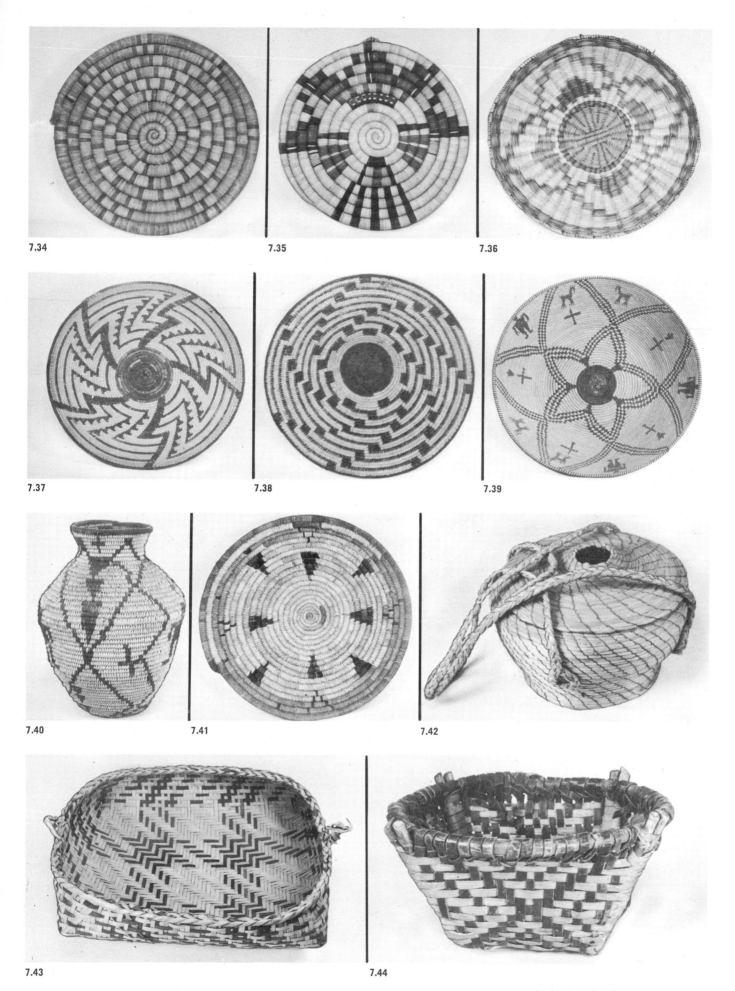

7.34

7.35

7.36

7.37

7.38

7.39

7.40

7.41

7.42

7.43

7.44

Pottery

Pottery was made in about a quarter of the area of North America, but that quarter included some of the more thickly inhabited country: the Southwest, including southern California below the Tehachapi Mountains; and the eastern half of the United States, extending a little up rivers into the Plains and somewhat into eastern Canada. Elsewhere, pottery was made only in minute quantities, if at all.

There are two great divisions of Indian pottery: Eastern and Southwestern. The pottery in both areas has left hundreds, or perhaps thousands, of whole or restored specimens and uncounted millions of potsherds. It is not tactful to say that much the better ware was made in the Southwest; let us say it was more sophisticated and further developed, perhaps from more contact in prehistoric times with the master potters of Mexico. The Southwest pottery is also much more colorfully and intricately decorated than Eastern pottery, so that it makes possible much more dating and fixing of design areas.

As art, much of the Eastern pottery is drab and plain, with an overall tone of muted gray. However, this is not to say that it had no lively artistic range, because there are hundreds of striking and often beautiful examples to prove otherwise. The Southwest, however, has supplied a richer and more varied selection, possibly because of the greater quantities of pottery made there. The only comment about art elsewhere than in the East and Southwest is that the Eskimos sometimes made creditable designs in the bottoms of somewhat clumsy pottery lamps.

Eastern Pottery

Decoration of Eastern pottery was attained in several ways. Much was ornamented sculpturally with figures of mammals, fishes, reptiles, birds, and persons superimposed or incorporated into the whole vessel. Some, notably in the middle of the Mississippi Basin, was painted. All over the East other pottery was incised, etched, stamped, or otherwise impressed with designs, sometimes simply with marks of string, basketry, scratching, thumb prints, etc. Some Algonkian pots were made more intricate by a square collar rim, usually ornamented, added to a round pot base. Similar experiments recur in the southeast.

A great deal can be told about the origin, both late and early in time, of this pottery because of its art character. Some design areas associated with the residence of Indians at the time of Columbus' landing are identifiable, and references are often made to Caddo, Iroquois, and Cherokee pottery styles. But much of the identification is complicated by the great movements of peoples in the past, so that many definite "schools" of design and pottery construction overlap or underlie others.

Southwest Pottery

Complicated as the description and analysis of Eastern pottery is, a short yet adequate summary of Southwest pottery is virtually impossible—whole books have been compiled on parts of its many phases. One can only present a few of the basic factors:

1. The origins and beginnings of Southwest pottery are somewhat obscure, as to whether it was developed spontaneously or was learned from the south. In the zone occupied by the prehistoric Basket Makers, the specimens which might be termed "mud vessels" rather than pottery appeared some 1700 years ago. Those which evidence knowledge of the basic principles of mixing and firing show up with dating of some 1500 years ago.

2. Almost from the beginning, methods of ornament and construction started off in ever-widening directions of patterns, colors, and forms. They then changed consistently within groups. Because of this, it has been possible to do precise dating by ceramics and potsherds in the Southwest. Such dating has not been possible to any such an extent elsewhere.

3. Pottery with the coils showing, called "corrugated," is an older form but has been retained largely for its merits in cooking. Ingenious ways of rippling, alternating, wiping, etc., these coils have often resulted in pleasing art results.

4. The wealth of ornament and design which was attained by the use of simple black on white, and later by colors on white and colors in combination, defies summary. It might be noted that pottery which used three or more colors is called "polychrome pottery."

5. Southwest pottery can be separated into two eras: pre-European and modern. The modern Indian pottery is frequently beautiful, and it is on display in all art museums that have room for it. But it differs from that of the older era in sophistication as contrasted with true folk art, in its influences, and in being an individual rather than a tribal expression. Therefore, rightly or wrongly, it is regretfully omitted from this book.

7.45   **7.46**

7.47   **7.48**

7.49   **7.50**

Eastern Pottery

7.45 Woodland culture pot
7.46 Aztalan bowl (photos courtesy
Milwaukee Public Museum)
7.47 Loop-handled jar, Van Buren County,
Tennessee (photo courtesy United States
National Museum, Smithsonian Institution)
7.48 Restored engraved vessels from
Moundsville, Alabama (photo courtesy
United States National Museum,
Smithsonian Institution)

7.49 Polished black Caddo bottle,
Arkansas, with typical curved and cross-
hatched engraving
7.50 Painted red and white water bottles
with same sort of curling design as (7.49);
also Arkansas, heights (left to right) 11 and
10 inches (United States National Museum
photo, Smithsonian Institution)

7.51

7.52

7.53

7.54

7.55

7.56

7.57

7.58

7.51-7.58 Effigy pottery of the Eastern Woodland Indian country, home of the Mound Builders, in the collection of B. W. Stephens, Quincy, Ill.: (7.51) dog (?) with curly tail, height 6½ inches, Dunklin County, Mo.; frog (7.52), 5 inches, Mississippi County, Ark.; three human figures; (7.53) from New Madrid County, Mo., height 6 inches; (7.54) Poinsett County, Ark., height 5½ inches; and (7.55) Scott County, Mo., 4½ inches; turkey (?) effigy bowl (7.56), Poinsett County, Ark., 10 inches wide, 8 inches high; (bottom) (7.57) duck (?) bowl with possum on tail, Poinsett County, Ark., 10 inches wide, 8 inches high; and (7.58) a fish, Dunklin County, Mo., 6 inches high (photos courtesy B. W. Stephens)

Types of Southwest Pottery
7.59 Old corrugated pot with rippled ribbon ornamentation; one of the earliest forms, which was continued in use for cooking
7.60 Intricate angular design black on white bowl from Angell, Arizona; black on white was one of the earliest color combinations
7.61 Black on yellow Jeddito ware, an early Hopi region form; decoration on both outside and inside of bowl not a general practice
7.62 Design similar to (7.61) on interior of a red, black, and white polychrome bowl found near the edge of Roosevelt Lake, Arizona, in the Payson area

7.59

7.60

7.61

7.62

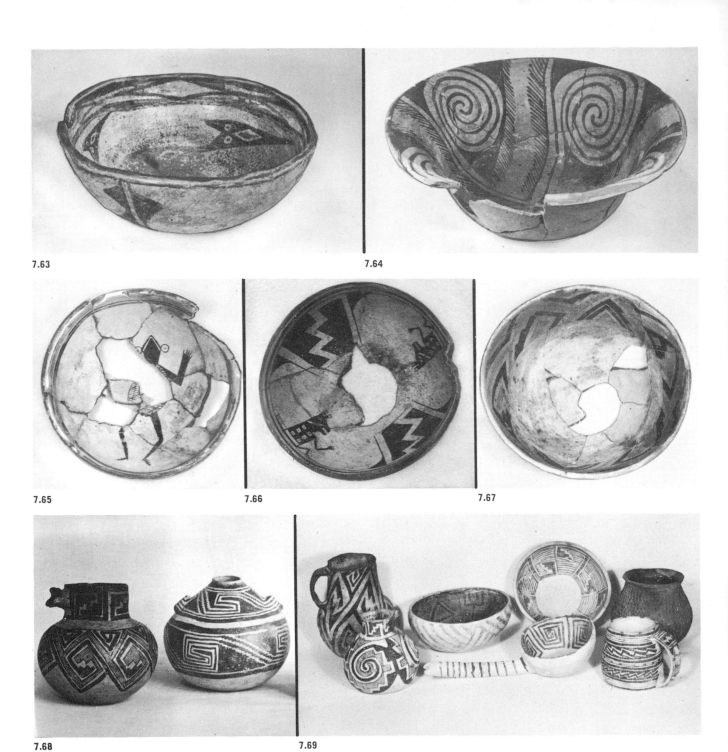

7.63

7.64

7.65

7.66

7.67

7.68

7.69

7.63 Old Zuñi-style design from a New Mexico site; exact location not recorded; showing reddish-black design on a white background, also ornamented on outside as well as inside

7.64 Typical curling red on buff theme recurring in Hohokam pottery from near Phoenix, Arizona

7.65-7.67 Mimbres ware; one of the most notable of old Southwest pottery forms; found in the Mimbres Valley, New Mexico: (7.65) and (7.66) typical pictorial bowls for which this pottery is famous; (7.65) showing combination of animal (coyote) and geometric design; (7.67) geometric pattern; these remarkable for precisely ruled lines resembling those made by a ruling pen. Mimbres bowls are characteristically "killed" (usually by poking a hole through the bottom), the ejected fragment apparently being thrown away, as it is seldom, if ever, found.

7.68-7.69 Various forms of Southwest Anasazi culture pottery in the Southwest Museum, Los Angeles, collections; Anasazi covers Basket Maker and Pueblo cultures from about A.D. 100 to the present (photos courtesy the Southwest Museum, Los Angeles, California).

7.70 Indented corrugated jar, Blue, Arizona; Cat. No. 245,599; United States National Museum (courtesy Smithsonian Institution)

7.71 Very thin-walled red ware, jar with polished black interior and incised design, pitcher with gold mica binder and coil finish, Gila River Valley, Arizona

7.72 Black on white pitcher, Mesa Verde style, Pueblo III, Anasazi culture

7.71

7.70

7.72

Art in Other Materials

Whereas art by present-day North American standards is confined to what is produced especially for aesthetic purposes, such as paintings, sculpture, and building ornamentation, it was not so restricted by the First Americans. They applied it to anything they made. Its role in basketry and pottery have just been summarized. In addition to these mediums, it was expressed in artifacts of stone, copper, ivory, horn, bone, shell, wood, and quillwork and beadwork.

The quantity of artwork in any one of these mediums and its percentage in relation to the total work in that medium or to the work done in other media is impossible to even guess. No contemporary records were kept by the pre-Columbians, and as their civilization was gradually destroyed, most of their artwork decayed or passed into oblivion. What survives in the more imperishable materials is no guide at all, except to the possible quantity in one medium. Much stone, pottery, copper, shell, bone, and other materials have survived from Mound Builder days, from decaying freshwater pearls to ornamented artifacts, but we have no way of knowing if those who built the mounds were major artists in quillwork, arrangement of feathers, carving of wood, and so on in the perishable elements.

Because attention has been directed to the artwork of the Northwest Coast Indians in recent years and because much of such work is carving in wood, these Indians are likely to be regarded as the master woodcarvers of the pre-Columbian population. However, a few art objects in wood that were recovered under unusually fortunate circumstances at Key Marco, Florida, tell us spectacularly that there were Indians at the other side and end of North America who were able, and possibly superior, rivals, but whose works and identity are all but obliterated and forgotten.

However, there are more than enough imperishable objects remaining from the prehistoric past, and enough perishable ones made late enough to be preserved, to tell us that the pre-Columbians, within the limitations of the technical knowledge and materials available to them, were the active equals of any peoples in the world in their aesthetic pursuits in the field of art.

Art in Stone
7.73 Ram carved out of lava, and steatite turtle with bowl on its back, Arizona
7.74 Hohokam (Arizona) ceremonial pot (?) made of lava, with a snake around the rim and dancing figures around the sides
7.75 Hard sandstone bowl with a ram's head on the edge
7.76 Prehistoric and historic period pictographs; left, a man, moon(?), and bird cut into a water-worn pebble; right, a catlinite tablet showing a tipi, man smoking pipe, Indian and white man shaking hands, and a flag on a fort; apparently a memento of a Plains Indian peace settlement
7.77 Birdstone from Indiana; black slate
7.78 Semitranslucent flint blade labeled by Moorehead as Flint Ridge material, 8¼ inches long
7.79 Effigy pipes; left, brownish steatite, seated figure holding pipe bowl; right, black stone frog
7.80 Banded slate artifacts; a tube, or large bead, and a gorget, the latter identified by Moorehead as from Kentucky

7.73

7.74

7.75

7.76

7.77

7.78

7.79

7.80

7.81   7.82   7.83   7.84

7.85   7.86

7.87   7.88

7.89   7.90

7.81-7.84 Northwest Coast artifacts: (7.81) slungshot club head, or weight, with whale etched on surface; (7.82) portion of a stone club with fish head; (7.83) scraper with face and bands etched on it; (7.84) slate totem pole of the type much illustrated in art books; Haida Indians

7.85 Haida black slate plate with killer whale designs and white bone insets around the edge

7.86 Western Indian arrowhead "masterpieces"; top left, northwestern California, top right, central California; center left, California della serrate, and part of a brown obsidian point from Goose Lake, northern California; bottom left, Priest Rapids (Columbia River) type of agate point; right, black agate(?) "dagger point," Columbia River

7.87 So-called "slave killers" from northwestern California made of polished black slate; these are effigy clubs once found in some numbers on Gunther Island, Humboldt Bay, but also found individually in northern California and the Columbia River area of Washington and Oregon.

7.88 Black steatite bowl in river canoe form, with some decoration, lower Klamath River area in California

7.89 Black steatite bowls, left from northwestern California, others from southern California coast; right one inlaid with shell beads

7.90 Chumash or Canalino arrow shaft straightener decorated with incised lines and knobs on end; black steatite

7.91-7.92 Banner stones in the National Museum of the Smithsonian Institution showing the varied range of forms and the wide range of territory; sixteen Eastern Woodland states are represented.

Left group (7.91), specimen numbers and states: (top row) 16681, Ill.; upper, 6626, Pa.; lower, 11528, Conn.; 16681, Ill.; (second row) 61857, Va.; upper, 248092, Ind.; lower, 8024, Ga.; 13151, N.Y.; (third row) 136996, Ind.; 97834, Ind.; 298370, Pa.; (bottom row) 88586, N.C.; 17901, Conn.; and 6214, N.J.

Right group (7.92) specimen numbers and states: (top row) 98026, Ind.; 62033, Mo.; 61899, Tenn.; (second row) 306990, Ark.; 173204, Tex.; 9099, Ind.; (third row) 58516, La.; 147748, Pa.; 30191, Ill.; (bottom row) 171873, Ark.; 9100, Ind.; 90714, Ohio

(Both group photos courtesy of Smithsonian Institution, National Museum)

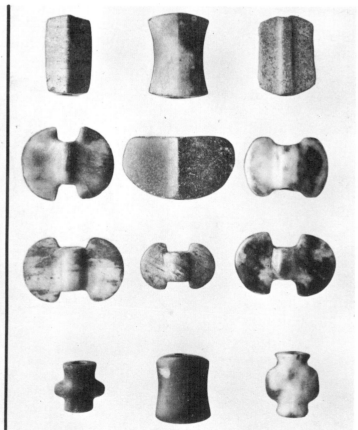

7.91

7.92

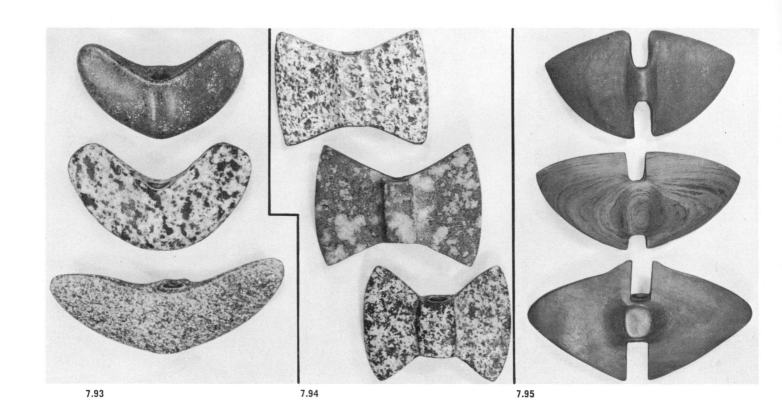

7.93   7.94   7.95

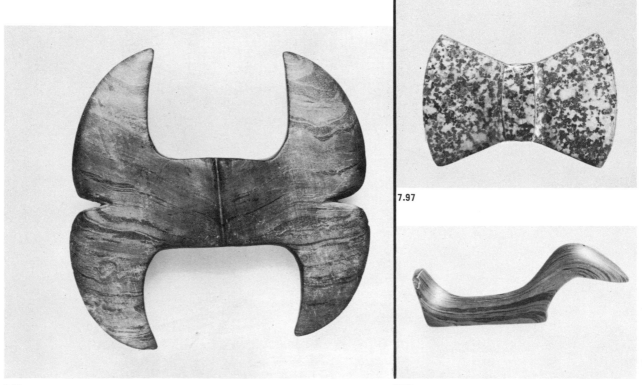

7.96   7.97

7.98

7.93-7.95 Close-ups of banner stones in the collection of B. W. Stephens, Quincy, Ill., illustrating variations of the wing type, and artistic choice of materials and craftsmanship in construction; left group (7.93), crescent type: top, Scott County, Ill.; 3 inches wide; center, Greene County, Ill., 4½ inches; bottom, Franklin County, Mo., 5¾ inches; center group (7.94), Wisconsin bow-tie type: top, mottled granite, Madison County, Ill., 4 inches; center, porphyry, Calhoun County, Ill., 4¾ inches; bottom, mottled granite, Calhoun County, Ill.; right group (7.95), butterfly type, all banded slate: top, Richland County, Ohio, 5¼ inches; center, Ross County, Ohio, 6 inches; bottom, Darke County, Ohio, 6½ inches (photos courtesy of B. W. Stephens, Quincy, Ill.)

7.99

7.100

7.101

7.96 Close-up of symmetrically banded slate double-crescent banner stone
7.97 Spotted granite "bow-tie" type of banner stone
7.98 Banded slate birdstone (photos (7.96), (7.97) and (7.98) courtesy Milwaukee Public Museum)

7.99 Axe blade with fluted decoration, an art style apparently originating in Wisconsin (photo courtesy Milwaukee Public Museum)
7.100 Carved granite bowl found under the waters of the Columbia River, a typical example of the newly discovered Columbia River art style (photo from picture in "Stone Age on the Columbia River" by Emory Strong, Binfords and Mort, Publishers, Portland, Oregon)
7.101 Southeastern Woodland Indian steatite pipes; left, Wythe County, Virginia, 6 inches long; right, Fulton County, Georgia, 5½ inches long; in the B. W. Stephens collection (photo courtesy B. W. Stephens, Quincy, Ill.)

7.102

7.103

7.104

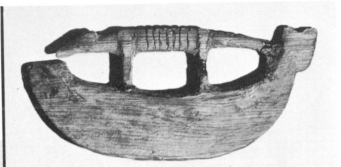

7.105

7.106

7.107

7.108

7.109

Northwest Coast Indian wooden bowl;
conventionalized bear effigy

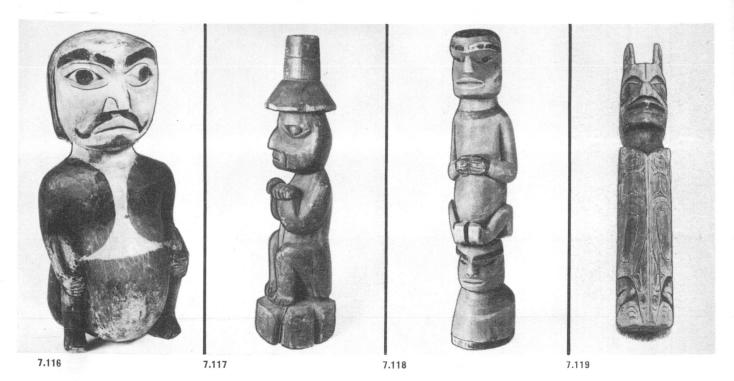

7.116   7.117   7.118   7.119

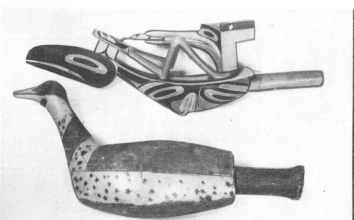

7.120

7.121

7.116   Caricature figure of a European (Russian?) emphasizing physical appearance and demeanor that the Indians found funny

7.117   Chief with hat having two top sections; these used to emphasize importance

7.118   Figure seated on figure, a conventional idea

7.119   Hawk, the body shaped to the roundness of the staff (?) from which the figure was cut off; Haida-style carving

7.120   Northern and southern style rattles; upper, a favorite form of northern Northwest Coast Indians, involving a bird with a shaman(?) receiving "power" from a frog held in the beak of a kingfisher, and a conventional hawk on the "belly"; lower, a painted Nootka style rattle representing a local sea bird

7.121   Wooden whale pendant, head painted in black and red

Eskimo and Northwest Coast Wooden Receptacles

7.122   Eskimo trinket box or paint box in the shape of a seal holding another seal on its belly

7.123   Carved dish, Haida style, seems to be a seal with flippers at one end and head at other

7.124   Carved and painted bowl representing a bear; black, red, and natural wood

7.125   Puffin bowl, head and beak accurately represented, with mammal whiskers for head crest

7.126   Carved black wood bowl inset with bone and abalone shell

7.127   Eskimo bowl with lines and deer painted inside. Food bowls constructed with bent wood sides set on a separate wood base

7.128   Polished brown wood with bone insets, showing sewing at the joined corner; other corners kerfed and bent

7.129   Carved and painted bowl; this and bowl in (7.128) of Haida design

Art in Wood

7.102 Wooden mask or figurehead of a deer found at the Key Marco site in Florida, which, with other artifacts of great artistic merit found at this site, tells us that many beautiful art objects may have been produced by these and other "savages" of North America, which have not survived because they were perishable and were not preserved by the fortunate surroundings in which the Key Marco artifacts were found (photo courtesy Bureau of Ethnology, Smithsonsian Institution)

7.103 Sauk-Fox spoon obtained from John Young Bear of the Mesquokie gens, and burl wood bowl obtained from John Green Hill, Chippewa medicine man

7.104 Wooden mortar, Yakima Indian type, Columbia River culture (photo from picture in "Stone Age on the Columbia River" by Emory Strong, published by Binfords and Mort, Portland, Oregon)

7.105 Mat creaser, Sauvies Island, Columbia River, showing the exposed rib motif that recurs in Columbia River art style (photo from picture in "Stone Age on the Columbia River" by Emory Strong, published by Binfords and Mort, Portland, Oregon)

7.106 Menomini war club of the often gracefully curved Woodland Indian ball-head type

7.107 Choctaw drum, Louisiana (courtesy Smithsonian Institution, B.A.E., Neg. 1102-b-7)

7.108 Algonkin birchbark container; Quebec, Canada (courtesy Museum of the American Indian, Heye Foundation)

7.109 Another Key Marco example of fine art, reminiscent of Egyptian statuary of cat gods (courtesy Smithsonian Institution)

Northwest Coast Totemic Art in Wood

7.110-7.112 Varieties of totem poles; center one (7.111) with doorway hole at base, perhaps a replica of a pole forming the center ornament of a house front; the bear in (7.112) represents a flood legend of the Indians around Sitka, Alaska, that the bear led chosen ones up from the flood —and back down—as indicated by his footprints, seen here on sides of totem pole.

7.113-7.114 Sections of a shaman's wan left (7.113), an octopus; right (7.114), a kingfisher(?)

7.115 Polished cedar paddle with wha effigy; Haida style

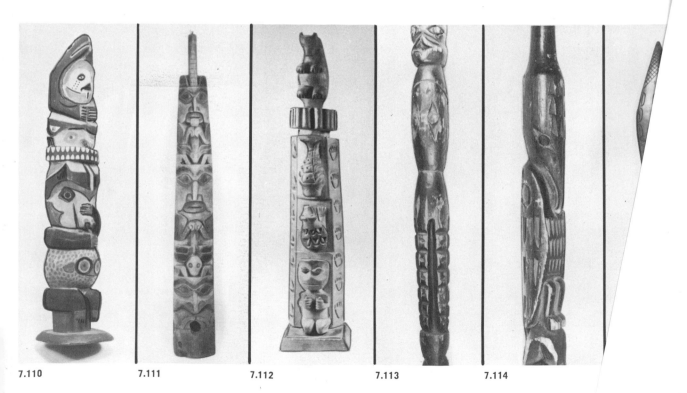

7.110   7.111   7.112   7.113   7.114

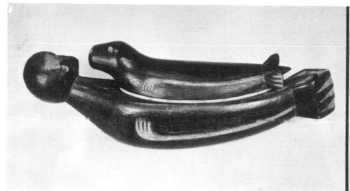

7.122

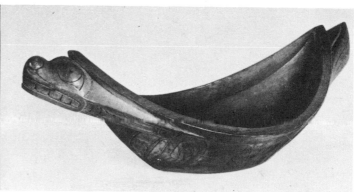

7.123

7.124

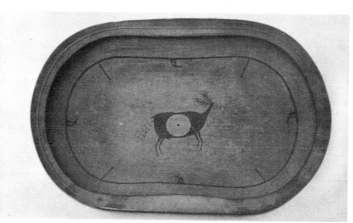

7.125

7.126

7.127

7.128

7.129

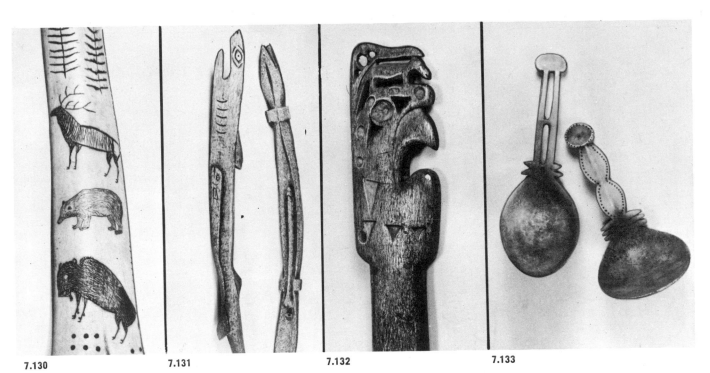

7.130   7.131   7.132   7.133

7.134

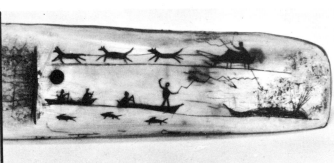

7.135

7.136

7.137

Art in Ivory, Bone, Horn, Shell, Copper, and Paint

7.130 Plains Indian etchings on an elkhorn quirt handle; elk, bear, buffalo, trees, and tally marks

7.131 Alaskan Indian effigy wands with miniature accompanying figures, whalebone

7.132 Totemic effigy on whalebone club picked up on the east side of Unimak Island, Alaska; apparently once had insets of bone, shell, or beads

7.133 Elkhorn spoons, Yurok-Hupa culture, northern California

7.134-7.135 Two sides of Eskimo ivory artifact with hunting, traveling, and village life scenes

7.136-7.137 Sections of three sliced ivory tusk pictorial artifacts; upper four in the two illustrations showing umiaks with sails, village and herding scenes; lower in both illustrations showing fanciful double-ended walrus figures attended by nonchalant birds

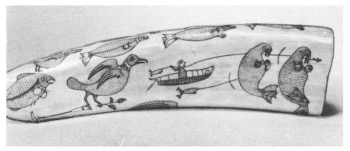

7.138

7.139

7.140

7.138 More sophisticated drawings of birds, fish, sealskin floats, man harpooning walruses, and trap on bird's foot

7.139 Boats and "goings-on" inside an igloo; recumbent figure the object of attention by three others; storage structure on top of igloo

7.140 Top, umiak and sail, rack of drying fish(?), huts, man, and seals; bottom, Eskimo-style map showing contour of coast line, perhaps where a hunt took place

7.141 Eskimo ivory buttons, not, however, to button garments, but to ornament them; note variations of seals.

7.141

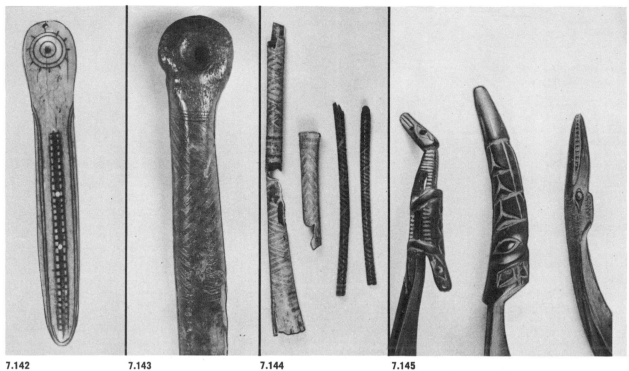

7.142   7.143   7.144   7.145

7.146   7.147

7.142 Ivory ornament for front of Eskimo wooden hunting hat
7.143 Engraved handle of central California dagger, or strigil
7.144 Engraved broken bone whistle and ear tubes, central California.
7.145 Totemic carved handles of black horn spoons, Northwest Coast
7.146 Spindle whorl for nettle-fiber spindle; design Haida in character
7.147 Shaman's (?) pendant, whalebone with red paint in deeply cut carving; oddly suggestive of Central American execution

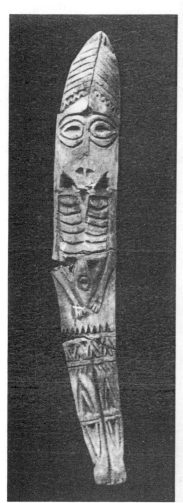

7.148   **7.149**   **7.150**

7.148   Bone or antler figure, Wishram,
Columbia River
7.149   Antler statuette, Sauvies Island,
Columbia River; both this figure and
(7.148) typical of Columbia River art style;
note exposed ribs, the eye treatment, and
prominent navel, features not accented in
conventional "pretty" art; (7.148) and
(7.149) are pictured in "Stone Age on the
Columbia River" by Emory Strong, Binfords
and Mort, Publishers, Portland, Oregon.
7.150   Iroquois bone comb, Monroe County,
New York (photo by Museum of the
American Indian, Heye Foundation)

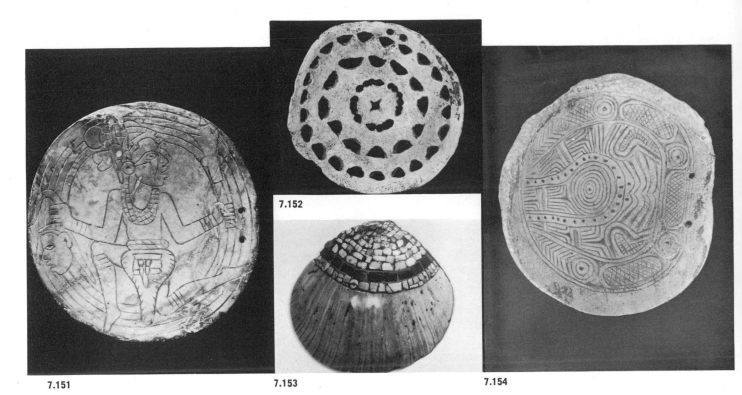

7.151   7.153   7.154

7.152

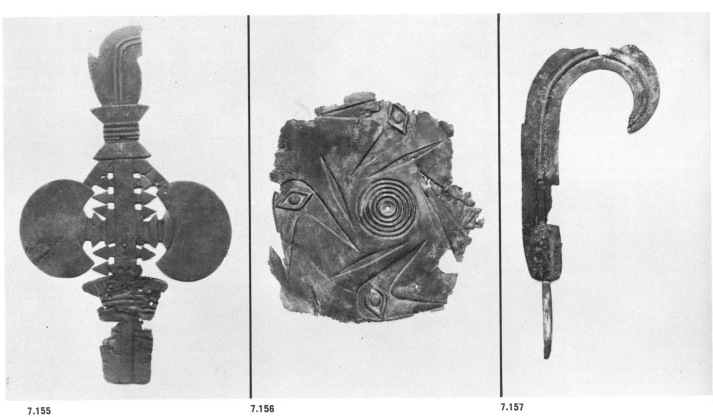

7.155   7.156   7.157

7.151 Shell gorget depicting a man (priest or chief?) holding a severed head in one hand and a scepter or mace in the other; Sumner County, Tennessee
7.152 Pierced shell gorget (3¾ inches diameter); Georgia
7.153 Red shell pendant decorated with turquoise and lignite mosaic (3 inches diameter); Pueblo Bonito, New Mexico
7.154 Shell gorget with conventional spider design (5½ inches diameter); Tennessee (photos (7.151-7.154) courtesy Museum of the American Indian, Heye Foundation)
7.155 Copper headdress ornament; Nashville, Tennessee (11⅝ inches long)
7.156 Portion of a sheet of copper with an embossed design of birds around concentric circles; Spiro Mound, Oklahoma (10⅜ inches long)
7.157 Copper hair plume; Spiro Mound, Oklahoma (10¾ inches long) (photos (7.155-7.157) courtesy Museum of the American Indian, Heye Foundation)

7.158 Carved and painted figures on an Eskimo musical instrument
7.159 Horse and buffalo painted on a miniature buckskin tipi
7.160 Centipede and decorative band on an Apache "fiddle"
7.161 Portion of a tent lining with painted designs; Plains Indian (photo courtesy Robert H. Lowie Museum of Anthropology, University of California; Cat. No. 2-5583)
7.162 Painting of Plains warriors on rawhide; trail of hoof prints indicates it may be a mnemonic painting and thus part of the basis of written language (photo courtesy Robert H. Lowie Museum of Anthropology, University of California; Cat. No. 2-4816).
7.163 Northwest Coast Indian harpooner's cape; woven rush or sea grass with painting in native pigments; probably Kwakiutl, as this tribe pays high honor to the harpooner who stands at the bow of a canoe and harpoons a whale.

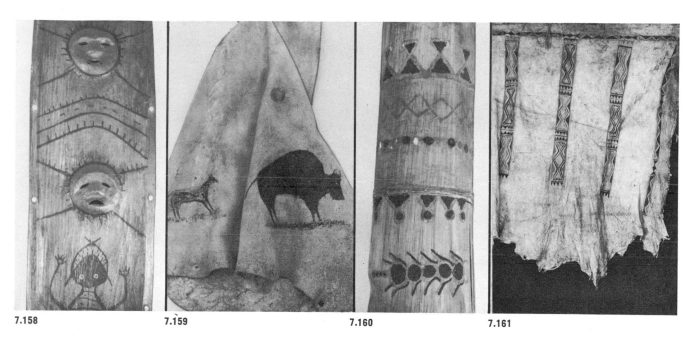

7.158   **7.159**   **7.160**   **7.161**

7.162

7.163

7.164

7.165

7.166

7.167

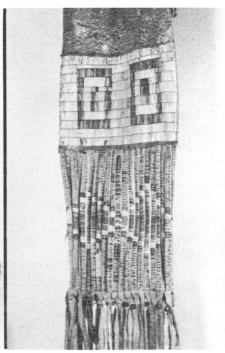

7.168

7.169

7.170

7.171

7.172

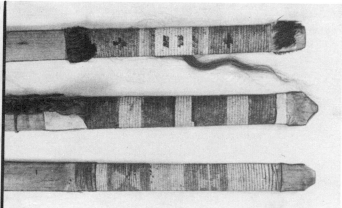

7.173

7.170 Fine quillwork belt made by Canadian Indians; buckskin base and beaded edging
7.171 Woodland Indian decoration on the collar of a thick skin (moose?) gun case; much braiding
7.172 Saddlebag, Plains, with quilled bands on side, and beading on flap and ends
7.173 Quilled pipestems with colored hair and feather ornamentation added; finely braided quillwork

Quillwork
7.164 Box lid, bark, with floral quillwork in various colors; Ottawa Indians
7.165 Bark case (cigar?) with pictorial quillwork and rolled grass edging; upper a squaw tending a pot on a tripod; lower a squaw following a brave or a white man, both dressed in costumes and smoking pipes suggesting French influence; perhaps French-Canadian area
7.166 Plains Indian quilled bag in sun-ray or tipi circle designs
7.167 Completely quilled Plains bag; coin on other side indicates a date in the sixties or seventies; buckskin base
7.168 Section of a pipe bag all in quilling, Plains Cree
7.169 Pistol holster with quilled ceremonial figures and a deer head, or deer-head mask

7.174

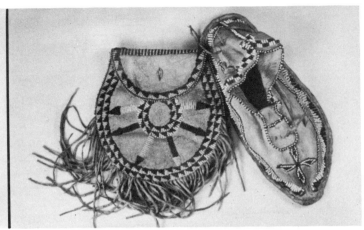

7.175

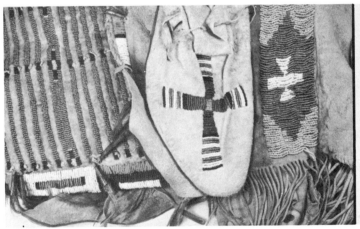

7.176

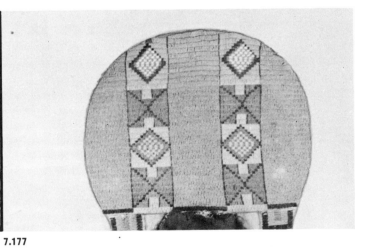

7.177

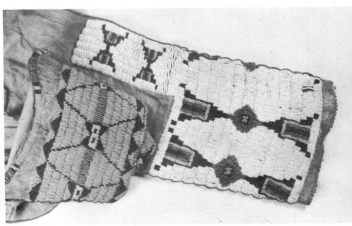

7.178

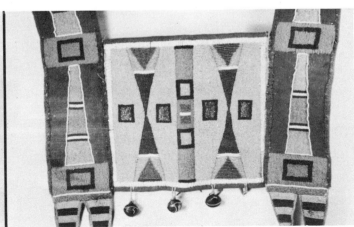

7.179

Beadwork

7.174 Major methods of solid Plains beading; left, overlaid stitch; right, lazy stitch; producing in the one case a flat surface, in the other, a ridged surface

7.175 Style of beading used by Indians of the southern Plains, in lines and ribbons; Apache, Comanche, etc.

7.176 Comparatively simple designs common to northern Plains Indians; simple bands, bars and oblongs, plain star (Maltese cross shape), and simple strips with geometric figures

7.177 Blackfoot Indian style, with designs composed of numerous tiny checkers

7.178 Sioux style, with spidery lines and attenuated figures on much solid beading, usually in lazy stitch

7.179 Crow-style beading, marked by much use of long triangles and often associated with red cloth backgrounds

7.180

7.180 Varieties of floral beading used by the Woodland Indians and to some extent by the northern Plains Indians; direct pictorial floral work, suggesting embroidery on church vestments; conventionalized and semiconventionalized floral forms; overlaid stitching

7.181 Eastern Woodland; left, Algonkian-style white bead curves on ankle flap, and band and diamond design; right, heavy pictorial floral beading

7.181

8 Pre-Columbian Music

Indian and Eskimo music crossed Bering Strait and came by other possible routes from Asia, and is Oriental in its scales and arrangements. Its relation to European music is the same as that of a Chinese band or orchestra to one of our conventional bands or orchestras. That is, unless a person with a European music background has learned how to appreciate Oriental music, Indian and Eskimo music can hardly be more than systematic noise to him. It is interesting to note that enthusiasts who are unaware of this disparity between Indian music and European music, essay to sing and dance Orientalwise in imitation of the pre-Columbians, whereas they would not think of trying to do the same with Chinese or Japanese songs and dances.

The pre-Columbian musical instruments used to produce this Asiatic-style music were, of course, similar to those still used in Asia. An example of this is illustrated by an incident: A Japanese gardener chanced to be present when a Winnebago love flute was unpacked from the mail. He appeared to be surprised and delighted, and when given the instrument to play, he blew crooning sounds on it that quite plainly meant homeland music to him. Perhaps he was "talking" the same message to his sweetheart at home that the Winnebago played to his inamorata at the upper reaches of the Mississippi.

There are two major difficulties in identifying these pre-Columbian musical instruments. One is that some of them could be used only as noisemakers in the company of other sources of sound. Could these be called musical instruments? Asking leave to waive argument, they are so included here with certain exceptions. These exceptions present the second difficulty. Some noisemakers were not intended for musical use at all, but were, as previously indicated, game callers or decoys. Some have been treated as such, but the incidence of error can be pretty wide because first-hand information has disappeared. A case in point is what the Northwest Coast Indians call a "two-voiced" whistle. If one of these has two voices that mimic two renditions of widgeon cries, is it a game caller or is it still one of the "musical instruments" that used to punctuate a medicine man's or shaman's chantings?

Perhaps such difficulties are trivial, except in placing artifacts in categories. Moreover, they are familiar in European music, wherein some musicians have used such things as cap pistols, washboards, and saws in orchestrations.

One further item is pertinent: whereas the pre-Columbians had numerous varieties of both percussion and wind instruments, anthropologists have been unable to discover use of any stringed instruments—except for a simple musical bow mildly used by a few California tribes. What seem to be exceptions are apparently adaptations of European stringed instruments: a sort of guitar which was used by the Eskimos and a so-called "fiddle" played by the Apaches.

Percussion Instruments

Percussion instruments are the ones that produce sounds by hitting one thing against another. Drums and rattles were the percussion instruments most used by nearly all tribes of pre-Columbians all over North America.

Drums were made with single and double heads stretched over hoops or cylinders. However, the single-headed ones were commoner. They were beaten with hands, wands, and sticks, usually to emphasize the rhythm of whatever ceremony was in progress. Sometimes the drumming to rhythm was accomplished with means other than true drums. The Kwakiutls made a baton fashioned exactly like a club with which they beat endwise on a plank or canoe. Some California Indians laid a plank across a hollow in the ground and beat their feet on it. Some Pueblo Indians drummed on baskets. Other Indians made a drum by stretching a leather head over a pot.

Rattles were more diverse in appearance than drums, and a continent-wide collection of them would display an endless power of individual invention among their makers. They divide into two types: those that make noise with pellets inside a hollow container, and those that make their noise by rattling objects against one another—commonly, dangling objects.

Rattling noises could also be produced by objects dangling on the persons of dancers and musicians when the wearers shook themselves or stamped. Such objects include tinklers on skirts, strings of cocoons, turtle shells on the legs, etc.

Drums

8.1 Eskimo drum ornamented with painted figures

8.2 Northwest Coast drum with typical conventionalized bird figure painted on it

8.3 Plains drum, faded green, red, and white star design; all of these (8.1-8.3) are single-headed drums.

8.4 Plains Indian drum suspended on a three-standard stand; drum and stand covered with rawhide and ornamented with cloth and beads; the head is novel in that the fur is left on.

8.5 Three single-headed drums, the largest used by Priest Rapids Indians on the Columbia River in Washington, showing mode of tightening rim; others Plains Indian drums

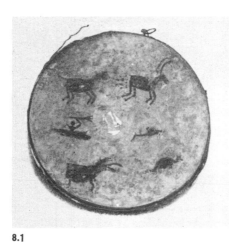

8.1

8.2

8.3

8.4

8.5

Other variants that made similar noises included: wands split partway into several slender divisions broomlike in appearance, which gave a sort of rustling rattle; sticks split in two or three parts to create clapping noises; notched sticks, called "moraches," used by the Southwest Indians who played them by rubbing a bone or another stick back and forth over the notches; and, perhaps, a number of other equally ingenious devices to spur on melody.

Wind Instruments

Indian wind instruments are generally extensions and variations of whistles. Because they were usually made of bone, they have survived in considerable numbers.

The simplest extension of a whistle was the addition of ventholes, making a flute of it. A variation on this was to place a sliding stopper over the main venthole. Sometimes, as in many Plains flutes, both of these devices were incorporated. Another method of getting more than a single note was to fasten two or more whistles together in a row like a Panpipe.

Efforts have been made to determine if the placing of ventholes was done to fit the notes of a scale, but so far the results have been negative.

As previously noted, there is considerable chance of error in guessing whether a whistle was a musical instrument, an auditory game decoy, some form of signaling among Indians during battle, or a noisemaker for disconcerting patients under treatment by shamans.

Pre-Columbian Music 195

8.6

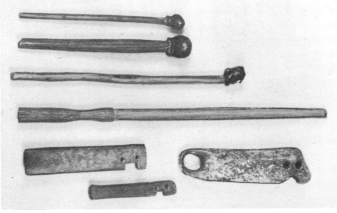

8.7

8.8

8.9

Rattles

8.10 Basketry rattle enclosing fragments of shells; a type originating in northern California

8.11 Menomini Indian rattle; rawhide container shaped like a small box; turtle claw attached to handle

8.12 A carved and painted wooden "raven rattle" popular among the Northwest Coast Indians

8.13 A cocoon and feather rattle of the sort made and used by California Pomo Indians and their neighbors

8.14 Two carved wooden effigy rattles made by Northwest Coast Indians; upper, wolf; lower, face with frog crawling on it; frog ornamented with inset abalone

8.15 Nootka-style bird effigy rattle; art style directed at a more natural-looking figure of a bird

8.16 Plains rattle using carved bits of hoofs on a stick covered with buckskin and ornamented with a beaded dangler

8.17 Northwest Coast Indian two-ended rattles; upper with puffin beak danglers, lower with bits of hoof danglers

8.18 Turtle shell rattles designed by Pueblo Indians to be fastened on the legs; rattling enhanced by cut hoof danglers

8.19 Apache rattle strips; buckskin bands with cocoons attached to be tied to the persons of the users

8.6 Pueblo Indian double-headed drum; ceremonial dance figures painted on head

8.7 Another Southwest Indian double-headed drum stretched over a hollow piece of tree trunk

8.8 Four Indian drumsticks and three Eskimo ivory drum handles with notches for attachment to the rim of the drum. The Eskimos used a thin wand for a drumstick and hit against the rim of the drum. Indians used plain sticks, or sticks with knobs, usually padded, as shown.

8.9 Etching on ivory of a quartet of Eskimo drummers, showing manner of holding drums and using drum wand

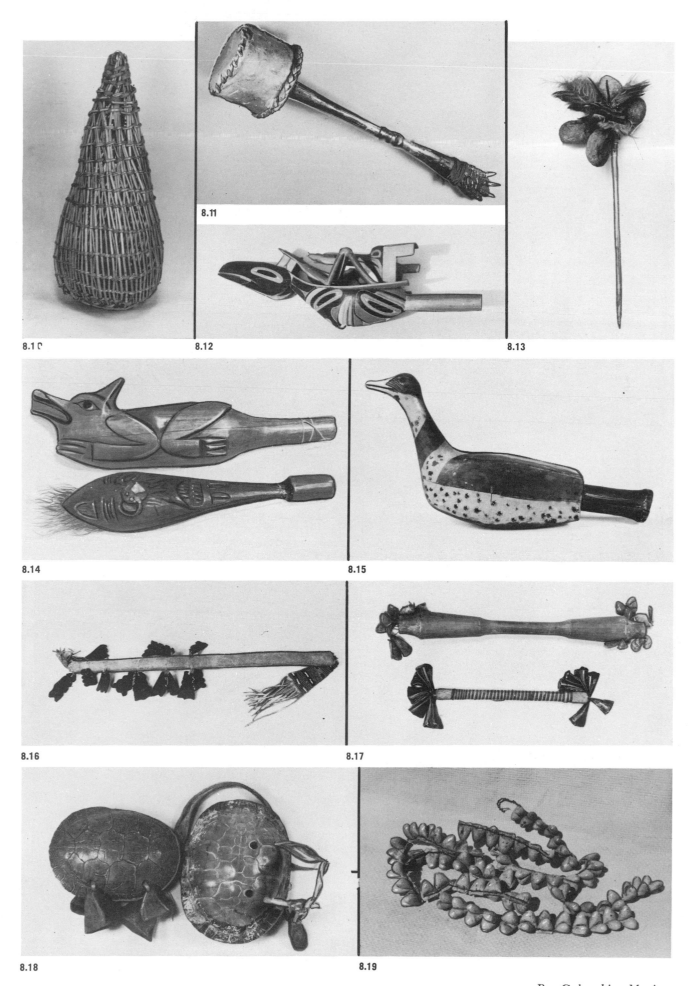

8.10

8.11

8.12

8.13

8.14

8.15

8.16

8.17

8.18

8.19

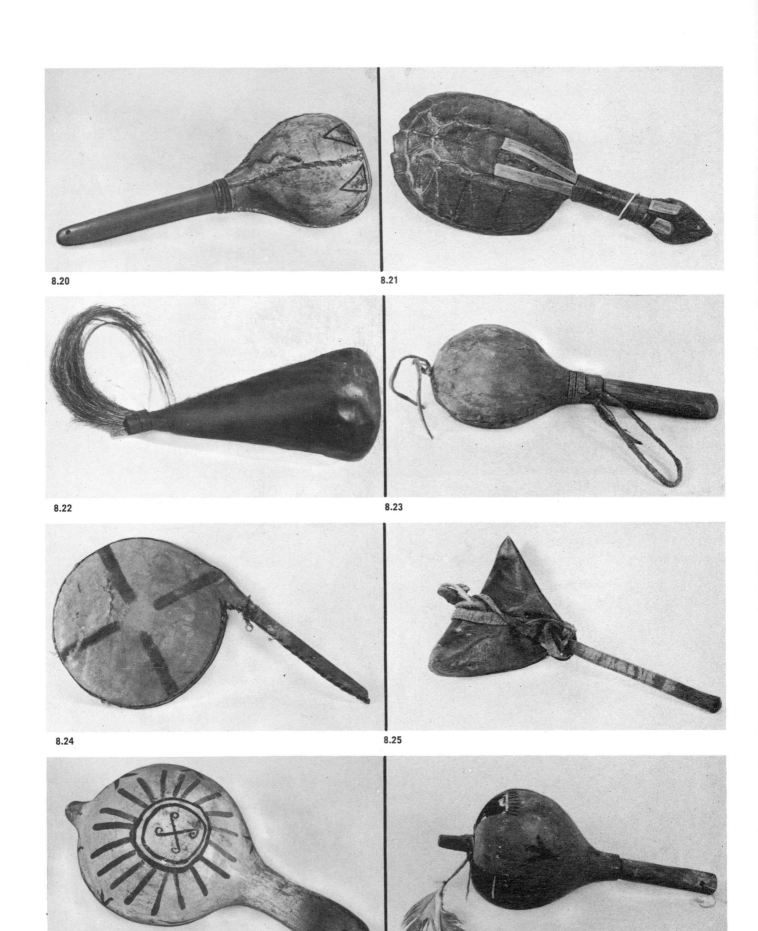

8.20

8.21

8.22

8.23

8.24

8.25

8.26

8.27

8.20 Plains Indian gourd with rawhide covering and with the gourd partially cut off at the end across which the stretched hide acts as a tympanum

8.21 Iroquois turtle shell rattle of the type much used in false-face society activities

8.22 A Plains Indian type of rattle made by filling a wet rawhide bag with sand and letting it dry out stiff in the desired shape, the sand then being poured out the handle end

8.23 A Kutenai rattle, rawhide head and wooden handle

8.24 A flat disk-shaped Plains rattle made of rawhide stretched out to cover and be sewn around a wooden handle

8.25 Two halves of a buffalo's hoof attached to a wooden rod; Plains Indian

8.26 Pueblo Indian pottery rattle with holes for attaching feathers or other danglers as seen in (8.27)

8.27 Typical Pueblo Indian rattle made by transfixing a gourd on a stick and painting it

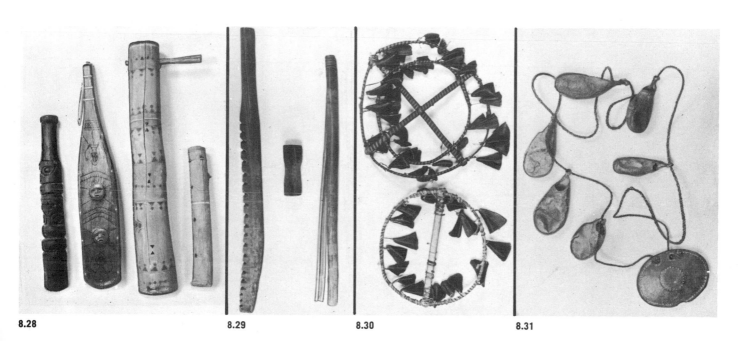

8.28   **8.29**   **8.30**   **8.31**

Various Musical Instruments

8.28 Unusual instruments, (a) a carved Kwakiutl baton which was pounded endwise on a plank or canoe in lieu of a drum; (b) an Eskimo stringed instrument, apparently imitating a European or Asiatic stringed instrument, hollow body like a violin or guitar, note division bars, and a pick for strings; (c) two Apache "fiddles" played with a bow like a violin; stringed instruments, except for a minor instance of a musical bow, are not believed to be of pre-Columbian "vintage."

8.29 A notched billet of wood, called a "morache," rubbed with the short billet, used by Indians of the Southwest to make a washboardlike sound; and a Pomo (California) Indian split-stick clapper

8.30 Hoop rattles used by Northwest Coast Indians, deer toe danglers

8.31 A cocoon necklace rattle with a carved wooden instrument that may be a form of whistle; provenience unknown

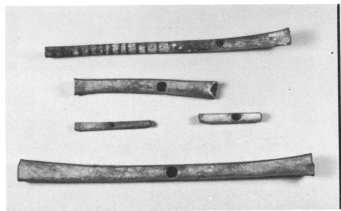

8.32

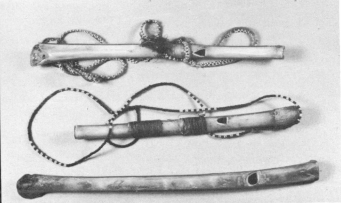

8.33

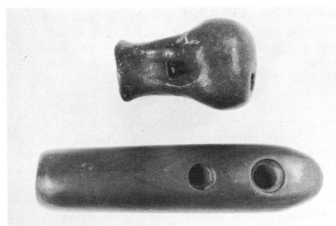

8.34

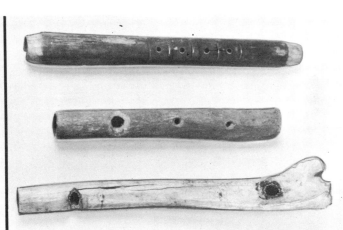

8.35

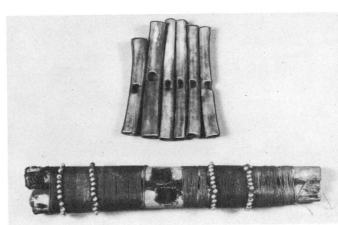

8.36

8.37

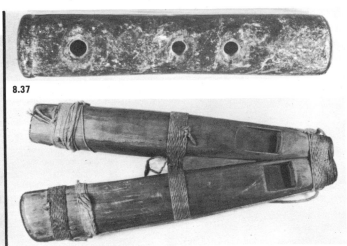

8.38

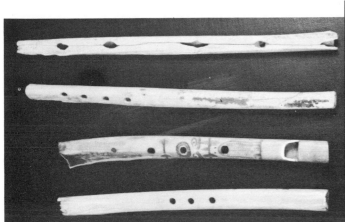

8.39

8.40

8.41

8.39 Four bone whistle-flutes, upper two, Mississippi Valley; third, Northwest Coast, with etched ornamentation; and bottom, northwestern California

8.40-8.41 Mississippi Valley wooden flutes and whistles: top (8.40) solidly beaded; next, a Winnebago "love flute"; below, an Omaha flute; and (8.41), a Plains Indian flute with a vent-control device in addition to six holes. The two bottom flutes in (8.40) are also equipped with vent regulators. The effigy control piece on the flute in (8.41) suggests a possible use for some of the stones of problematic identification.

Wind Instruments

8.32 Bird-bone whistles; top from a grave in Kansas, others of California origins

8.33 Two Plains Indian bird-bone "war whistles" for making "cries" or signals in combat, and a California whistle with one end of the bone plugged up

8.34 A pottery whistle, origin unknown; and a banded slate whistle which appears to be of Eastern Woodland origin

8.35 Three flutes; top, Pomo wooden flute; center, California (labeled) bone flute; and a large bone flute from the southern California coast area

8.36 A Panpipe arrangement of whistles from a burial in central California, and a Yuki (north central coast of California) double whistle made of reeds

8.37 A Canalino (Santa Barbara coast) stone whistle made of green variegated steatite

8.38 A Northwest Coast double whistle said by the Indians to have "two voices"; a form sometimes used for music and apparently sometimes for game calling

9 Toys

There are few things that sadden one so much as the sight of a child's toy lying in the flotsam of war; one cannot escape a feeling of guilt and shame. The aura of this feeling is associated with most of these artifacts made by Indian parents for their children in the days before the European tidal wave rolled over toys and tots alike.

As artifacts, toys are among the rarities, but their occurrence everywhere indicates that they were once as common as are toys among our children—and perhaps just as destructible. Those that have survived because of their materials—tiny stone axes, pottery animals and dolls, ivory birds, etc.—together with those made of more fragile materials—basketry cradles, miniature bows and arrows, buckskin dolls, etc.—have come to us from later times when the white man's destructiveness had waned. They tell us that there was no dearth of love and affection for the children of the First Americans.

Among less certainly identified examples and remnants, there would appear to be more toys and fragments of toys than are commonly recognized. One of these forms is the tiny arrowpoint. The minute stone or ivory points of a sheaf of arrows made in historic times by Indians or Eskimos for their children, suggest to us that similar points found archaeologically in considerable numbers may be all that is left of pre-Columbian children's bow-and-arrow sets. In this light, doubtless many collections contain artifacts that are obviously or possibly toys.

Toys
9.1 Eskimo ivory toy ducks, or water birds
9.2 Southwest prehistoric pottery dogs; southeast Arizona, Wide Ruins, and provenience unknown
9.3 Eskimo ivory toys, center, a seal hunt with figures on pins housed in a wooden box; bottom, dogs and a sled
9.4 Toy ice scoops and a trident spear
9.5 A toy bow and arrow outfit (Sioux) with tiny flint heads on the arrows
9.6 Eskimo bows and arrows with ivory tips, and a toy spear with ivory tip lashed on sidewise
9.7 Eskimo dolls and two doll heads, ivory and wood
9.8 Plains Indian buckskin dolls, two men and three women
9.9 Southwest Indian dolls; a prehistoric pottery figure, and three Kachina dolls made of carved and painted cottonwood
9.10 Four dolls; Eskimo wooden jumping-jack type with "innards" painted on; Mohave pottery doll, painted, with a head of horsehair; Plains Indian doll with buckskin body and clothing, human hair, bead nose ring, earrings, and other bead decoration; wooden painted Kachina doll

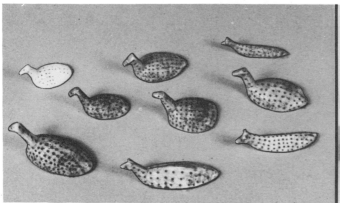

9.1

9.2

9.3

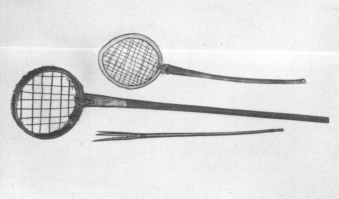

9.4

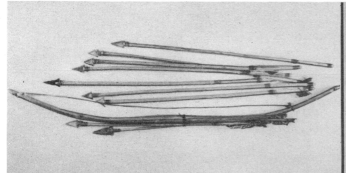

9.5

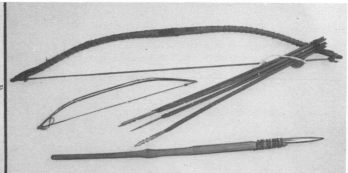

9.6

9.7

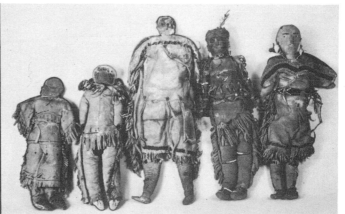

9.8

9.9

9.10

9.11

9.12

9.11 Eskimo ivory and wood toys; miniature root picks, miniature boat, toy sealer's outfit of harpoon, line, float board, and atlatl; and, top right, an ivory top

9.12 Stone and pottery toy utensils; top three, plain bowl, Hohokam bowl, and Mimbres bowl; bottom, Southwest pitcher; California Canalino steatite olla; and Eskimo pottery toy lamp

9.13 Stone miniature tools and utensils; pestles, hand mauls, dishes, and a pestle and mortar; all California

9.14 Eskimo stone-bladed woman's knife, two Eskimo lamps, a grooved axe (1 inch long) from New Jersey, and a beveled adze blade, provenience unknown

9.15 Basketry toy utensils; pitched water bottle, winnower, and two basket hoppers

9.16 Basketry burden baskets, left, Arizona; right, California; and center, two baby carriers, left, Hupa, and right, Yokuts

9.13

9.14

9.15

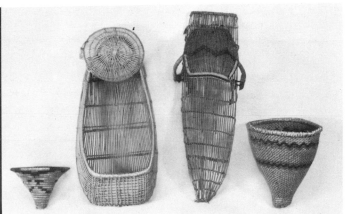

9.16

10 Games and Sports

The common idea that Indians were basically a dour and savage lot preoccupied with thoughts of mayhem and murder is of value only as a device to assuage the feelings of guilt that must occur now and then in connection with the white man's treatment of them. Actually, even the most warlike Indians spent much of their leisure time having fun, particularly with games—a fact commented on many times by early travelers among them when their old ways still existed.

Their gaming devices were many and ingenious. They can be divided into two general classes according to our standards: one that some of us would call harmless and wholesome—games of amusement and skill; the other that some of us would call ruinous and bad—gambling games. Both were equally widespread and intricately developed, though gambling was pretty much confined, as it is with us, to adults.

Games of Skill and Amusement

Interest in games of skill, particularly in athletic contests, is still a major feature of life in North America, though the chief artifacts for its feeding today are passive, in the forms of seats, sports pages, radios, and TV. In pre-Columbian days, however, all these latter blessings were absent, and the numerous forms of skill contests involved participants with or without spectators clustered about them, as in modern golf matches.

Two of the most popular of group contests still survive in more organized and standard forms: lacrosse and hockey. Both were played with many and wide variations all over North America where playing fields were available, and white spectators who have witnessed contests in the old ways of playing testify that they often make football seem ladylike. While the two games mentioned were major forms of group sports, there were others: notably kickball games in which stone balls were sometimes used. It must also be remembered that much of what we would call warfare was regarded by Indians as fodder for sports rather than the front page. The practice of tallying by touching foemen with coupsticks was called "counting coups," and various other "stunts," such as stealing a canoe, horse, or woman, also rated on a warrior's score.

In other games involving skill along the lines of our track-meet events, there were several popular inventions. One of these which was played over much of the Indians' territory is called by anthropologists the "hoop and pole" game. It is a variation of the basic skill of throwing a dart or spear, and it might have come from the days when the Indians' ancestors used spears and darts, rather than bows and arrows. The hoop was a rolling target: in some cases a plain hoop, in some a netted hoop, and in others a disk. If most of the discoidals found in the Eastern Woodland area are allowed to have been adjuncts of this game, one can see that it was extremely popular. The pole, wand, or dart was thrown to hit or come to a stop near the hoop.

Another game of skill of wide distribution was a "holes and pin," or "toss and catch" game. This used a long needle or awl attached by a string to some object that it could pierce and catch. Both Indians and Eskimos used variations of this gaming device.

From artifacts involved in sports, such as the big group contests and feats of individual skill, the range went through devices for mild amusement, such as tops and buzzers, into the realm of toys.

10.1

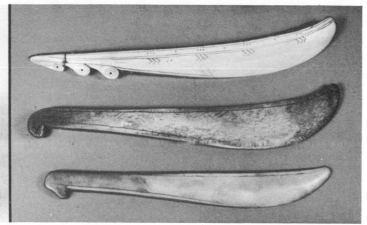

10.2

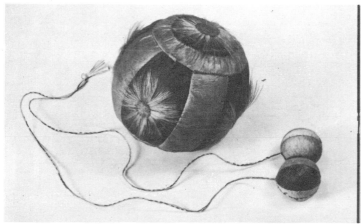

10.3

10.4

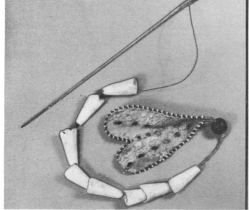

10.5

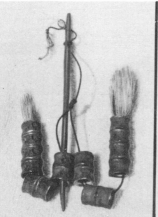

10.6

10.7

Games

10.1 Eskimo ivory top with incised ornamentation

10.2 Eskimo ivory snow knives, used to carve and cut snow, as more southerly children cut and dig dirt

10.3 Eskimo ornamented leather-covered ball and a game consisting of two small leather balls on strings, the object being to set the two rotating in opposite directions at the same time (easier said than done)

10.4 Plains Indian bone and sinew cordage buzzers; strings put through two holes in the buzzer after being twisted around each other can be pulled so as to keep the buzzer rotating with a buzzing noise.

10.5-10.7 Three versions of a widely popular game involving tossing an object and catching it on a pin; (10.5) Chippewa, with bone cones and a pierced buckskin flap; pin exactly like a needle; (10.6) Northern California, fish vertebrae on sinew cord, decorated with fur tassels; (10.7) Eskimo, small animal pelvis bored full of holes

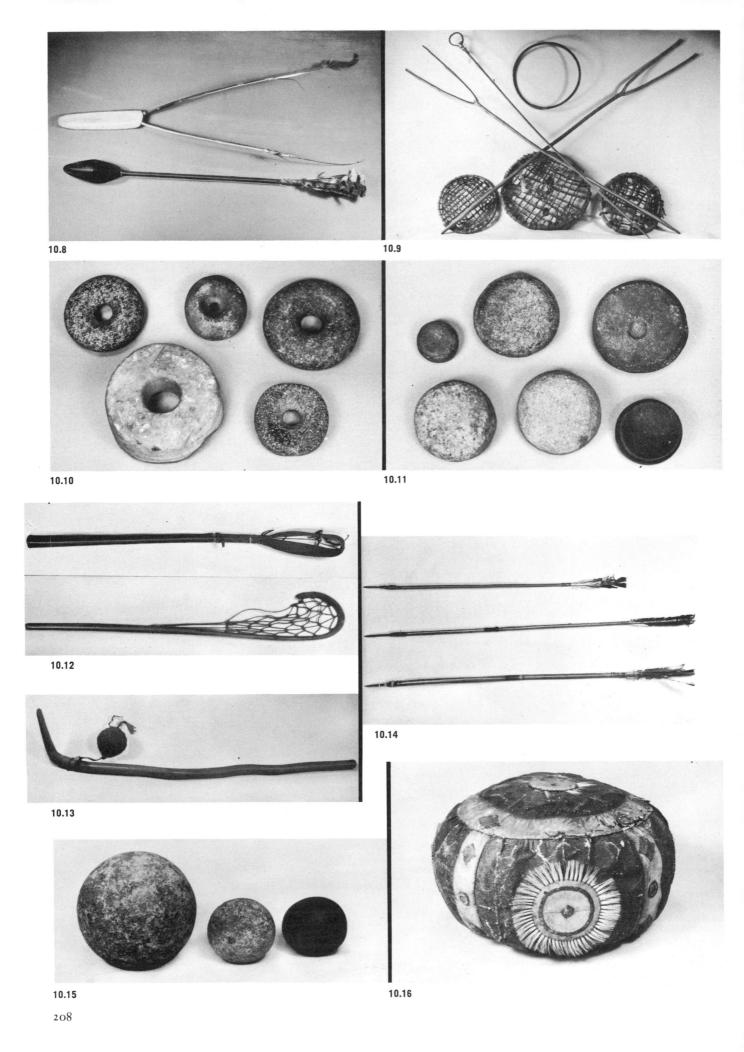

10.8

10.9

10.10

10.11

10.12

10.13

10.14

10.15

10.16

Games of Skill

10.8 Snow snakes, designed to slide on ice and snow for distance and placement; a favorite gaming device among both Plains and Woodland Indians. Snow snakes assumed many forms, including a rather large spearlike pole which, when skidding on the snow, resembled the movement of a snake, hence the general name.

10.9 Another widely popular game set consisting of a hoop and pole; the netted hoops typical of the Plains; plain hoops, and "discoidals" of all sizes and varied materials were used everywhere.

10.10 "Doughnut stones" from California and the Southwest suitable for use in the hoop-and-pole games

10.11 Eastern Woodland "discoidals," of which the same is true; some credited to use in a game called "chungkee"

10.12-10.13 Two kinds of sticks used for games: (10.12) sticks used for singularly ungentle forms of lacrosse, the ball being tossed about and caught by the pockets in the sticks; (10.13) an Arapaho hockey stick and ball

10.14 Three heavy-ended darts (not arrows), in this case with metal tips, thrown for accuracy, placement, and distance by Plains Indian tribes; perhaps a leftover from outmoded uses of darts and spears thrown by hand and by atlatls

10.15 Stone balls from various areas; one of their uses, along with wooden balls, was to be kicked around by teams of Indians in a sport called the "kick" game.

10.16 Eskimo large stuffed leather-covered ball thrown about in various games in the Arctic

Games of Chance

Besides noting the Indians' delight in sports and recreation, many observers of their lives under the old régime have testified to their passion for gambling. Venting this has left two classes of artifacts: those used in guessing games, and dice.

The guessing games all resembled what we have come to know in our rural folklore as the "shell and pea" game. One person or side hid something, and the other person or side tried to guess its location and in some cases its identity. The basic set for such games was a pair of bones, sticks, or pebbles; one marked, the other not. Another simple group of equipment was a pair of moccasins and a pebble or other such object. From these, the equipment grew apace until many sticks and auxiliary factors were involved.

Dice games were the same as Europeans' games in that the dice were tossed and the count was on the uppermost markings when they came to rest. But if the Indians ever made the familiar dotted cubes, they were but one of a hundred or more variations in both shapes and markings. Plains Indians favored five dice, three marked one way on one side, two another way on one side. These were made of wood, bone, stone, or fruit pits. Yokuts Indian women used eight half-acorn hulls or walnuts stuffed with gum or asphaltum, which they tossed up to fall on ornate trays to the accompaniment, spectators tell us, of language that would arouse the envy of Macbeth's witches.

But perhaps one should draw a veil over this side of Indian life lest we get the idea they were, in this form of sin, our equals.

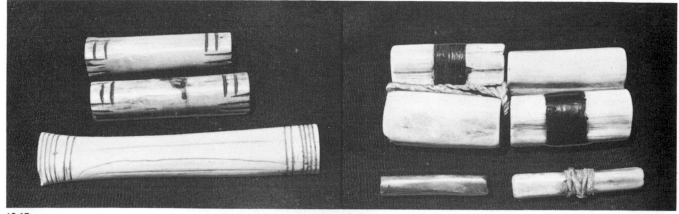

10.17

10.18

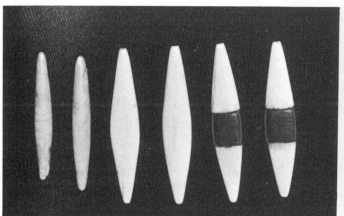

10.19

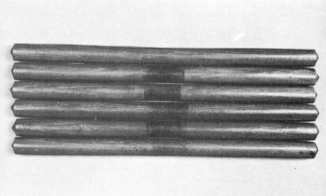

10.20

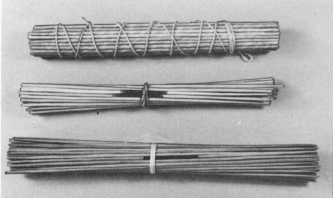

10.21

10.22

Guessing Games

10.17 Hollow bone billets used in the moccasin game; being hidden in the toes of moccasins, the opponents to guess which ones

10.18 Guessing bones used in varying numbers from two on, to be hidden in combinations for guessing; upper, an old pair long used by Chief Shluskin of the Yakimas and made of bear bones; lower pair from central California Indians

10.19 A pair and a quartet of Plains-style guessing bones; two with black bands and two plain making a popular combination

10.20 A larger number of wooden rods with five black banded and one plain, used by the Wiyot Indians of California

10.21 A popular form of guessing sticks among the Yurok-Hupa cultures of northwestern California; usually with one black banded stick and a handful of plain ones

10.22 Hupa bone guessing game set, exact nature of use obscure, but apparently similar to other sets

10.23 A popular Diegueno (California-Mexico tribe) guessing game involving wood and bone billets on strings; four dark wood and four white bone in this set; in background, tally sticks used to count scores

10.24 Carved wood disks used in games popular among the coast Salish gamblers, particularly on the Olympic Peninsula in Washington State, the distinctions being in partial, entire, and no blackening of the rims

10.25 A set of more than sixty guessing rods with their case, a form popular among the Northwest Coast Indians; the rods being differentiated by combinations of colored bands; sometimes seen as analagous to the property bands on arrow shafts

10.26 Another set identified as Haida by painted Haida designs on the buckskin case

Dice

10.27 Arapaho stick dice, with a variety of painted and incised markings, same on both sides

10.28 Buffalo horn gambling bowl, Plains Indians, with a set of bone dice

10.23

10.24

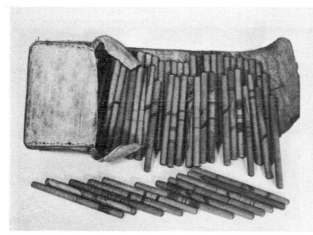

10.25

10.26

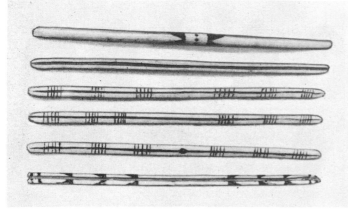

10.27

10.28

II Smoking

All methods of using tobacco, including chewing, snuffing, eating, and drinking, were known to the pre-Columbians. In fact, they were known to them long before 1492, as such uses of tobacco were discovered by Europeans along with the New World.

There were more than a dozen kinds of tobacco available, though only one, *Nicotiana tobacum*, has been developed into the many brands advertised today. These various kinds of tobacco were cultivated more widely than any other plant in North America. Tobacco was grown in all the maize areas, over practically all the United States, and somewhat north of the Canadian border.

Most tobacco was used in pipes. The Northwest Coast Indians chewed a mixture of tobacco and lime, their pipes being post-Columbian productions. The only cigarettes, if they could be called such rather than a form of wooden pipes, were short lengths of cane stuffed with tobacco. They were smoked in the Southwest from Basketmaker times on. The Eskimos and Northwoods Indians had no pipes, although the Eskimos did make a kind of snuff. Aside from these exceptions, the pipe was "it."

Pipes were made in a practically endless variety of shapes, but all can be divided into tube pipes and elbow pipes, with an occasional in-between hybrid. Tubular pipes, believed to be the older form, prevailed in the West; elbow pipes in the Woodland Indian areas of the east; and both forms in the Plains and intermountain plateau.

Materials were: stone or pottery, particularly for pipe bowls; wood, especially for pipe stems; bone, usually for mouthpieces in the West but sometimes for a whole tube pipe; and ivory, for the post-Columbian Eskimo pipes.

Eastern Pipes

The Eastern and most Plains Indian pipes are prevailingly elbow-shaped and are mostly pipe bowls rather than pipes—especially in archaeological material. Although they are remarkable for a bewildering display of individual ingenuity, there are a number of regional shapes that are discernable. Some shapes occur again and again all over the East and the Plains.

Perhaps the best known pipe found in its complete form is a Plains Indian pipe with catlinite (a red clay also known as pipestone) bowl and a flat, round, or square wooden stem. This has been loosely called a "peace pipe," but only a few were actually used ceremonially, the term coming from a practice of passing a pipe around during friendly discussions.

Other forms, mostly as bowls only, are known to collectors of smoking gear as Micmacs, monitors, disks, Iroquois, biconically drilled, etc., according to their shapes, and a number of forms are recognized as originating in certain localities because of the shapes of their stems and bowls and their materials.

The most spectacular form of Eastern pipe is the effigy pipe. Those made by carving or molding a figure of a person, mammal, fish, or other creature seem to be sculptures first and pipes second, but most show evidence of use for the latter. When the figure is a human being, they are sometimes called "image" or "idol" pipes. Effigies were also put on the other forms as decoration, from vague scratches to finished figures.

Sometimes it is forgotten that the earliest European pipes were copies of Indian models from the eastern seaboard. Usually associated with Virginia and Sir Walter Raleigh, the now old-fashioned clay pipe of the Old World plainly shows its ancestry in the New World.

Western Pipes

The tube seems to be less open to variation than the elbow form, but Western pipemakers succeeded in developing nearly as many distinct varieties as did the Eastern Indians. Although the Southwest may have been the first area to see the use of pipes—which date back to Basketmaker times there—its pre-Columbian pipes did not vary much from a stubby Basket Maker tube to a later, often rather clumsy, cigar-shaped tube.

On the Coast, however, variety began at once in southern California with pottery pipes in somewhat trumpet form and often having suspension fins. On the southern coast, there were polished steatite cigar-shaped pipes, sometimes ornamented with beads. One site in the latter area produced effigy pipes of elaborately grotesque shapes.

11.1

Interior California Indians made wooden pipes which have nearly all vanished and polished steatite tubes which have survived in mounds and sites. The latter, smoked with bird-bone mouthpieces, sometimes run to lengths over twelve inches.

In northwestern California, a wooden tube was made with a stone bowl inset in the end. On the Columbia River, tube pipes were now and then elaborated until they assumed a wineglass shape.

The works of art in wood and black slate created by Northwest Coast Indians are post-Columbian as are the ivory pipes made by the Eskimos. The latter have a distinct resemblance to Oriental pipes, hinting that the world-girdling tobacco habit that followed Columbus' return to Spain may have completed its circuit among the previously nonsmoking Eskimos, thus ending where it began, in North America.

11.2

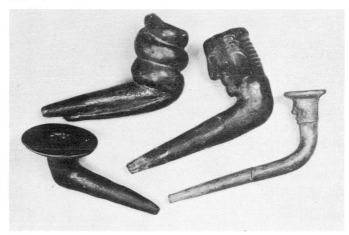
11.3

Southwest, Eastern Woodland, and Plains Pipes
11.1 Oldest forms of pipes in the Southwest; a stubby bowl form found in Basket Maker sites and a cigarette-like cane pipe with the tobacco separated from the smoker by a holed joint in the cane
11.2 A pottery pipe of a rather clumsy form found in the Southwest, this from the Mimbres area in New Mexico, and a stubby lava form, provenience unknown
11.3 Trumpet-shaped Iroquois pottery pipes, with effigies typical of the Iroquois area; the larger disk-rim pipe being a part of a false-face society mask outfit, used through a hole in a mask (see "Masks")
11.4 Atlantic seaboard form; this is Cherokee; steatite; the bulging bowl may have been the model from which early European pipes were copied.

11.4

11.5

11.6

11.7

11.8

11.9

11.10

11.5 Kentucky biconical stone pipes; one of the varieties found in this state

11.6 Two northeast Indian types; Micmac and "beaver tail." The Micmac form was copied quite widely across the northern part of central North America; this example is Cree. The "beaver tails" are so called because of the flat, cross-hatched stem.

11.7 Varied forms; lower left, popular and known as a disk-bowl pipe, commonly having a rather tiny tobacco chamber

11.8 Another form of disk pipe made from the eastern Plains into northeastern California, both bowl and stem in the edge or rim of the disk, as shown in the split example; left one is Oto.

11.9 Eastern pottery pipes; upper, a curved monitor type with two stems

11.10 Other pottery forms; these associated with the central Mississippi Basin, notably Arkansas, where these come from

West Coast Pipes

11.11 Varieties of pipes found on the Columbia River in Washington and Oregon; top, a local form which in a more exaggerated development is called an "hourglass" form; center of stone with a clay pipe form of bowl and a fin, quite restricted in area to the central Columbia; bottom, an unusual tiny steatite pipe from Umatilla, Oregon

11.12 Typical northern California wooden pipes with long rodlike stems and bulblike bowls, used until recently by the Pomos and their neighbors

11.13 Seven typical northwest California pipes from the Yurok-Hupa cultures, wooden bowls with inset superimposed steatite bowls; two inlaid with shell and bone; these pipes are pre-Columbian but apparently are a fairly recent development, as the stone insets are seldom found in burials.

11.14 Northern California types of similar shape to those in (11.13), but monolithic; top and bottom, prehistoric Wiyot pipes with very thin walls

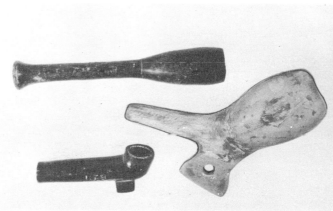

11.11

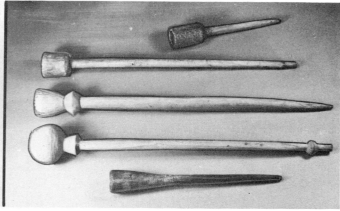

11.12

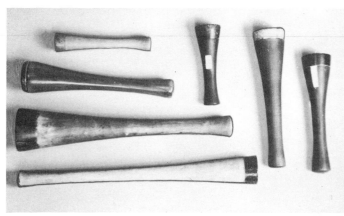

11.13

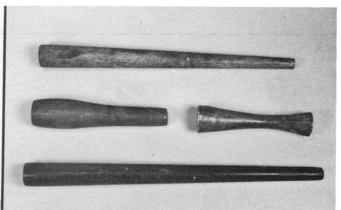

11.14

11.15

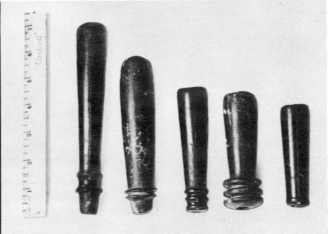

11.16

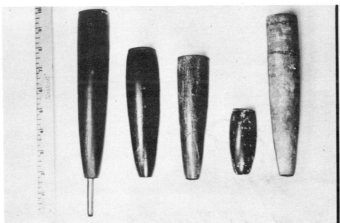

11.17

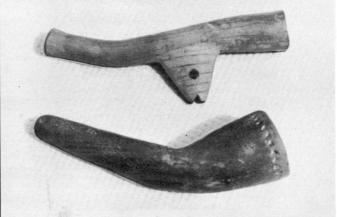

11.18

11.15 Long forms of California central valley steatite tube pipes, longest nearly 12 inches

11.16 Shorter forms of the same; 3½ to 7 inches; ringed decoration of mouthpieces typical

11.17 Chumash (Santa Barbara coastal) forms of tube pipes, more convex than central valley forms and with no decoration of mouthpieces; one with bird-bone stem

11.18 Diegueno pottery forms, showing local tendency to bend, and a form of fin peculiar to this tribal area

Effigy Pipes and Other Unusual Forms

11.19 Eastern effigy pipes; left, brown steatite, a southeastern Woodland form; others pottery effigy pipes associated with the Arkansas area and vicinity

11.20 Sandstone effigies, frog, Kentucky, and fish, Iowa

11.21 Turtle effigy pipe, steatite, Fraser River area, Canada

11.22 Frog effigy pipe of unknown origin; hard black stone, not steatite; showing features of both Northwest Coast and "Mound Builder" pipes

11.23 Northwest Coast Indian wooden effigy pipe, profusely inlaid with abalone fragments and touched up with painted red markings; metal bowl; pipes are a post-Columbian development in this area, where tobacco was chewed in prehistoric times.

11.24 Eskimo ivory pipe and pipe bowl, with etched scenes of Eskimo life; also a post-Columbian development

11.19

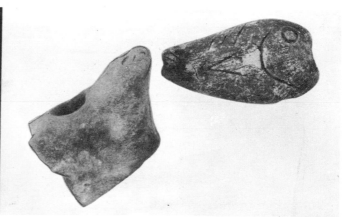

11.20

11.21

11.22

11.23

11.24

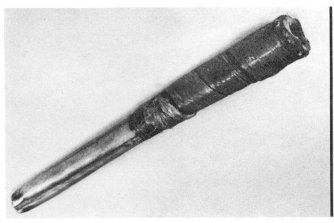

11.25

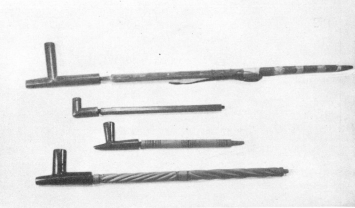

11.26

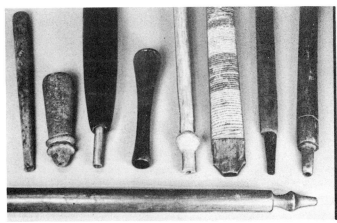

11.27

11.28

11.25 Plains Indian bone pipe wrapped with ribbons of sinew; not unusual but seldom used in comparison with other forms

11.26 Typical Plains Indian pipes with catlinite bowls and carved stems; longest more than thirty inches, with a quilled stem

11.27 Mouthpieces of various forms of pipes showing the great variety developed by the Indians; seventh pipe exceptional because, while it is not evident, the wooden lip part is protected by an auxiliary steatite covering piece, presumably to prevent wear by the teeth; third pipe has a bird-bone mouthpiece.

11.28 Close-ups of braided quillwork pipestems created by Plains Indians, usually on long pipes of ceremonial, or "peace pipe" nature, and often associated, as were their personal tomahawks, with warrior chief poses in early photographs

Tobacco Accessories
11.29 Plains Indian pipe bags with beaded panels and quilled bases of fringes; an important "show-off" possession of all Plains Indians who wished to maintain importance, and whose status made them recipients of products of top skill in beadwork, tanning, quillwork, and construction

11.30-11.31 Tobacco containers (11.30) of "ordinary" Indians, and Eskimos; (11.31) Hupa-Yurok culture tobacco basket with lid held on by an ingenious drawstring device

11.32 Pipe containers or bags for Yurok-Hupa pipes, leather pouches with thongs to wrap and tie around them when the pipes were stored

11.33 Plains pipe tampers and, bottom, kinnikinnick chopping knife; top, the fancy butt, only, of a tamper, carved and at one time fully quilled. The chopper was used on a wood or horn board.

11.34 Eskimo snuff mortars and pestles; used to make a form of snuff out of Arctic tundra moss

11.35 Eskimo snuff-boxes and bone tubes for sniffing snuff. The Eskimos learned smoking after 1492, probably from Asia, judging by the forms of their tobacco pipes—thus completing the circling of the globe by the tobacco habit started on its way, tradition says, by Sir Walter Raleigh.

11.29

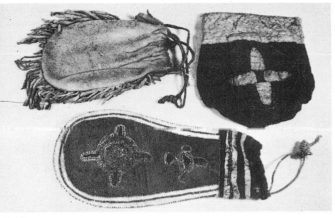

11.30

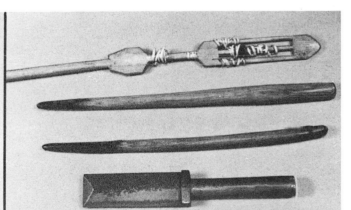

11.31

11.32

11.33

11.34

11.35

12 Travel

Although the great majority of Indians never got more than a few miles from their homes, there were whole tribes that were nomadic and covered wide areas in their wanderings. There were also many individuals who traveled alone or in groups to places far, indeed, from their homes. Emphasis has been placed on the journeys of Indian war and raiding parties, but the great number of trade items found in sites all over North America tells us that in pre-Columbian times native traders were in motion somewhere at all times of the year when weather permitted. Common sense tells us that their journeyings and the travels of peaceful groups and individuals must have been far in excess of the hostile movements.

Even in the frigid Arctic, the Eskimos were frequently on the move on land, and in constant travel on open water. Their journeys, in fact, included going abroad, for in season Bering Strait used to be dotted with umiaks to and from Siberia, though now they stay home by ukase of the Soviets.

One of the best evidences of extensive and continuous pre-Columbian travels is in the form of trails—some of them, in effect, roads and highways—that once laid their network over the continent. As is known, many of these were expanded and altered to become parts of the highway network created by New Americans. In considering these, however, we sometimes forget that there was also a liquid network in the form of streams and lakes; sometimes, especially in the maritime Northwest Coast, dominating the land trails.

Land Travel

Pre-Columbian land travel was of two sorts. One was within a tribal area: sometimes large areas, as in the case of Plains hunting grounds and the scantily furnished food reaches of the Nevada and other deserts; and sometimes small, as in the case of some California and New England tribes concentrated in pockets. The other was intertribal over major trails.

Although there were no special artifacts that distinguished one from the other, the impedimenta for travel in the vicinity of a village were much more varied and numerous. The tendency for distance was to travel light and live off the land.

The vehicles used in travel indicate northern origin and suggest that before the Eskimos came, human feet were the only means of locomotion and human backs and heads the only burden bearers. Wheeled vehicles were unknown.

In the Arctic, the Eskimos depended much on sleds and toboggans, chiefly to transport food and goods, but sometimes to carry persons, especially small children. The toboggan as a snow vehicle was adopted by the Canadian Northwoods Indians. Farther south, the sled degenerated into a simple contraption of an "A" frame placed on the shoulders of a dog, with the open ends dragging. This, known as a "travois," was enlarged by the Plains Indians for use on a horse and was the key to their expansion of village life over the wide areas in which they lived.

As aids to the feet in snow and ice country, artifacts include crampons and test staffs (resembling ski sticks) used by the Eskimos and snowshoes, also used by them and by most Indians in snow areas.

Water Travel

The variety of boats used by the First Americans is surprising, and while most of them are called canoes there are some that, as in the case of the Eskimo umiaks and kayaks, have to be given individual recognition with their special names. They divide roughly as follows: a later form, that was made with a covering over a framework; an older form, the dugout; and three special forms, rafts, sewn plank boats, and bullboats.

The kayak has lately reached worldwide use. It has a strong light frame over which a watertight skin is fastened that covers all but the paddler's hole. This hole, in turn, has a rim to which a waterproof covering for the paddler can be lashed, making the whole assemblage impervious to even a complete ducking. The umiak is simply a skin-covered boat with a framework large and sturdy enough to accommodate a number of people and sails.

Using similar frameworks, but covering them with bark, a variety of forms of light canoes were made and used from the Northwoods to the Algonkin country and south almost to the Gulf of Mexico, along the littoral of which the dugout canoe still remains in use.

Land Travel

12.1 First of the adjuncts to pedestrian travel among Indians and Eskimos shown here is a Plains Indian dog travois (12.1), perhaps an early form of the sled and adapted to use on horses in post-Columbian times; the dog travois being the only form of vehicle developed by the Indians before Columbus, except for some use of toboggans in the far north

12.2-12.3 Forms of Indian and Eskimo snowshoes, which assumed a great variety of forms in snow country and were adopted pretty much unchanged in character by Europeans

12.4 In the top picture, an Eskimo towing a sled and using the ice-testing staff shown in (12.5)

12.5 Point of a staff looking just like a ski staff but used more for testing snow and ice in terrain where pools of water could be concealed by light, fragile coatings; a plunge of feet into water being a serious matter in the extreme low temperatures of the Arctic. The back figure in the waterproof coat in (12.4) appears to be using two such staffs.

12.6 Ice crampons; Eskimos tied these under their boots on very slippery ice or snow, somewhat as chains are fastened on automobile tires.

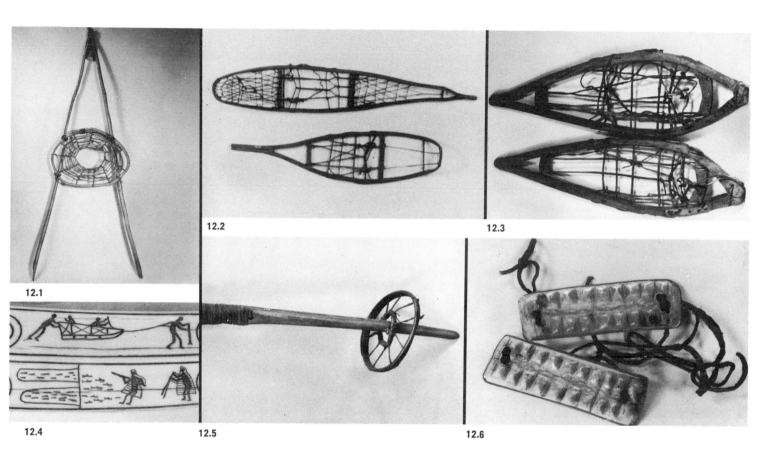

12.2

12.3

12.1

12.4

12.5

12.6

Roughly speaking, the province of the framework canoe is the same as that of tailored clothing. That it was not always used in the north, however, is indicated by a few examples of ancient dugouts found buried in bark canoe territory.

Meanwhile, dugouts were the mainstay not only of the mariners of the southern streams, bayous, swamps, and Everglades but also of the maritime tribes of the Pacific Northwest from Alaska to the redwoods of California and of most of the river tribes on the northern Pacific slope.

These were carved into many forms, from simple hollowed-out logs to the clipper-bowed whale-hunters' canoes that coped with the waves of ocean waters. They were small to large, from one-man jobs to big carriers that could transport huge loads of materials and many paddlers and passengers. Three specialized forms created by the Northwest Coasters deserve individual attention. The northernmost Indians used a form distinguished by overhang of both bow and stern; the central Indians, around Vancouver Island and on the Columbia River, also made their canoes with clipper bows, but they fashioned an abrupt vertical stern; and the Yurok-Hupa tribes at the southernmost tip of the Northwest Coast culture made their own versions of a snub-nosed squatty canoe, whose use was confined to travel on a broad river, mostly the lower Klamath River.

The bullboat was what is known in the Old World as a "coracle." It had a bowl-like frame over which a hide covering was stretched, and was used to cross rivers in the Plains Indian territory. It is a valuable piece of evidence for those who think Welsh immigrants settled in prehistoric America in a lost period of the past.

The raft was a craft used by the Indians living in the marshy floodlands of central California. It is sometimes called a "balsa" because of its resemblance to similar boats used by South American Indians. It was made

12.7

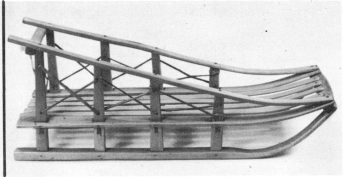

12.8

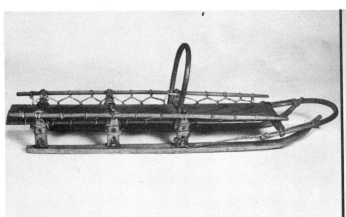

12.9

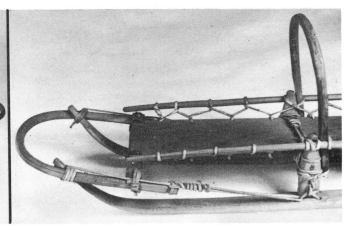

12.10

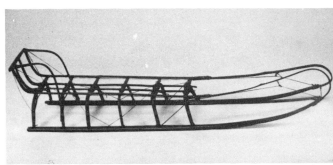

12.11

12.12

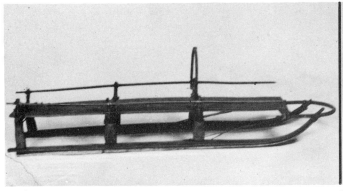

12.13

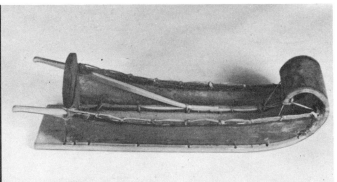

12.14

by constructing tule reeds into long, cigar-like bundles and tying them together in the shape of a canoe. The reeds eventually became waterlogged, but they floated for a long enough time to be useful, and they could easily be dried out in the sunshine for which California is famous.

The plank boat is a fascinating enigma, because no complete and intact specimen has been preserved. It was used by the maritime Indians of the southern California coast to make long voyages on the Pacific not only up and down the coast but between and among the offshore islands—where it was the key to the island lives of a comparatively dense population. Early visitors to the coast tell about seeing these canoes in use, but all that is left today is an occasional plank with holes at its edges.

The plank boat was a canoe fashioned by literally sewing together the needed number of small planks, presumably on a somewhat rigid keel. The holes and lashing were calked with asphaltum, of which there was a plentiful supply. This is a style developed and used by the South Sea Islanders, a good example being on view in the Bishop Museum in Hawaii. The temptation is pretty strong, even for the most stubborn opponent of prehistoric transpacific travel, to believe that at least one of the South Sea vessels, surely Polynesian, did make it across to give the early Canalinos the answer to how to live on the offshore islands.

Besides all these forms of canoes, of course, there were a few artifacts needed for their navigation: certainly paddles, and sometimes painters, bailers, and anchors.

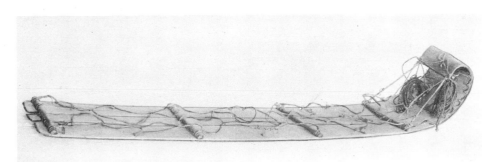

12.15

Sleds and Toboggans
12.7-12.15 Standard forms of Eskimo sleds and Indian toboggans used in the Arctic and subpolar regions: (12.7) and (12.8) variations of a medium-sized sled used primarily to carry household goods and personal effects in travel or to transport food to the igloo; (12.9) a larger transport sled, and (12.10) close-up of front of runners showing construction to absorb the shocks of bumps and hummocks; (12.11) and (12.12) another form of the same type of sled—this one originating in Siberia—showing a different shock-absorbing construction; (12.13) another freight sled; (12.14) and (12.15) Indian toboggans; the former from the upper Yukon River, and the latter an Athabascan vehicle (photo of (12.15) courtesy of the University of California, Robert H. Lowie Museum of Anthropology). It is perhaps superfluous to note that these vehicles usually were pulled by dogs.

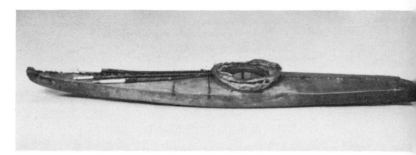

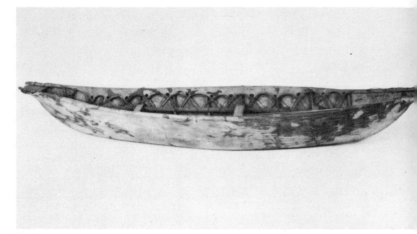

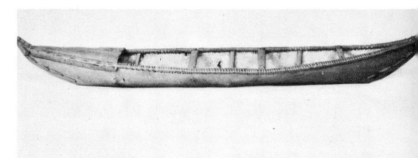

Kayaks, Umiaks, Canoes, and Other Craft

12.16-12.17 Eskimo kayaks; these are one-holed craft, the commonest form; some have two holes, and some three; the paddlers wear watertight covering that is battened around the manholes, so that it is possible, when properly equipped, for kayak and paddler to turn over, into, and under water and right the combination without shipping water.

12.18 An umiak, the Eskimo name for a skin-covered open boat

12.19 The seat hole portion of a kayak frame showing construction at this point

12.20 Northwoods form of birchbark canoe, indicating similarity to and perhaps imitation of Eskimo skin-covered craft

12.21 Bottom view of kayak framework

12.22 The most familiar form of birchbark canoe, standard in the northern Woodland area of the Eastern United States and copied elsewhere for many years by Europeans

12.23 A variation of (12.22), this from the Great Lakes country, with high bow and stern construction

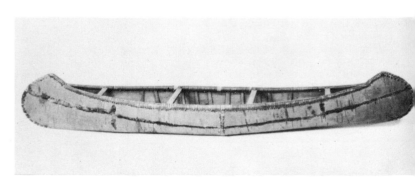

12.17

12.19

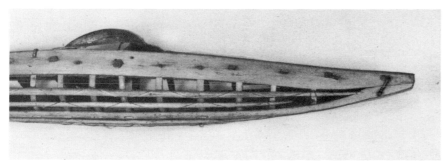

12.21

12.23

12.24

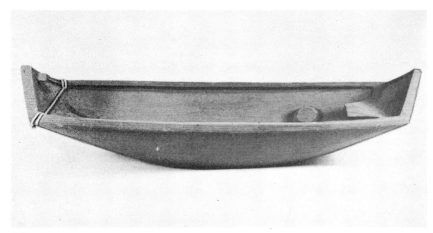

12.26

12.28

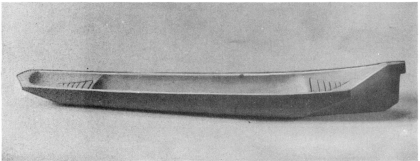

12.30

228

12.25

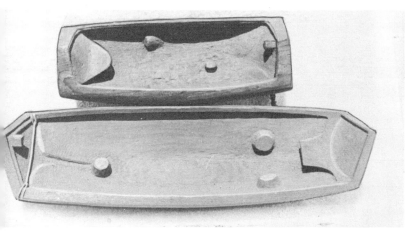

12.27

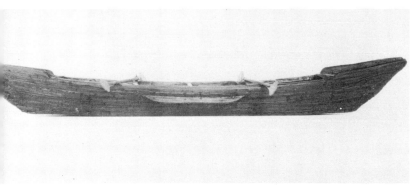

12.29

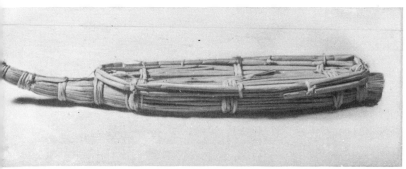

12.31

12.24 The southern form of Northwest dugout canoes designed for salt-water use, showing the clipper bow which, it is said, was copied by the early New England shipbuilders

12.25 Northern form of Northwest Coast dugouts, differing most noticeably in overhang of both bow and stern; ornate painting common

12.26 Northwest California, Yurok-Hupa culture, dugout form used chiefly on the lower Klamath River and adapted to river rather than deep-water travel

12.27 Interiors of such canoes showing the "heart" hummock conventionally carved into such canoes, seat carved into the stern, footrests, and conventional ornamentation of the bow, with reinforcement lashing on one

12.28 Prehistoric stone effigy of a southern California coastal canoe made of planks sewed together and caulked with asphaltum (courtesy California State Indian Museum, Sutter's Fort, Sacramento, California)

12.29 Model of such a canoe (12.28) with double-bladed paddles used by the Chumash Indians (courtesy Southwest Museum, Los Angeles, California). These were seagoing canoes, remarkable in the unlikely nature of their construction of pieces sewed together on an only slightly rigid keel. The basic idea of their construction is in evidence in South Sea Island craft, leading to valid assumption of copying from such sources.

12.30 Model of Seminole Indian pirogue, a dugout used to navigate the Gulf Coast offshore and inland waters, bayous, everglades, and swamps of the Deep South; the fin on the bow, evident as it is here, is not observable in usual pictures taken with the craft submerged.

12.31 A hybrid canoe-raft used by central California and Nevada lake Indians, constructed of tule reeds made into bundles and assembled in canoe shape; became waterlogged after some hours of use but dried out quickly in hot sun; this specimen a Paiute model (courtesy of the California State Indian Museum in Sutter's Fort, Sacramento, California)

12.32

12.33

12.32 A Plains Indian "bullboat," made like a bowl, rawhide over a framework, the result being like the Old World coracles, which, having been used in Wales, could be considered evidence of the migration of Welsh immigrants to America before Columbus; this popular legend is referred to in Lewis and Clark's Journal and considered credible by the two explorers (B.A.E. Neg. No. 3455-b).

12.33 Mandan Indian women using bullboats near a Mandan village (on bluff in background); copy from engraving in Maximilian's "Travels," 1843, Plate 16; original by Carl Bodmer, 1833 (B.A.E. Neg. No. 3444-b); (both photos courtesy Bureau of American Ethnology, Smithsonian Institution)

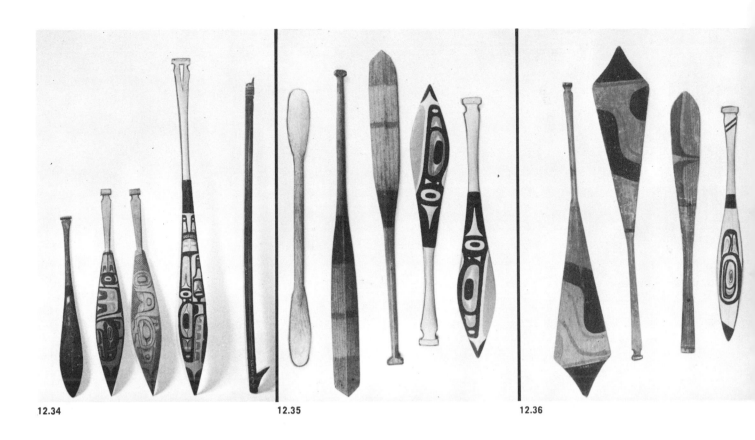

12.34   **12.35**   **12.36**

12.37

12.38

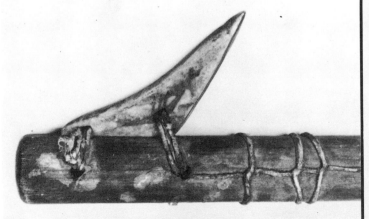

12.39

12.40

12.41

Boat Gear

12.34-12.36 Eskimo and Indian canoe paddles and, in (12.34), an Eskimo boat hook. Canoe paddles in pre-Columbian times were single- and double-bladed, the latter used by single-seat kayak paddlers and by the maritime tribes of the southern California coast navigating their sewed plank boats. The handles were managed by two methods; one, by using a crutchlike bar and accompanying grip, and the other, by simply gripping the paddle handle at spaced points. Blades were of a variety of shapes.

12.37-12.38 Canoe anchors: (12.37) Columbia River types; the open space on the grooved variety being a typical feature, probably conforming to a superstition as it serves no practical purpose; (12.38) northwest California types

12.39 Close-up of Eskimo boat hook spur; a necessary artifact for kayak and umiak paddlers to deal with the edges of ice sheets and floes

12.40 Eskimo kayak and umiak boat scraper to clean off detritus after beaching

12.41 Another canoe anchor, origin unknown but of northwest California style

12.42

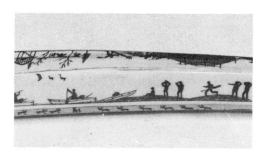

12.43

12.42-12.44 Eskimo pictures of umiaks and kayaks in use: (12.42) beaching an umiak, with another approaching; giving an idea of the size of such craft and the rigging of the sails; (12.43) kayaks, beached and afloat; the bundle on the cockpit of the beached craft is the waterproof material tied around the paddler's waist and the rim of the kayak well; (12.44) umiaks with and without sails; harpoons in the bows bode no good for the walrus.

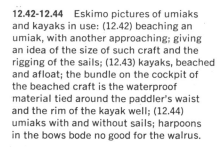

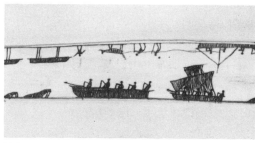

12.44

13 Combat

Indians and Eskimos before Columbus did not wage war on the organized and semipopular scale enjoyed by civilized European countries, nor did they fight as continuously as popular notions seem to have it. But there was fighting individually and in groups and occasional large-scale clashes, usually resulting from migratory invasion, for which special weapons, now artifacts, were constructed to supplement hunting weapons diverted to sanguinary use.

There were around twenty major types of clubs and axes and some were used exclusively for belaboring the persons of fellowmen. There were also several styles of stabbing daggers and dirks especially intended for gruesome use. And, of course, it did not take much to dedicate certain ordinarily used weapons for killing animals to use for killing human beings—especially bows and arrows and spears.

In the defensive line, shields were commonly carried by Plains Indians and by warriors of several tribes in other areas when on the warpath. Armor was known, but it appears to have been an individual creation rather than a general item in tribal arsenals.

Other artifacts connected with combat were trophies and symbols of achievement, the best known of which are scalps and war bonnets. In respect to the latter, it need be noted that in genuinely Indian use war bonnets were properly worn by only a few outstanding individual warriors among certain Plains tribes. They were an earned tribute to valor and not merely made and put on as is generally the case today among theatrical-minded Indians, and even among some humorless white men and, occasionally, women.

Combat
13.1 First of three pictures showing the development of the Indian tomahawk is of a stone axe blade in its pre-Columbian style setting; this specimen is of Plains Indian type but uses a form of axe blade familiar over a wide area of the Eastern Woodland country.
13.2 Iroquois belt-axe blade, a trade article of colonial vintage, around 1700; also called a "squaw axe," and used to split kindling and skulls impartially
13.3 Nineteenth-century pipe-tomahawk blade, made by Europeans for Indian customers and greatly cherished by the latter; the relationship to the earlier belt axes shows plainly in the shape and hang of the blade.
13.4-13.6 Nine of the many varieties of clubs created by Indians; most of these definitely identified with combat use: (13.4) left to right, Penobscot (Maine); Canalino (California); (13.5) Menomini (Great Lakes), a form used all through the Eastern Woodland area; Southwest Indian "potato-masher" type; Northwest Coast Indian (Unimak Island, Alaska) paddle-type club which could be considered a dull-edged sword with a totemic crest; (13.6) four Plains Indian "skull crackers"; two of pointed egg-head type and two slungshot type
13.7 Daggers; left to right, Pomo (California) stabbing dirk made of a section of elk antler; Eskimo stabbing dirk; two Northwest Coast Indian dirks, one of horn and the other of wood
13.8 Two northwest California dance wands, observed only in ceremonial and display use, but potentially stabbing weapons
13.9 A Plains Indian rawhide shield, minus the usual feather and other danglers and with the painted design much faded; thick hide stretched on a hoop, with buckskin arm loop and grip

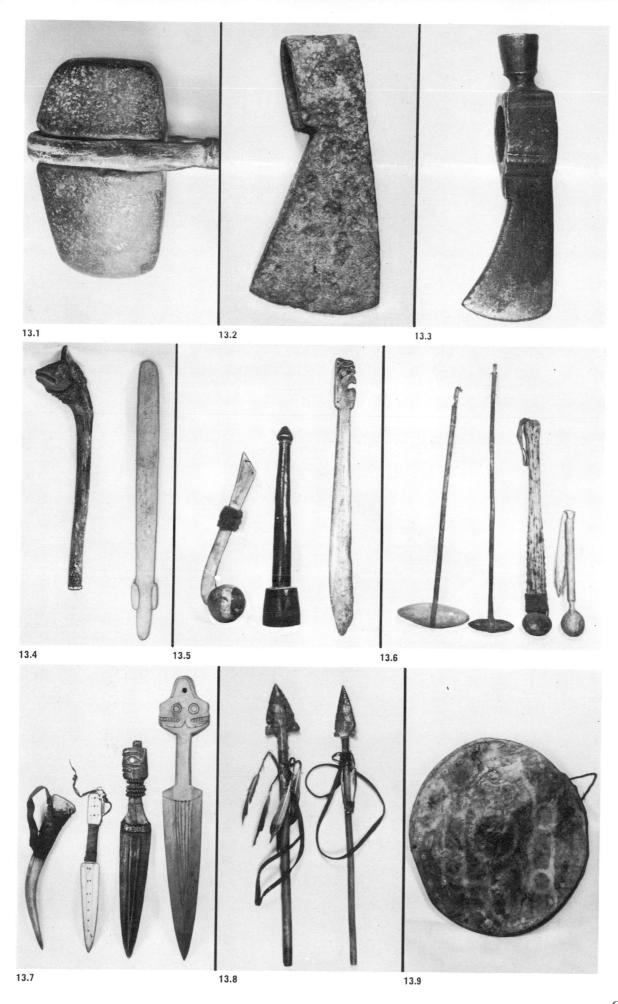

13.1

13.2

13.3

13.4

13.5

13.6

13.7

13.8

13.9

13.10   **13.11**   **13.12**

13.13

13.14

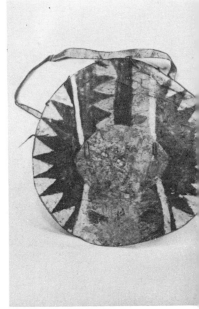

13.15

13.16

13.10-13.12 Plains Indian war trophies: (13.10) and (13.12) two war bonnets and (13.11) a scalp; the bonnets are based on caps, commonly the crown of an old felt hat, but can be rawhide or cloth. On a band around this is fastened a halo of feathers —usually eagle feathers—with feather danglers and, as in one of these examples, a long trail from the back, and a feather at the top of the crown; two cheek pieces of dangling material, and a forehead band, commonly beaded; the whole being the earned regalia of an exceptionally able warrior of proved skill and prowess, like the medals worn on the breasts of European soldiers. Wear by others and for theatrical purposes, although now commonplace, is therefore tinged with a ridiculous and childish effect. The scalp, with the pigtail and shell ornament of the unfortunate victim, is Plains style, with a rather small disk of "leather."

13.13-13.14 Typical Woodland Indian war clubs: upper (13.13); Sauk-Fox, ball-head type, 25 inches long; lower (13.14), Miami, "gun-stock" type with a spike, 29½ inches long (photos courtesy Museum of the American Indian, Heye Foundation)

13.15 Pueblo Indian rawhide shield with loop to hang over the back; appears to be a ceremonial item rather than a combat item

13.16 Eskimo land and sea battles depicted on an ivory pipe stem; center archers and spearmen(?) in opposing "armies"; the acrobatic figure is following the custom of more daring Eskimo warriors in showing his contempt for his opponents by his antics; recumbent figures may be doing likewise but appear to be casualties; lower, naval engagement with umiaks; it appears one vessel has been sunk with its crew; characters on shore may be infantry waiting to repel invaders in case their navy fails.

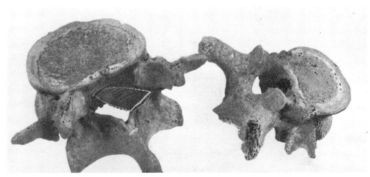

13.17

13.17-13.18 "Stone Age" casualties; arrowheads imbedded in vertebrae; (13.17) from neighboring burials near Marysville, California; both cases lethal as arrowheads struck the spinal cord; (13.18) left, also central California, in this case the bone had grown up around the juncture of the point and vertebra, indicating that the victim survived for some time after being shot; (13.18) right, from a cave burial in Kentucky

13.18

Bibliography

Bibliographies are too often made redundant by the author's seeming desire for length rather than suitability. It is this author's belief that for this book the appropriate bibliography should contain a few titles which are useful for much reference, and a few examples of books that quickly and easily inform about special aspects concerning artifacts. Many of these examples have bibliographies from which an interested reader may go on to other books of apparent interest to him, some of which, in turn, will also have bibliographies. In his visits to libraries, he can examine associated books that may please and inform him.

Before citing other books that will reward examination, mention should be made of:

DRIVER, HAROLD E., AND MASSEY, WILLIAM C. "Comparative Studies of North American Indians," *Transactions of the American Philosophical Society*, Vol. 47, Pt. 2, 1957.

The plan of the Studies is somewhat similar to that of this book, so that this book may to some extent serve as a volume of illustrations showing many of the artifacts mentioned in the course of the Studies.

General Coverage

DRIVER, HAROLD E. *Indians of North America*. Chicago: University of Chicago Press, 1961. A comprehensive examination of variations of culture patterns among Indians and Eskimos from Alaska to Panama.

HODGE, FREDERICK W. "Handbook of the American Indians," Bureau of American Ethnology. *Bulletin*, No. 30, 1907-10.

JOSEPHY, ALVIN M., JR. (ed.). *The American Heritage of Indians*. New York: Simon & Schuster, 1961. A history of the American Indians from prehistoric times to the present, accompanied by nearly 500 pictures, more than 100 in color.

MARTIN, PAUL S., QUIMBY, GEORGE I., AND COLLIER, DONALD. *Indians Before Columbus*. Chicago: University of Chicago Press, 1947. Based on culture areas.

RADIN, PAUL. *The Story of the American Indian*. New York: Liveright, 1944.

UNDERHILL, RUTH. *Red Man's America*. Chicago: University of Chicago Press, 1956.

WISSLER, CLARK. *The American Indian*. New York: Oxford University Press, 1938.
———. *Indians of the United States*. Garden City, N.Y.: Doubleday & Co., Inc., 1949. Based on language families.

Regional

AMSDEN, CHARLES AVERY. *Prehistoric Southwesterners from Basketmaker to Pueblo*. Southwest Museum. Los Angeles, 1949.

BIRKET-SMITH, KAJ. *The Eskimos*. New York: E. P. Dutton & Co., Inc., 1936.

DRUCKER, PHILIP. *Indians of the Northwest Coast*. Handbook Series No. 10, American Museum of Natural History. New York: McGraw-Hill (for the Museum), 1955.

FUNDABURK, EMMA LILA, AND FOREMAN, MARY DOUGLASS. *Sun Circles and Human Hands*. Luverne, Ala.: Published by the authors, 1957.

GODDARD, PLINY E. *Indians of the Northwest Coast*. Handbook Series No. 10, American Museum of Natural History. New York, 1924.
———. *Indians of the Southwest*. Handbook Series No. 2, American Museum of Natural History. New York, 1931.

HAMILTON, HENRY W. *The Spiro Mound*. The Missouri Archeological Society. Columbia, Mo., 1952.

JENNESS, DIAMOND. "The Indians of Canada," National Museum of Canada. *Bulletin*, No. 65, 1932.

JOHNSON, FREDERICK (ed.). *Man in Northeastern North America*. Andover, Mass.: Phillips Academy, 1946.

KIDDER, A. V. *An Introduction to Southwest Archaeology*. New Haven, Conn.: Yale University Press, 1924.

KROEBER, A. L. "Handbook of the Indians of California," Bureau of American Ethnology. *Bulletin*, No. 78, 1925. Truly a "bible" regarding California Indians.

LATTA. F. F. *Handbook of Yokuts Indians*. Bakersfield, Calif.: Merchants Printing and Lithographing Co., 1949.

LOWIE, R. H. *Indians of the Plains*. New York: McGraw-Hill (for the American Museum of Natural History), 1954.

McGREGOR, JOHN. *Southwest Archaeology*. New York: John Wiley and Sons, Inc., 1941.

NELSON, E. W. "The Eskimo About Behring Strait," Bureau of American Ethnology. *18th Annual Report*, Pt. 1, 1889. A "bible" for Eskimo artifacts.

NIBLACK, A. P. "The Coast Indians of Southern Alaska and Northern British Columbia," *Annual Report of the United States National Museum for 1888*, pp. 285-386.

RIGHTS, DOUGLAS L. *The American Indian in North Carolina*. Durham, N.C.: Duke University Press, 1947.

RITZENTHALER, ROBERT. *Prehistoric Indians of Wisconsin*. Milwaukee Public Museum. Milwaukee, Wis., 1953.

ROBERTS, FRANK, H. H., JR., "Archaeology in the Southwest," *American Antiquity*, Vol. 3, No. 1, 1937.

ROGERS, DAVID BANKS. *Prehistoric Man of the Santa Barbara Coast*. Santa Barbara Museum of Natural History. Santa Barbara, Calif., 1929.

SWANTON, J. R. "Indians of the Southeastern United States," Bureau of American Ethnology. *Bulletin*, No. 137, 1946.

UNDERHILL, RUTH. *Indians of the Pacific Northwest*. U.S. Indian Service. Phoenix, Ariz., 1945.

WISSLER, CLARK. *North American Indians of the Plains*. American Museum of Natural History. New York, 1927.

———. *North American Indians of the Plains*. Handbook Series No. 1, American Museum of Natural History. New York, 1941.

WORMINGTON, HANNAH M. *Prehistoric Indians of the Southwest* (3rd ed.). Denver Museum of Natural History. Denver, 1956.

Some Special Aspects

CULIN, STEWART. *Chess and Playing Cards*. United States National Museum. Washington, D.C., 1896.

———. "Games of the North American Indians," Bureau of American Ethnology. *24th Report*, 1903.

DOCKSTADER, FREDERICK J. *Indian Art in America*. Greenwich, Conn.: New York Graphic Society, 1961. A superbly illustrated presentation of Indian and Eskimo art, with an authoritative interpretation of the many phases of that art.

DOUGLAS, F. H. (ed.). *Indian Culture Areas in the United States*. Denver Art Museum. Denver, 1950.

KRIEGER, H. W. "American Indian Costumes in the United States National Museum," *Annual Report of the Smithsonian Institution for 1928*, pp. 623-61.

McGUIRE, J. D. "Pipes and Smoking Customs of the American Aborigines," *Annual Report of the United States National Museum for 1897*, pp. 351-645.

MASON, OTIS T. "Aboriginal American Basketry," *Annual Report of the United States National Museum for 1901-02*, pp. 171-548. Regarded as a "bible" on the subject.

———. "Cradles of American Aborigines," *Annual Report of the United States National Museum for 1887*, pp. 161-212.

ORCHARD, W. C. *Beads and Beadwork of the American Indians*, Vol. II, *Contributions*. Museum of the American Indian, Heye Foundation, Southwest Museum, Los Angeles. New York, 1929.

PARKER, ARTHUR C. *The Indian How Book*. Doubleday Doran, 1928.

SALOMON, JULIAN H. *The Book of Indian Crafts and Lore*. Harpers, 1928. This and Arthur C. Parker's *The Indian How Book* give some idea of the construction of many artifacts.

WEST, G. A. "Copper, Its Meaning and Use by the Aborigines of the Lake Superior Region," Milwaukee Public Museum. *Bulletin*, Vol. 10, No. 1, 1929.

———. "Tobacco, Pipes, and Smoking Customs of the American Indians," Milwaukee Public Museum. *Bulletin*, No. 17, 1934.

WILSON, THOMAS. "Prehistoric Art," *Annual Report of the United States National Museum*, 1896, pp. 327-664.

Books Heavily Illustrated

DOCKSTADER, FREDERICK J. *Indian Art in America*. Greenwich, Conn.: New York Graphic Society, 1961. A superbly illustrated presentation of Indian and Eskimo art, with an authoritative interpretation of the many phases of that art.

FUNDABURK, EMMA LILA, AND FOREMAN, MARY DOUGLASS. *Sun Circles and Human Hands*. Luverne, Ala.: Published by the authors, 1957.

INVERARITY, ROBERT BRUCE. *Art of the Northwest Coast Indians*. Berkeley, Calif.: University of California Press, 1950.

JOSEPHY, ALVIN M., JR. (ed.). *The American Heritage Book of Indians*. New York: Simon & Schuster, 1961. A history of the American Indians from prehistoric times to the present, accompanied by nearly 500 pictures, more than 100 in color.

KNOBLACK, BYRON. *Banner-Stones of the North American Indians*. Privately printed. Author's address: 2016 Jersey Street, Quincy, Illinois.

MOOREHEAD, WARREN K. *Stone Ornaments of the American Indians*. Andover, Mass., 1917. Leans heavily toward Eastern forms.

———. *The Stone Age in North America*. New York: Houghton Mifflin Co., 1910. A two-volume "classic," although somewhat out of date and sparse on Western artifacts.

TOWNSEND, EARL C., JR. *Birdstones of the North American Indian*. Privately printed. Author's address: 5008 N. Meridian, Indianapolis, Indiana.

Index